Debts to Pay
A Fresh Approach to the Quebec Question

John F. Conway

D0218155

James Lorimer & Company, Publishers
Toronto, 1997

James Lorimer & Company Ltd. acknowledges with thanks the support of the Canada Council and the Ontario Arts Council in the development of writing and publishing in Canada.

Canadian Cataloguing in Publication Data
    Conway, John Frederick
    Debts to pay
    Rev. ed.
    Previously published under title: Debts to pay: English Canada and Quebec from the conquest to the referendum.
    Includes bibliographical references and index.

    ISBN 1-55028-545-9 (bound)
    ISBN 1-55028-544-0 (pbk.)

    1. Canada – English-French relations. 2. Quebec (Province) – History – Autonomy and independence movements. 3. Canada – Politics and government. 4. Canada – History. I. Title.

FC144.C65 1996   971.4   C96-932301-8   F1027.C65 1996

James Lorimer & Company, Publishers
Egerton Ryerson Memorial Building
35 Britain Street
Toronto, Ontario
M5A 1R7

Printed and bound in Canada

CONTENTS

For Patricia Vivian Conway Robitaille,
born, 17 November 1940 at Moose Jaw, Saskatchewan,
died, 6 March 1988 at Montreal, Quebec,
who attempted a reconciliation of the two nations
in her personal life

In days of yore, from Britain's shore,
Wolfe the dauntless hero came,
And planted firm Britannia's flag,
On Canada's fair domain.

Here may it wave, our boast, our pride,
And joined in love together
The Thistle, Shamrock, Rose entwine
The Maple Leaf for ever!

from "The Maple Leaf for Ever"

Alexander Muir, 1890

Je me souviens.

Quebec's national motto since 1883

I am convinced that much of our
problem is simply that people do
not know enough about their history...

Joe Clark
Minister Responsible for Constitutional Affairs
Globe and Mail, 31 December 1991

Those who cannot remember the past
are condemned to repeat it.

George Santayana

PREFACE

When I was growing up in Moose Jaw, Saskatchewan, we regularly sang "The Maple Leaf for Ever" during morning assembly at Empire School. It was not until much later that I noticed that the *fleur-de-lis* was not allowed to entwine with the rose, shamrock, and thistle. That it was not is not, of course, surprising. During those days the song was English Canada's unofficial anthem, usually sung with more gusto than "God Save the King."

Quebec and the entire "French fact" were more or less absent from my direct experience, except when we studied history (and those classes never left any doubt that the best thing that ever happened to New France was the Conquest). I can't recall meeting a French Canadian from Quebec during my childhood, but I heard a lot about them. And we had our local, semi-assimilated variety. I learned the usual epithets — pea-souper, frog. A lot of the prejudice we absorbed in my home mixed Orange hostility to Rome with ethnic contempt. What I learned about French Canadians was either uniformly negative — disloyal to Britain and Canada, untrustworthy, unwilling to fight in the war while our boys died, lazy, backward, priest-ridden — or patronizing — overly emotional, good-natured, simple. Both these stereotypes were also portrayed in the movies I went to see at the Royal Theatre — French Canadians were either evil villains or happy-go-lucky, good-hearted buffoons.

There was one jarring exception to this general attitude. Like most working men in Moose Jaw in that era, my father joined in the harvest. He used to bring home stories of the French Canadians he met who had come out on the harvest trains to help take off the wheat. At the time it didn't strike me as odd that these men he worked with were quite different from all other French Canadians. They worked hard, did their fair share, were easy to get along with, and enjoyed a good time.

Like most English Canadians, I was shaken out of my ignorance about Quebec by the Quiet Revolution. At university I was exposed to books and courses on Quebec. I heard touring speakers like Pierre Bourgault and René Lévesque. I followed political events in Quebec avidly. I travelled to Quebec. On my first extended trip there in 1965 I learned something of both the anger and the reasonableness of the people when I discovered that my inability to speak or to understand French provoked hostility only until the Quebeckers in question learned I was not from either Montreal or Ontario, but from the West. Then they would warm up. It was okay to be an English-only speaker from western Canada.

On my last extended trip to Quebec in the autumn of 1987 for language training at Laval University I learned something of the determination of the Québécois in securing their nation. This was a period when many in English Canada, and not a few in Quebec, were gleefully crowing that Québécois nationalism was dead for at least a generation. The Québécois were too busy earning money, and they had even voted Tory in 1984, an unthinkable act! Yet I failed to find any evidence of this death of nationalism. Quite the contrary. I was in Quebec City when René Lévesque died, and I was amazed by the massive outpouring of deep love and grief for the man and strong support for his ideals.

I've put my children in French immersion. I have learned enough French to function haltingly at professional meetings. I do not want Quebec to separate. Yet I know that my linguistic gestures are not enough, are not even what Quebec wants. I believe today, just as I believed at the height of the Quiet Revolution, that Quebec will eventually separate unless English Canada offers a serious accommodation to Québécois nationalism. The temporary breathing space provided by the narrow October 1995 referendum result may be our last chance. The next federal and Quebec elections will clarify just how much time we have. And it may not be much. This is an appeal to my fellow English Canadians to open their hearts and minds to Quebec in an effort to help save the Canada we know and love.

ACKNOWLEDGEMENTS

The manuscript was read by historian Dr. Lorne Brown, University of Regina, and by Diane Young, Editor in Chief at James Lorimer and Company. The idea was also discussed at length with Jim Lorimer. Their suggestions helped to produce a better book. The copy-editing expertise of Jane Fredeman greatly improved the final text. Cheryl Heinnemann and Leanne Overend typed the manuscript, showing constant patience with my interminable changes and revisions. To all six, to my family, and to my many students and colleagues, both in Quebec and English Canada, with whom I have debated the "Quebec question" over the years, my heartfelt thanks.

NOTE

The use of the term "English Canada" may bother some readers, but it is still the most convenient and historically accurate term. The facts are clear. Canada is composed of two nations: the Québécois nation, with the province of Quebec as its political and constitutional home; and the English-Canadian nation, with a considerably stronger political and constitutional home — nine provinces and two territories. The latter also has hegemony in the House of Commons, the Senate, and all other federal institutions and a well-protected minority status in Quebec. Canadians have now agreed to add a third nation to the equation of Canada's constitutional design, the aboriginal or first nations.

About 70 per cent of Canada's current population is of British or French extraction, or some combination thereof. Those of British extraction make up the largest single population bloc, often an overwhelming majority, in every province except Quebec. In Quebec, about 80 per cent of the population is of French origin. Granted, the English-Canadian nation is characterized by a high degree of tolerance of ethnic and cultural diversity, and this diversity has continued to transform and enrich it. Perhaps we will soon reach the point when we can drop the adjective "English" and just speak of the Canadian nation. The Québécois nation is similarly undergoing transformation as diverse ethnic and cultural groups adopt French as their language of work and education. Sixty-eight per cent of Canadians speak English, 23 per cent speak French, while only 8 per cent speak a different language at home.

The English-Canadian nation's distinctive roots remain in its British origins, now significantly modified, and the English language; the Québécois nation's distinctive roots remain in its French origin, also significantly modified, and the French language. All the other ethnic groups that have come to Canada have integrated, to varying degrees, to one or the other of these nations.

1

Dangerous Impasse

Canadians are living through a death-watch as the country slowly ebbs and fails. Those aware of the coming end seem powerless to stop the decline; sceptics accuse them of babbling incoherent and fantastic remedies. Many, especially the media, appear blithely unaware that death is in the air. Those with the power to reverse the trend — incumbent politicians in Ottawa and the nine English-Canadian premiers — are perversely more interested in assisted suicide than curative measures, expressing public pride at refusing to discuss a constitutional resolution. Any reasonable person will recognize that the end is near and will come very rapidly if present trends are confirmed in the next federal and Quebec elections, due at the latest in 1998 and 1999 respectively. The next sovereignty referendum in Quebec will likely take place, barring an electoral upset in Quebec, in 2000, a dangerously symbolic year. The new millennium could very well begin without Canada as we have known it.

Supporters of the Charlottetown Agreement told Canadians that approval would bring an end to constitutional bickering, the beginning of national reconciliation. The defeat of the Agreement on 26 October 1992 in both Quebec and English Canada, and the deep divisions provoked by the referendum campaign, are damning testimony to a monumental miscalculation on the part of our political elite. The Charlottetown referendum became the first upheaval in what became a sustained and rolling political earthquake that has shaken Canada to its foundations. Echoes of the referendum reverberated in the results of the 25 October 1993 federal election. The two parties that campaigned strongly against Charlottetown were rewarded by their regional electorates. In Quebec, where sovereigntist sentiment surged, the Bloc Québécois took 54 of 75 seats with 49.3 per cent of the popular vote and became, ironically, Her Majesty's Loyal Opposition in the House of Commons. In the West, the Reform Party won 51 of 86 seats with 38 per cent of the vote, annihilating the Tories and almost doing the same to the NDP in the region. Forty-six Reform seats are in Alberta and British Columbia, the seed-bed of the greatest hostility to Quebec in English Canada. Thus the two extreme factions in opposition to Charlottetown fared well — the Reform Party in the West, which argued that Charlottetown gave Quebec too much, that Quebec should learn to love Canada or leave it; and the Bloc, which argued that Charlottetown gave Quebec nothing of significance and sovereignty was now the only dignified option for the Québécois nation. Clearly, between these two positions there is no middle ground and if they have their way, each for their own reasons, we will witness the end of Canada.

The rolling political earthquake impacted again during the 12 September 1994 provincial election in Quebec. Though the Parti Québécois won a victory only by a narrow popular vote — less than 1 per cent — Jacques Parizeau won a comfortable majority of seats (77 of 125) easily enough to move, as promised, to a quick referendum on sovereignty. Despite this narrow victory, in which many in English Canada sought delusional solace, the pro-sovereignty popular vote in Quebec, had in fact edged up to 51.2 per cent when one added in the vote won by Mario Dumont, the former leader of the Young Liberals in Quebec, now leader of the pro-sovereignty Action démocratique du Québec (ADQ). This was a significant gain over René Lévesque's 1976 victory with 42 per cent.

The final seismic shock resulting from the Charlottetown fiasco occurred on 30 October 1995, when 49.4 per cent of Québécois voters supported a much harder sovereignty question than that presented by Lévesque in 1980. This was an incredible indictment of the failure of federal leadership — both in Ottawa and in the nine English-Canadian provincial capitals — which seemed incapable of offering anything but a campaign of political, economic, and territorial threats against a sovereign Quebec during the weeks preceding the referendum vote. The inescapable fact was that Quebec sovereignty had come ominously close to winning the magic number required in any democratic system, 50 per cent plus one vote.

Canadians should not underestimate the seriousness of the current political situation. In the 1993 federal election, the people of Quebec gave the Bloc Québécois 49.3 per cent of the vote and 54 of 75 seats in the House of Commons. Thus, in our constitutional, parliamentary democracy, the legitimate democratic voice of the people of Quebec in Ottawa is sovereigntist — an unprecedented fact in any federal system that hopes to survive. In the 1994 provincial election, the people of Quebec gave the PQ a clear majority of seats, control of the National Assembly, and a secure and comfortable parliamentary mandate to govern the province. A majority of voters — when those supporting the PQ and ADQ are combined — also voted for candidates who explicitly favoured sovereignty. Had more than 50 per cent in Quebec supported sovereignty in the 1995 referendum, the political trajectory toward a sovereign Quebec would have been virtually irresistible. By any legal, constitutional, or moral argument premised on the principles of democracy, Quebec's sovereigntist leaders would have had a mandate to proceed, and to proceed by a unilateral declaration of independence if Ottawa tried to thwart the democratic will of the citizens of the province. Foreign governments — led by France — would have had little difficulty in quickly recognizing a sovereign Quebec when sovereigntists democratically and constitutionally represented the people of Quebec, a majority of whom would have voted for sovereignty by referendum.

How did we reach this impasse? Though the conflict between English Canada and Quebec has been with us since the Conquest in 1759, its currently sharp expression exploded with the death of the Meech Lake Accord in 1990. Many Québécois interpreted the failure of Meech as a rejection of their minimum demands. When Meech died, public opinion in Quebec hardened on the option of either sovereignty or a satisfactory renewal of federalism. In English Canada, positions also hardened as a result of the death of Meech. During the period following its failure, sympathy for Quebec fell to a low ebb, where it has remained. The meteoric rise of the Reform Party reflects the way many English Canadians have hardened their hearts against the concerns of the Québécois. The party leapt almost overnight from relative obscurity in the 1988 election to prominence in English Canada. Reform's support remains wholly concentrated in English Canada, especially in the West, and Reformers have shown little interest in offering themselves as candidates in Quebec, although they have toyed with the idea of appealing to extreme elements among Quebec's non-francophone minority.

Though Preston Manning and the Reform Party got their start in the late 1980s by voicing western alienation and demanding a Triple-E Senate, much of Reform's national rhetoric has been carefully designed to capture the minority strain of anti-French, anti-Quebec bigotry that has always ebbed and flowed in English-Canadian politics. Manning's position on Quebec was probably given its most disturbing expression in a speech he made in April 1991 in New York, counselling Americans to look to the U.S. Civil War in order to understand what was happening in Canada. He spoke of the Civil War as the "model for secession." In that speech, Manning came perilously close to suggesting civil war as a possible outcome in Canada's constitutional crisis. During Manning's one foray into Quebec during the 1992 Charlottetown referendum campaign, he spoke at the Loyola campus of Concordia University in the heart of anglo-Montreal. In the sole incident of a speaker requiring police protection during the campaign, he reiterated his determination to confront the separatists head-on, forcing the Québécois "to choose once and for all" between Canada and independence. He has maintained that hardline position ever since — Quebec must accept Canada largely as it is or leave it — and there would be little room for Quebec's unique national aspirations in the so-called "New Canada" envisioned by the Reform leader. Manning, more than any other English-Canadian politician, has actively embraced the role of undertaker, eager to have possession of Canada's corpse after Quebec's departure.

At the opposite end of the spectrum from the folksy right-wingers of the Reform Party are Canada's mainstream anglophone intellectuals. During the Quiet Revolution and the Lévesque era, these thinkers, particularly those in the centre and on the left, were largely sympathetic to Quebec. Though unable to persuade Ottawa and most provincial governments that Quebec needed some special constitutional accommodation, English-Canadian intellectuals played a significant role in tilting public opinion toward a softer line on Quebec. This positive attitude largely ended with the free trade election of 1988, when many intellectuals in English Canada were angered and deeply disappointed by Quebec's strong support for Brian Mulroney and free trade, particularly by the aggressive support of Québécois nationalists. The events at Oka in 1990, which provoked sympathy for the Mohawks across English Canada but hostility in Quebec, further undermined the progressive reputation of Québécois nationalism among the English-Canadian intelligentsia.

In a sense, Québécois nationalism lost an influential ally — a sort of fifth column — in English Canada. At the same time, the minority intellectual current in English Canada that had always been hostile to Québécois nationalism was pushed to prominence. Books that formerly would have had only a narrow appeal — Mordecai Richler's *Oh Canada! Oh Quebec!*, for example — became best-sellers. Views that would have formerly been largely beyond the pale were taken seriously: Canada would be better off without Quebec; military force ought to be contemplated to keep Quebec in Confederation; a separating Quebec would be carved up and partitioned; an independent Quebec would not be welcome in any post-separation economic or other association; and so on. Before free trade and the collapse of Meech, intellectuals who took such positions were seen as cranks. In the Meech aftermath, they were taken seriously, a fact that indicates how far the polarization had gone. These poisonous voices resonated on the fringes of the No campaign in English Canada during the Charlottetown referendum, and a year later played a central role in the success of the Reform Party in Alberta and British Columbia during the 1993 federal election campaign.

The referendums of October 1992 and 1995 have passed. Instead of a reconciliation, the two solitudes have not been so hunkered down in their respective enclaves since before the Quiet Revolution or the bitter World War I Conscription Crisis or perhaps even since the hanging of Louis Riel. The Bloc Québécois and the Reform Party represent the logical extreme of each solitude, looking inward and brooding over its own grievances. Perhaps one could take a fatalistic view, arguing that this outcome was inevitable, that it has been coming ever since the Conquest. But many of us do not share that view. Rather, we believe that history, both long past and recent, informs us that English Canada must largely shoulder the blame for our present circumstances.

The Bloc Québécois and the Parti Québécois reflect a conviction, present in Québécois nationalism from the beginning, that in order to save the Québécois nation, a separate, sovereign state must be constructed. Ever since René Lévesque was spurned by the Quebec Liberal Party and proceeded to build the Parti Québécois, that conviction has been a clear provincial choice for the Québécois.

But in the past, it was a choice only exercised in the secure context of simultaneously choosing among the Conservatives, Liberals, or NDP in federal elections. Now, with the Bloc Québécois holding a clear majority of Quebec seats in the House of Commons and showing no signs of losing support, the situation is dangerous. It was one thing to joke during the Lévesque-Trudeau era that the Québécois wanted an independent Quebec within a strong federal system. The election of sovereigntists who represent the people of Quebec at both the provincial and federal levels is no joking matter. Quite simply, the federal government now has much less political legitimacy in Quebec or in world councils when dealing with the Quebec question. We witness this reality daily in our politics, whether it is the manifestations of contempt, derision, and lack of support for Prime Minister Jean Chrétien in Quebec, or the arrogant ease with which the prime minister of France can travel to Quebec and assure the Québécois of France's support for whatever destiny the people of Quebec may choose.

After Meech, Charlottetown, and the October 1995 referendum, Canada has entered a period of serious political instability and rancour, a period that could witness the departure of Quebec. It need not come to pass, just as what has happened since the Quiet Revolution need not have happened, and perhaps it is not too late to learn from our history in order to avoid repeating past mistakes. During the Quiet Revolution, when English Canada opened up to Quebec as never before, there was an opportunity to renegotiate Confederation. English Canada refused to do so. After Lévesque lost the referendum in 1980, there was another opportunity to renegotiate Confederation. English Canada again refused. After the failure of Meech, there was another chance. Initially, the wide-open process that culminated in the Charlottetown Agreement raised many hopes, but then the English-Canadian premiers intercepted the process and badly fumbled the ball. British Columbia's minister responsible for constitutional affairs, Moe Sihota, put it most graphically when he said Quebec's Premier Robert Bourassa "ran into a brick wall formed by nine other governments...[that] said: 'Look, there is no way you are going to get special status...'"

Once again, English Canada has failed to rise to the challenge of the Quebec question, harshly refusing to make the accommodations for which Quebec has been asking, episodically from the Conquest onward and most insistently for the last forty years.

What Quebec wants is straightforward: that English Canada affirm an acceptance of the right of the Québécois to national self-determination and that negotiations begin to reconstruct Canada's constitutional order in ways that give Quebec the special powers it needs to protect and enhance the Québécois nation. That was what the Royal Commission on Bilingualism and Biculturalism more or less told us in 1967. That was what the Task Force on Canadian Unity told us in 1979. That was what Lévesque first asked of the Quebec Liberal Party and then of Canada through the PQ. And that's what Bourassa, who may well go down in history as the last credible federalist in Quebec provincial politics, asked in 1992 when he warned us against "domineering and authoritarian federalism."

After the English-Canadian premiers and Ottawa arrogantly and unsuccessfully presented Charlottetown to Quebec on a "take it or leave it" basis, warning there would be no new offers or concessions, a campaign of intimidation against the Québécois began, in a desperate effort to deflect them from the sovereigntist course. Warnings about partition, territorial claims, the establishment of ethnic enclaves, the possible enforcement of a general principle of the infinite divisibility of a separating Quebec (a piece each for the Cree, the Innu; pieces for the allophones, the anglophones; perhaps a chunk including communities in western Quebec; and so on), no negotiations, no association, no legal or constitutional path to sovereignty despite any democratic decision by the Québécois, economic reprisals, these and more were all tossed into Quebec politics like so many bombshells. The campaign of intimidation failed, as affirmed in the federal and provincial election results in Quebec. And only a last-minute gesture of conciliation by Ottawa and English Canadians narrowly forestalled a victory for the Yes side in the 1995 sovereignty referendum. As a result, the federation totters on the edge of the abyss, and Quebec and English Canada are face to face in a polarized standoff in which the options have been dangerously clarified and simplified for the Québécois as never before since 1837–38: surrender or sovereignty.

A large part of the problem is that English Canada and Quebec premise their actions on two very different versions of the same history. English Canada recalls the Conquest of 1759 as a simple battle on the Plains of Abraham. Quebec recalls it for what it was, the final military confrontation in a long, bloody military campaign that stretched from Acadia up the St. Lawrence. English Canada recalls the uprising of 1837–38 almost as a comic-opera sideshow in the irresistible march to responsible government. Quebec recalls 1837–38 as another bloody suppression of the Québécois nation. English Canada celebrates Confederation in 1867 as the birth of a nation. Quebec views it as the imposition of a two-layered constitutional stranglehold on national aspirations. English Canada sees the hanging of Louis Riel as unfortunate, an event best forgotten, and ambivalently contemplates making Riel a hero. Quebec views the hanging of Riel as yet another English-Canadian declaration that the French ought to stay locked up in Quebec. And so it goes, each solitude with its own version of the same history, even up to the present.

English Canada now believes the imposition of the *War Measures Act* in 1970 was a regrettable, if understandable, overreaction. Quebec considers it as another military occupation designed to subjugate, to warn, and to humiliate. English Canada sees the victory of the federalist option in the 1980 Quebec referendum as an affirmation of Quebec's commitment to Canada. Quebec, contemplating all the broken promises made during that referendum campaign, views it as yet another example of English Canada's political duplicity. English Canada sees the isolation of Lévesque in 1981 as another small gambit in the constitutional chess game in which Quebec's leader was outmatched by the English-Canadian team. Quebec regards it as an affront to the Québécois nation, as a deliberate slap in the face. English Canada was divided on Meech and Charlottetown. Some regarded both accords as craven surrenders to blackmail by Québécois nationalists while others regarded them as reasonable and generous offers to Quebec. Quebec regarded Meech as a bare minimum on which English Canada choked and Charlottetown as yet another effort by English Canada to impose unilateral constitutional solutions.

English Canada has not yet been able to go through the process of recognizing the oppression of the Québécois — and other francophones — and undertaking a resolute effort to make amends. It has gone through such a process to atone for the oppression of aboriginal people. Now we appear prepared to pay our debts. Similarly, Canadians have acknowledged the reparation owed to Japanese-Canadian victims of the infamous World War II internment. And we have gone part way from time to time with the Québécois. Indeed, many English Canadians believe that we admitted our oppression during the Quiet Revolution with the Commission on Bilingualism and Biculturalism. They believe we proceeded to pay our debts amply, perhaps too amply, to the Québécois — French power in Ottawa, official bilingualism, allowing French to become the language of work and education in Quebec, various economic development concessions. But the Québécois do not agree, and they never have. English Canada's most recent effort, finalized at Charlottetown and forcibly presented to both Québécois and English Canadians on a "take it or leave it" basis, has finally served to deepen the divisions both within and between the two solitudes.

The idea that Quebec is oppressed is a hard sell in English Canada. Canadians have many diverse grievances and oppressions that are uniquely rooted both in the design of Confederation and in our free-market political economy. Confederation was, after all, a scheme hatched and carried out by the British Colonial Office to salvage the fortunes and futures of the traditional colonial elites in Britain's possessions in North America. It involved the construction of a sea-to-sea federation that would remain loyal to Britain while containing the troublesome French fact. Confederation was a last resort for our elites, who had stumbled from option to option and crisis to crisis after the defeat of the rebels in 1837–38 and whose separate futures would doubtless have culminated in their falling into the tender embrace of Uncle Sam. Confederation had only minority popular support throughout the British colonies, except in Canada West (Ontario). Atlantic Canada, British Columbia, and the Prairies all continue to have grievances rooted in the political and economic design of Confederation. It is, therefore, understandably hard to win sympathy for the Québécois nation from the poor and unemployed of Cape Breton or Newfoundland, from Saskatchewan farmers driven off the land because of low prices and debt, from B.C. lumber and mining communities that live through booms and busts always mindful that a total shutdown is possible.

But that sympathy must be won if we want Canada to survive. Whatever the grievances and the regional oppressions faced by English Canadians, we must never forget what sets the oppression of the Québécois apart. No other province or region has faced the routine use of military force, or the threat of such force, throughout its history. No other province or region can claim to be the political and constitutional homeland of a unique nation with its own language, culture, and history. And the Québécois and the aboriginal nations are the only "peoples" or "nations" who can claim that their defeat and oppression laid the basis for the emergence of Canada as we know it. The Québécois nation exists, justifiably festering with historical grievances and resentments arising from unjust treatment by English Canada. These are the facts that English Canada refuses to face and avoiding them has been the object of an elaborate constitutional dance begun long before 1867. The dance must end; the facts must be faced. And if we in English Canada want Canada to survive we must set about paying our debts to the Québécois nation, a nation we continue to deny at Canada's peril.

2

Quebec as a Defeated Nation: The Conquest

The first historical fact to be remembered is the military conquest of Quebec. The Conquest must colour our interpretation of all subsequent events. It was much more than the defeat of the French by British forces in a contest for North America, a contest whose geopolitical outcome was only a matter of time. The Conquest was also the defeat of a nation — the *Canadiens* — a people who no longer saw themselves as French citizens on a temporary sojourn in the New World. They had in fact built a new *habitant* culture from which, for most, there was no going back.

English Canada no longer celebrates the Conquest. One rarely hears the "Maple Leaf for Ever" any more. School children do not recite 18 September 1759, the date of the final surrender of Quebec City to the British, as a singular founding event in Canada's history. But the fact of conquest is not ignored. It is duly recorded as the inevitable outcome in a continental struggle between the 60,000 to 70,000 French, largely in Acadia and New France, and the more than 1.5 million British, largely in the Thirteen Colonies. And, it is also noted that this was more than a local continental skirmish; it was a confrontation between the French and British world empires, a confrontation only finally resolved at Waterloo.

Historians in English Canada often refer to Versailles' neglect of New France and indifference to the growing gap between the French from France and the Québécois. In this context, the quip by Montcalm's aide Bougainville is often quoted: "It seems that we are of a different nation, even an enemy one." These historians also frequently recount stories about the generosity of the British conquerors and the good, even kindly relations between the British troops and the people of Quebec City, especially during that first terrible winter of 1759–60.

General James Murray, Wolfe's replacement as commander of the troops and the first governor of Canada, was generous and humane in victory, once referring to the Québécois as "the bravest and the best race upon the Globe." Scarce food and fuel were shared, and troops who misbehaved were punished severely. During the worst of the winter, the British troops, ill prepared and poorly equipped for the harshness of the climate, suffered terribly from the cold and hunger, over a thousand troops dying. The kindnesses of the conqueror were repaid by the conquered. The Ursuline nuns — who had tended the mortally wounded Montcalm and buried him in their convent's walls (their museum today contains his relics, including his skull) — knitted knee warmers for the bare-legged Highlanders. Such events should be remembered and celebrated, but so should other, less admirable actions. They are not well remembered in English Canada, but they are among the Québécois.

This final war to conquer France in North America continued from 1754 to 1760, and until the last year the British did not fare well. Indeed, until the spring of 1760 neither the French nor the British knew for certain who would win the final day, since that depended on which country's supplies and reinforcements arrived in the St. Lawrence first. Montreal had not been taken, and the French army of seven thousand (including three thousand *Canadien* militiamen) had regrouped there and intended to retake Quebec City. General Murray had only three thousand troops fit to fight. The British fleet arrived first, and Montreal surrendered in September 1760.

However, because their campaign had gone badly until 1759, the British took some desperate measures. About fifteen thousand French lived on the Nova Scotia peninsula, which was ceded to Britain by the 1713 Treaty of Utrecht. Angry that many Acadians remained actively loyal to the French cause and fearful that a majority might share similar sentiments, the English decided in 1755 to exile the Acadians forcibly and disperse them throughout the Thirteen Colonies. The orders were brutal — the Acadians were rounded up by military units, those who evaded deportation were deprived of shelter and food by the torching of their homes and crops. In this way, an estimated six thousand Acadians were dispersed, their land seized without compensation and later redistributed to loyal British settlers, largely from New England.

Before the battle on the Plains of Abraham, a frustrated Wolfe ordered a scorched-earth policy, burning homes, villages, and farms along the St. Lawrence and shooting any *Canadien* who carried a gun. Further frustrated by Montcalm's effective defences at Quebec City, Wolfe had the city bombarded from across the river, a tactic without military merit that served only to inflict terror and suffering on the city's civilian population. The later generosity of Governor Murray could not completely erase such events from the collective memory of the Québécois. And the fact that Murray was forced out in 1766 by the minuscule but powerful bloc of British merchants, who chafed and bridled under the restrictions on their right to exploit Britain's newest possession freely, could not have been reassuring to the Québécois, who, above all, feared sharing the fate of the Acadians.

After the Conquest, the British occupation had two faces, military and economic. Of the two, the military occupation was the milder, and the economic occupation would have been harsher, but for Murray and his successors. The newly arrived British merchants wanted to make profits, and they anticipated easy plunder. The profitable fur trade of New France was rerouted from French to British hands and from French to British ports. But the merchants wanted more. Because the Québécois could not hold office, the British merchants sought an elected assembly and other rights of British subjects. Had they been successful, the Québécois would have been delivered, shackled, to a pitiless commercial fate. But Governor Murray, and later Governor Guy Carleton, who once described the British merchants as "the scum of the earth, masquerading as its salt," refused to accede.

Upon reflection, this contrast — the economic occupation held in check by the military occupation — makes sense. The British merchants had little interest in agriculture, except insofar as it fed land speculation. Their primary interest was the fur trade and the resulting commercial traffic across the Atlantic. Furthermore, for them, the Québécois were merely a source of cheap labour to staff the fur trade, a small but significant captive market, and the annoying occupiers of potentially profitable land. If the merchants could have exiled all the Québécois they considered either surplus to their pecuniary needs or impediments to profit, they would have done so without a second thought. After all, the Québécois were not only conquered and therefore subject, but they were also French and Catholic. On three counts, therefore, they were of little consequence.

The British military, and later the governors appointed from London, were concerned with both day-to-day and long-term order in the context of the long-range global interests of the British Empire. They were acutely aware that a handful of British occupiers could never hold the colony against a united, determined, and aroused population. As military commanders and politicians, they knew that the population had to be placated and reassured that their worst fears were groundless and that the local leaders had to be won over at least to passivity and indifference. Wisely, therefore, they turned a blind eye to the practice of the Catholic religion and dealt with the population in the French language. The law was administered as fairly and as reasonably as possible under the circumstances. Charity was given. Kindnesses were shown.

Thus, even though the Royal Proclamation of 1763 outlined what appeared to be a Draconian program of forced assimilation, its implementation was another story altogether. The Proclamation clearly intended to re-make the new colony in the mould of British colonies. It imposed English civil and criminal law and customs and the use of English. Catholics were effectively barred from public office because of the oath requiring allegiance to the British monarch as head of church — the very oath that had provided the pretext for the exile of the Acadians. In this way, the Québécois were excluded from all influence in the society and effectively enjoyed no status as citizens. The size of the colony was severely reduced: the northern boundary now ran northeast from Lake Nipissing to Lake St. John and thence up the north shore of the St. Lawrence; the southern boundary ran due east from Lake Nipissing across the St. Lawrence and thence up the south shore of the river. The Proclamation also promised the introduction of an elected assembly — which would effectively have been English and Protestant — in an effort to promote an influx of British settlers. Legally, the Proclamation was implemented, but only imperfectly, and life for the ordinary Québécois went on much as before. Introducing an assembly was left to the governor's discretion, a discretion Murray and Carleton chose not to exercise.

While it may be true that the Conquest and its aftermath were benign by the standards of the day and that the governors did hold in check some of the more rapacious tendencies of the British merchants, these facts should not deflect us from the long-term sociological consequences of the Conquest. Québécois society lost its leadership or, as some have put it, suffered "decapitation." The British victory led to the dismantling of the French political and administrative apparatus, the displacement of the French and Québécois merchant élite, and the emigration of many of the old landowners. How many actually returned to France and how many remained or returned later to be absorbed in a transformed and defeated society is the subject of scholarly controversy. Sociologically it makes little difference. These elements largely ceased to exist as leaders with real power in the larger community, and those who remained, remained on the conqueror's terms.

British domination led to a massive rural retreat during which, like other conquered people, the Québécois turned inward and hunkered down in their parishes. Since their society was deprived of effective secular leadership, the Church and the local priest became a key focus of community life, a central source of leadership, and a rampart for linguistic and cultural resistance. With no significant outside contact, Québécois society became increasingly homogeneous and rural, rooted in a subsistence economy and overseen by British masters. The extent of the "ruralization" of Québécois society was dramatic and quite contrary to world trends: at the Conquest it is estimated that 25 per cent of Québécois were urban dwellers. By 1825 only 12 per cent were urban, and in Quebec City and Montreal the British were in the majority. This rural character of Québécois society remained predominant until World War II.

Cut off from the usual sources of population renewal and growth available to colonial societies through immigration, the Québécois commenced what has come to be known as "the revenge of the cradle," which saw the Québécois population, from the Conquest to the Quiet Revolution two hundred years later, increase eighty fold, rising from sixty or seventy thousand to five million, not counting the loss of another million or so to immigration to the U.S. Today, Quebec has the lowest fertility rate in Canada, a fact serving to increase the anxiety of the Québécois.

These, then, were the survival responses of a conquered nation determined to thwart the conqueror's plans. Certainly, the hope that the Québécois would ultimately be swamped by a huge British immigration was misplaced, at least initially. The slowness of British immigration combined with the relentless rate of natural increase of the Québécois to make clear that "the French fact" was in Canada to stay. The imposition of the English language and English laws, customs, and administration had been met with passive resistance, and long-run prospects of a significant rate of assimilation appeared more and more elusive as the Québécois nation remained vital. Thus conqueror and conquered reached a potentially unstable standoff. British power and British numbers could never withstand the Québécois should their resistance become active. This concern was always foremost in the minds of the wiser among the British, and it became even more central as the Thirteen Colonies moved from defiance to rebellion.

Under the circumstances, the loyalty of the Québécois could not be counted on, and even elements among the British merchants contemplated throwing in their lot with the American rebels. As relations deteriorated between the Thirteen Colonies and the British, Governor Carleton moved to forestall revolt in Quebec. The informal pact the British had made with the Québécois clergy and the remnants of the French merchant and landowning élite, was carefully cultivated in order to ensure that the Québécois masses were not swept up in the coming American contagion. Now, however, the Québécois leadership, forever conservative but also nationalist, demanded a *quid pro quo* — the worst of the chains binding the Québécois nation would have to go. Furthermore, the bases of the Québécois leadership would have to be consolidated since the Québécois as a whole did not blindly love their élite.

The *Quebec Act* of 1774 was adopted just in time, only months before open military hostilities broke out between British troops and American rebels. The Act was a complete reversal of the policies embodied in the Royal Proclamation of 1763. The Québécois nation got its language, its old civil law, and the freedom to practise its religion. With official, legal status, however, Québécois leaders were a step removed from their community, especially since they led by British selection rather than by Québécois election and therefore became more securely a part of the British apparatus of domination than before.

Furthermore, the *Quebec Act* explicitly forbade an elected assembly — "it is at present inexpedient to call an Assembly" — and established an appointed council to advise the governor. In this way, the overall governance of the Québécois remained essentially despotic. The British had, deliberately or otherwise, misinterpreted the Québécois' earlier resistance to an elected assembly from which they would be excluded as a resistance to elected assemblies in general. No one asked them if they wanted an assembly elected fairly by both Québécois and British residents, nor did their conservative leaders propose such a radical measure. The Québécois were not yet considered fit to enjoy the rights of Englishmen. In a final act, both to please the Québécois and to put the American rebels on notice, the *Quebec Act* also restored the boundaries of the colony to their pre-Conquest dimensions. The new Quebec included all the land around the Great Lakes north to the Height of Land, south to the Ohio, and east to the Mississippi, and the colony was extended on the north shore to Labrador and on the south shore flush to the American colonies. The fact that much of this territory was part of future expansion plans of the Thirteen Colonies was far from accidental. The new province of Quebec was therefore made up of equal measures of desperation and expediency on the part of London.

The *Quebec Act* was sufficient to ensure the passive neutrality of the Québécois during the American War of Independence. Contrary to some British expectations, the Québécois did not jubilantly hail this measure as a great victory — it was not — especially for the ordinary Québécois. But it was enough. While many sympathized with the American cause and not a few joined the Americans to fight the British, the Québécois, as a nation, did not rise up and join the Americans to throw off the British yoke. But neither did they join the British. When the Americans invaded, the Québécois not only refused to join the American cause but also actively resisted efforts to conscript them to fight on the British side. They did not view the Americans as enemies and invaders, treating them more often as a first wave of bothersome tourists creating noise and disturbances in their tranquil communities. The Québécois did not want to fight on either side. Many, of course, did agitate on behalf of the Americans, and some suffered excommunication as a result. Others did act as guides for the Americans and even fought with them. Consequently, the neutrality of the Québécois remained uncertain until the very end. The *Quebec Act* of 1774 and the alliance the measure cemented among the British, the Church, and landlords was enough. But had Montgomery and Arnold's winter 1775 siege of Quebec City been successful and had Quebec City surrendered to the Americans as Montreal had, Canada's and Quebec's stories would have been entirely different.

The *Quebec Act* granted the Québécois a portion of their national rights. It also briefly consolidated the conservative leadership bloc among the Québécois while setting in motion a process that ultimately undermined it. Professions that served the people and their culture were now legitimate: teaching, law, medicine, and the notariat joined the priesthood, which resulted in the growth of an alternative secular and middle-class leadership potentially more independent and progressive than the old bloc. These professional occupations, and to a lesser extent the Québécois merchant class, provided a fertile field for ideas and ideals spawned by the American and French revolutions. Though the British continued to select Québécois office-holders "from a group...of 'followers' of the English," as the early Patriote Pierre Bédard put it in 1814, alternative leaders with substantial popular support began to emerge from among the new Québécois middle class. Only the lack of an elected assembly prevented these leaders proving their legitimacy, and then, when an assembly was granted, the absence of responsible government kept them from office with real power.

The victory of the Americans had a final echo in Quebec with the arrival of the United Empire Loyalists to settle in the Eastern townships, the Gaspé, and what was to become Ontario. These were the most loyal of British subjects, having faced and passed the ultimate test of civil war and having lost everything as a result of their commitment to Britain and the Empire. Of the estimated forty thousand Loyalists who came to British North America, most went to Nova Scotia, but a large group of about seven thousand arrived in Quebec and provided that colony with its first British population of any great significance.

The Loyalists both sustained and subverted the traditional British colonial merchant élite. They sustained the élite just by being there in numbers as ballast to the large Québécois population. They also sustained the élite by their deep pro-British patriotism, their anti-Americanism, and their anti-republican conservatism. Their demands for loyalty to the British flag and Empire were implacable, and their standards were high. In payment for their losses, the Loyalists received an immediate tangible stake in the colony. Each Loyalist was granted one hundred acres of land, as well as another fifty acres for each additional person in that family. But the Loyalists who came to Quebec were largely farmers and therefore committed to further immigration and agricultural settlement. They found little support among the British merchant élite, whose vision was still limited by the blinders of mercantilism. The Loyalists also brought with them the expectation that they would enjoy the rights of Englishmen, including the election of assemblies and the right, as owners of property, to participate actively in the political life of the commonwealth. Inevitably, there was a clash of interests between the merchant élite and the Loyalist farmers, who were joined by other British immigrants who anticipated a well-settled agricultural society firmly based on a loyal landowning yeomanry. The contradiction between the commercial designs of the British merchant élite and the agricultural designs of the Loyalists and those who joined them on the land could not be long contained merely by appeals to patriotism and loyalty.

The growing British population was unhappy both with the *Quebec Act*'s considerable concessions to the Québécois in law, language, and land tenure and with its explicit prohibition of an elected assembly. Furthermore, they did not see the prospect of an assembly elected generally by both British and Québécois electors as a solution. They wanted British institutions, rights, laws, and customs. And they wanted English to be the language of daily life, business, and politics. These things the British population could never have without turmoil and controversy as long as they were confined in a political home with the Québécois. The Québécois, for their part, newly confident and assertive as a result of the assurances in the *Quebec Act*, and more and more led by a more progressive middle-class leadership, were attracted to the idea of an elected assembly to provide a representative political voice for the Québécois nation. The demand for an elected assembly therefore united the British and the Québécois against London and the local administrative élite. But they were very much divided on the other issues.

A reconciliation of sorts was achieved with the *Constitutional Act* of 1791. The Act imperfectly divided the British and Québécois populations into Upper and Lower Canada, respectively. The line of division, just west of Montreal, included in Lower Canada a small but powerful British minority. The Act allowed for elected assemblies, but appointed governors and councils. The rights of the British minority in Lower Canada were well protected: the appointed governor and a majority of the appointed council remained British, and the boundaries for election to the assembly were craftily drawn to give considerable over-representation to the British minority. For example, the Québécois, making up well over 90 per cent of the population of Lower Canada, were apportioned about 70 per cent of the assembly seats, while the British minority were granted the other 30 per cent. This practice of providing considerable over-representation to the British minority in the assembly only finally ended during the October Crisis in 1970. Nevertheless, in Lower Canada the stage was set for confrontation as the assembly rapidly became the democratic voice of the Québécois nation, or at least of those with property, and the appointed governor and council more and more took on the character and appearance of external impositions, which, of course, they were.

Since the *Quebec Act* was not repealed, the effect of the *Constitutional Act*, which was in fact passed as an amendment to the *Quebec Act*, allowed each colony to decide which provisions of the *Quebec Act* would continue to be in effect. Needless to say, Upper Canada quickly opted out and established a truly British colony. Lower Canada, however, retained the comforts granted to the Québécois by the *Quebec Act*, while making careful arrangements to secure and protect the privileges of the British minority. At least in that sense, long before Confederation, Quebec was recognized as an atypical and "distinct" British colony. The forerunner of modern Quebec was therefore born in 1791, having been conceived in 1774.

The Québécois moved into the nineteenth century with some remarkable gains. They had been granted concessions that made clear that London had finally abandoned the notion of making the "French fact" disappear through a combination of assimilation and British immigration, and they had secured their civil law, language, and religion. Though their homeland had been considerably reduced with the creation of Upper Canada, the very act of creating Lower Canada provided the Québécois with a geographical and constitutional homeland. Lower Canada was the territory in which the Québécois nation resided. The granting of elected assemblies — something that London could not very well give to British Canadians without giving it to the Québécois — provided the nascent structures necessary for the democratic evolution of the Québécois. The only things that separated the Québécois nation from full mastery in their homeland were the appointed British governor and council, a powerful, privileged, and dominant British minority, and British military might. To some of the more progressive middle-class leaders among the Québécois, who enjoyed growing popular support, responsible government and real national independence were only a small if momentous step away.

3

The Re-conquest and Isolation of Quebec

The four decades following the *Constitutional Act* of 1791 occupy an uncertain place of honour in Canada's official history as the era dominated by the struggle for democratic and responsible government in Upper and Lower Canada. The Québécois of Lower Canada and the English Canadians of Upper Canada were largely united in this struggle, which pitted elected assemblies against the Family Compact and the Château Clique.

There was much that united the middle-class democratic movements in the two colonies: anger at and hatred for a corrupt economic and political oligarchy, which ruled as if the colonies were the personal fiefdoms of its members; fury at distant colonial masters in London who failed to respond to petitions with speed and justice; the affliction of an unworkable political system based on elected assemblies with the limited power of supply and appointed governors and executives jealously holding all political and administrative authority — ensuring the impasse that inevitably occurred; the desire for colonial economic policies designed to encourage immigration, local industry, and agricultural settlement, as opposed to the oligarchy's increasingly irrational determination to cling to the old mercantilist strategy. These grievances, in retrospect, made the Rebellions of 1837–38 inevitable.

There was, however, a central issue that divided the democratic movements in Lower and Upper Canada from each other. In Lower Canada the movement was both nationalist and democratic, inevitably shaped by the resentment among the Québécois majority of the national oppression of British colonial rule and its local expression through a privileged, powerful, and arrogant English minority. In Upper Canada the basic democratic issues were unclouded by the issue of national oppression, and, as a result, both the Rebellion and its aftermath were much less bloody and bitter.

In Upper Canada the conflict between the assembly and the Family Compact was a more clear-cut constitutional question. The Family Compact dominated the London-appointed governor and his executive council. Furthermore, the gulf between the élite, the assembly members, and the electors was not complete. The élite enjoyed some popular support and maintained a strong loyal presence in the assembly, and elections were not always foregone conclusions. The Reform movement won majorities in the assembly in 1828 and again in 1834, but only a minority in 1830, and in 1836 was defeated, amid charges of fixed votes, unfair counting, bribes, and intimidation. Apparently, the governor's appeal in 1836 to British loyalty and patriotism was effective. The electorate's loyalty was uncertain and wavering to be sure and it was severely tried by London's refusal to accept the call for responsible government. But it was sufficient to hold most Upper Canadians, indeed most Reform sympathizers, back from leaping into the abyss of armed insurrection.

Most of the key grievances of the Upper Canadian Reformers had to do with matters of economic policy. The basic antagonism involved the Reformers' desire for an aggressive pursuit of policies to encourage immigration, agricultural settlement, and industrial development. The Family Compact, on the other hand, favoured continuing the emphasis on commerce within the British mercantile system. The Reform opposition, composed of farmers, nascent industrialists, small merchants, and the middle-class professionals who serviced them, resented the priorities of the colonial state: the pre-eminence of commercial policy; the use of public funds for expensive, commercially oriented public works (particularly canal building); and the absentee speculative ownership of vast tracts of land. All of these were seen as enormous obstacles to the progress desired by both the Loyalists and their descendants and the new immigrants.

The Reform movement's concerns were well documented by Robert Gourlay in his *Statistical Account of Upper Canada* published in 1822, a book that resulted first in the author's banishment and then his eventual trial and imprisonment for almost four years. In preparing his book, Gourlay asked thirty-one questions of each township in order to collect data. It was the thirty-first question that got him into trouble: "What, in your opinion, retards the improvement of your township in particular, or the province in general; and what would most contribute to the same?" This question, and the other thirty, were posed to the resident landowners of each township, obviously the leading "respectable" citizens. Everywhere the complaints were the same: a monopoly of land ownership by absentee owners and a lack of settlers with the capital needed to purchase land.

In Upper Canada a new society was emerging, based on agriculture and small industry. It was composed largely of landholding farmers locked in a structure of government and economy over which they had little or no control. Even when their representatives came to dominate the assembly, the appointed council remained in the hands of the dominant merchant class. This élite group had appropriated for themselves much of the land as its value increased. It was the land monopoly issue more than anything else that sparked the Rebellion. Indeed, the increasingly irreconcilable political conflict between the legislative and executive branches of government merely reflected this conflict between the new agricultural and industrial majority and the old mercantile minority, which blatantly used its control of the colonial state to defend its privileges. Lord Durham later agreed and reported the "deep-seated impediments in the way of industrial progress," including "the possession of almost the whole soil...by absentee proprietors, who would neither promote nor permit its cultivation, combined with the defective government which first caused and has since perpetuated the evil." It is not therefore surprising that William Lyon Mackenzie's 1837 Navy Island Proclamation most prominently promised freedom of trade and the redistribution of land when independence was won.

Independence, however, was not won. The Rebellion failed miserably. The military confrontation involved only a few skirmishes in 1837, the major one occurring at Montgomery's Hotel on the outskirts of Toronto, and a number of cross-border raids during 1838 by Reformer partisans who had fled to the United States. The military outcome was never in doubt: the Reform forces were outnumbered, outgunned, and very badly led. Canadians thereby learned the lessons learned by European revolutionaries that same decade. You do not storm barricades and topple governments with ideals, passion, and a just cause alone.

The repression was severe but not brutal, involving few casualties and no widespread punitive lootings or burnings against populations sympathetic to the Reform cause. Two military leaders — Peter Matthews and Samuel Lount — were tried and hanged, after being hugged and kissed by a tearful executioner. During the 1838 raids four captured Reformers were summarily executed after they surrendered. Nine others were tried and executed, and about sixteen were transported to Australian penal colonies. In total, some 855 fighters were officially named as arrested or escaping arrest. Most had their sentences of death or imprisonment commuted.

The 1837–38 Rebellion in Upper Canada is not accorded a great deal of honour in English-Canadian history. When seeking heroes from the event, English Canada has tended to honour those who sided with the authorities against the Reformers. A notable exception, of course, was the leader, William Lyon Mackenzie, though he has hardly been lionized in Canadian history. The Rebellion is very often viewed as the unnecessary actions of impatient hotheads whose extremism probably slowed down rather than speeded up London's benevolent devolution of responsible government to British North America. Often the Rebellion in Upper Canada is painted as faintly ridiculous, involving a great deal of bombast, a lot of running and hiding, and very little shooting. No significant historical monument memorializing the Rebellion in Upper Canada exists, with the exception of that to the executed leaders Lount and Matthews located in the Toronto Necropolis.

The Rebellion in Lower Canada was a different matter. The national question dominated every other issue contested. While Mackenzie envisioned an independent confederation of colonies if the Rebellion succeeded, Louis-Joseph Papineau, the Patriote leader, played coy with Mackenzie and toyed with the vision of an independent Québécois nation state emerging from success. Papineau and his followers favoured a democratic republican form of government. They did not embrace proposals for universal male suffrage, which were called for by the radical elements, nor did they embrace some of the more thoroughgoing anti-seigneurial and anti-clerical tendencies. Thus the democracy envisioned was imperfect and designed primarily to transfer political, economic, and social power from the English minority, and their British colonial masters, to the Québécois middle classes.

On the land question, Patriote concerns were different from those of the Reformers, since land and nation were inevitably emotionally intertwined in Lower Canada. The Patriotes were concerned about a land shortage resulting from both overpopulation and the fact that British immigrants with capital were taking up more and more land. Emotions concerning the land issue were intensified by the fact that the rural retreat after the Conquest had tied the survival of the nation to the land and the *habitant* way of life. Furthermore, British immigration into Lower Canada was viewed as ominous, particularly in the context of the recurring British dream of obliterating the French by drowning them in an irresistible tide of immigrants. The fact that the major urban areas were now dominated by the British minority and were the centres where economic, political, and administrative power was held largely by the British did little to alleviate this fear. While the Reformers' economic program might be characterized as wide-open frontier capitalism, that of the Patriotes was very much that of a capitalism managed in ways to sustain and nurture the nation, and the developments allowed must not be so uncontrolled that they could threaten the nation's foundation. Though there was a radical wing in the Patriote party that wanted to go beyond the moderate policies to a more popular, anti-clerical and anti-seigneurial program, they only began to reach ascendancy in the dying days of the Rebellion and then only because of their military courage and dedication to the cause.

There were other fundamental differences between the Upper Canadian Reformers and the Lower Canadian Patriotes. Both movements opposed the colonial system as a corrupt and un-democratic barrier to economic progress. But the Patriote complaints could never be separated from the fact that they suffered under a British colonial regime and that the Québécois nation — the overwhelming majority of the population — suffered endless national oppressions and humiliations. Those few Québécois co-opted into positions of power and privilege were denounced as *les gens en place*, and such promotions were counted against those who took them. The British minority dominated the economy, particularly in trade, industry, and finance, the sectors of growth, dynamism, and progress. The relentless pressure of this British domination and encroachment denied land to many Québécois, drove others into emigration to the United States, and left the Québécois excluded from the economy in the growing cities. All this fit into the sense of national grievance and could only intensify Québécois fears that the long-run project of the British was the ultimate extinguishment of the Québécois nation, or at least its reduction to the status of a rootless minority in what was formerly its national home. The Rebellion, therefore, was seen as more than a fight for democratic and responsible government. It was also seen as the necessary means, first to save and then reassert the Québécois nation's right of primacy of place on the soil of Lower Canada. Perhaps such emotions alone are sufficient to explain the Patriotes' greater courage, determination, and more general willingness to die for the cause in comparison to their counterparts in Upper Canada.

The Patriotes enjoyed much deeper popular support than that commanded by the Reformers in Upper Canada. After almost a generation of struggle for national recognition and democratic political reform, there was no doubt about the population's support for the Patriote party. In the 1827 election, the Patriotes won an overwhelming election victory, reducing the English party opposition to four. Many of the Patriote assembly members were of British origin, but they were committed to both the democratic program and the struggle for national independence of the Patriotes. In the general election of 1834, held to the tune of Papineau's denunciation of "the aristocracy of the banks, the government and trade," and fought on almost entirely nationalist grounds, the Patriotes swept in with 77 per cent of the vote, winning seventy-eight seats (forty-one of these by acclamation) to the English party's nine seats. Just prior to the election, the assembly adopted Papineau's "Ninety-two Resolutions," a passionate distillation of Patriote grievances and remedies. The government of Lower Canada reached a stalemate between the appointed British-dominated executive and legislative councils and the elected assembly, which controlled public funds.

Commencing after the 1834 election, the Patriotes held a series of huge rallies demonstrating their popular support. Clearly, Papineau and the Patriotes were determined to use the decisive 1834 election results and their palpable support to force concessions from London. Popular anger against the British minority and Québécois "traitors" increased, scuffles broke out, tensions mounted. The situation was further worsened by an economic crisis. A drastically lower harvest resulted in a sharp rise in the price of bread and in the cost of living. The economic downturn adversely affected all sectors of the economy and increased popular anger as farmers plunged into debt, workers could find no work, merchants saw profits fall, and professionals adjusted to shrinking incomes. Meanwhile, grain that could not be found for local consumption could be found for the export market. The situation became a classical pre-revolutionary one, with political and economic grievances coming together into a hardening of positions and a widespread anticipation of a looming final confrontation. At this point, the impasse could have been broken, and the Rebellion avoided, had London agreed to serious reforms toward responsible government. Instead, on advice from the local British élite, London acted provocatively when the British House of Commons adopted Lord John Russell's infamous "Ten Resolutions" in the spring of 1837. The resolutions in effect rejected any concessions to the Patriote reform program, while stripping the elected assembly of its powers. The message was clear. Not only was London rejecting any reform in response to the years of tireless democratic agitation culminating in an unmistakable expression of popular will, but it had also decided to strip the Québécois of what little political power they enjoyed, the very instrument that had allowed them to mobilize and shape this expression of the nation's will. It was a provocation that could have had only one outcome, presenting the Patriotes with a stark choice: abject surrender or insurrection.

That the Patriotes had not seriously planned insurrection from the beginning is well known. No military preparations of any significance had been made. A Patriote militia had not been organized, though some Patriote activists secured positions in the established militia. Military plans had not been made. Talk of military action usually occurred as mere rhetorical flourishes in flights of political oratory. Typically, such talk was not followed up with any practical actions. These were not serious revolutionaries, though they were in love with the idea of revolution and naively convinced that revolution was justified in the circumstances.

The Church, long suspicious of the anti-clerical tendencies among the Patriotes, and the government took counteraction quickly and ruthlessly, catching the Patriote leadership off guard. The Church announced that there would be neither absolution nor religious burial for those rebelling against constituted authority. The Patriotes were denounced from the pulpits as "heathens, hypocrites, and manipulators." This effort to shatter the Patriotes' popular support largely failed, since many local priests did not comply with the bishop's directives. But the message could not help having some inhibiting effect. There was now a yawning gulf, according to the Church, between the rebels and devoted God-fearing Québécois. The government banned public meetings, called in troops, and commenced military preparations. Arrest warrants for Patriote leaders were prepared, but most went quickly into hiding. The ranks of the magistrates and militia were purged of known and suspected Patriote sympathizers. London and the local government had opted for a final, military solution of both the present crisis and the previous decades of impasse.

The actual two-year civil war in Lower Canada was quite extensive, involving a number of pitched battles between poorly armed Patriotes and British regulars and volunteers. In most major battles the Patriotes were poorly led. The only significant Patriote victory occurred at St. Denis in the early phase of the war. Very soon, however, the war became a punitive expedition as British troops, particularly the volunteers with years of scores to settle, embarked on a campaign of killing, looting, and burning. At St. Charles, surrendering Patriotes were killed, and the village was burned. St. Denis was also burned to the ground in reprisal for being the site of the early victory. Patriote leader Dr. Jean-Olivier Chénier died during the defeat at St. Eustache. His body was put on display at the inn, it was rumoured that his heart was cut out, and the village was torched. Outnumbered Patriotes at St. Benoit offered to surrender, but their offer was refused, and the village was attacked and burned to the ground. The burning of villages and farms became so general that the British military commander and later governor of Lower Canada, Sir John Colbourne, was nicknamed *Vieux Brûlot* (Old Arsonist), and when he was later made Lord Seaton, many Québécois deliberately mispronounced his name as "Satan."

There are no precise figures for the total number of dead and wounded, but most accounts speak of hundreds. Of the estimated 515 locked up in jail at the end of the war, not counting those prematurely freed by Lord Durham, ninety-nine were condemned to death, and twelve were finally hanged. Fifty-eight were deported to penal servitude in Australia, and two were banished. Many hundreds fled into exile and later trickled back as pardons were granted. Chevalier DeLorimier, a Montreal notary who was among those executed, left a political testament in which he said, "I die without remorse; all that I desired was the good of my country, in insurrection and in independence...My efforts have been for the independence of my compatriots; thus far we have been unfortunate...I die with the cry on my lips: *Vive la Liberté, Vive l'Indépendance!*"

The full story of the uprising in Lower Canada is rarely recounted among English Canadians. We conveniently overlook it or diminish its significance. Among the Québécois it is different. The story is told and retold in all its detail. It is a deep part of the national heritage. The Patriotes are presented as heroes of the nation, and their names and the details of their lives are learned in school. Statues and monuments to the Patriotes dot the province. The most striking is that raised at St. Denis, the site of the only Patriote victory; topped by a Patriote partisan in fighting stance, it bears the simple inscription in French and English, "*Honneur aux Patriotes 1837.*" The events of 1837–38, and the agitations leading up to them, mark the birth of the modern Québécois nation. The fact that the nation was reconquered and suppressed by military force and the noose and that its leadership was broken and dispersed certainly slowed down its development. But the Québécois nation did not disappear despite continuing diligent efforts to make it do so.

Lord Durham's report on the events, issued in January 1839, was a scurrilous, anti-Québécois document that once again reflected the English determination to extinguish the French fact. The document blamed the rebellions on the Québécois and proposed, most importantly, that measures be taken to prevent the Québécois from ever controlling an elected assembly again. Since Durham himself, as a radical lord, was committed to responsible government and since it was inconceivable for him to deny democracy to Englishmen, he took local advice and recommended that the stillborn 1822 idea of a union of Upper and Lower Canada into one colony, Canada, be resurrected. The estimated 400,000 British in Upper Canada would combine with the 150,000 in Lower Canada, providing a working majority against the 450,000 Québécois. Durham also recommended that a policy of assimilation be adopted. The English language would prevail as the language of government and business. Excluded from the vital mainstream, the language and customs of the Québécois would be pushed to the margins of society where they belonged. Durham's view was that while the backward among the Québécois might continue their resistance by clinging to the old ways, the best and the brightest would be attracted to, and finally absorbed by, the opportunities and the progressive dynamism of a bustling, British-dominated colony. Furthermore, an aggressive encouragement of British immigration would doom the Québécois to the status of a declining minority.

London implemented many of Durham's recommendations with the *Act of Union* in 1840, which set the stage for the pattern that has continued ever since. The Québécois were locked up in a political and constitutional home they could never hope to control, a measure intended to ensure their long-term fate as a declining, marginalized minority. Upper and Lower Canada were united into a single colony with an elected assembly in which each former colony received forty-two seats. Thus, the seats for the old Upper Canada, combined with the over-representation provided the British minority in the old Lower Canada, would ensure a British-dominated assembly. French was denied official status as a language either of public record or of debate in the assembly. A very high property qualification was established for eligibility to run for election (in the old Lower Canada there had been no restrictions on who could run for the assembly and a fairly low property qualification determined eligibility to vote). Furthermore, money bills could only be presented to the assembly by the government. Durham's major recommendation — responsible government — was flatly denied. The governor and council were appointed, and there was no requirement for equal representation from the two former colonies in the appointed councils nor was there a requirement for the representation of both language groups.

London did not, however, go the whole route in national oppression. French civil law remained in place for Canada East (Lower Canada), and the religious rights of the Catholic church were respected, as was the principle of the local control of education. Thus, Canada was an administrative nightmare with two systems of law, two legal bureaucracies, two attorneys-general, and two school systems with two different languages of instruction. The *Act of Union*, then, pleased no one completely, but neither did it offend anyone completely. The Reformers were angry that responsible government was not granted, but they were pleased that Governor Lord Sydenham promised nearly responsible government by a careful selection of his council to ensure that its members had the support of the assembly. The British Tory bloc was happy to get union, an assured British majority in the assembly, and a postponement of full responsible government. The Québécois were angry, but they were marginally relieved that the national oppression was not as thoroughgoing as they feared. The

Québécois still had the right to elect representatives to the assembly, the comfort of their civil law, and the assurance that their key cultural and linguistic institutions — schools and the Church — would be permitted to carry on. But it was to prove a largely unworkable system, ensuring that deadlock would again inevitably result.

The biggest fear of London, Governor Lord Sydenham, and the local British élite was that the Reformers of Upper Canada and the Patriotes of Lower Canada might coalesce around another reform program and achieve control of the new assembly. For the first election the governor left nothing to chance or to the unfettered exercise of democracy. The high property qualification served to keep out some of the radical riff raff. In addition, the governor personally gerrymandered the electoral boundaries to reduce Québécois representation, and he actively campaigned in Canada West to encourage the election of moderate and/or conservative members. He also made clear he did not want too active a campaign, advising the public to "avoid useless discussion upon theoretical points of government." The tame press helped considerably in this effort to de-politicize the situation by warning the people "to shun as they would a pestilence the contaminating presence of an itinerant preacher of grievances...[and] to cast politics to the winds and devote themselves...to their farms and their warehouses as if...the turmoil of an election had never been heard by their peaceful firesides."

The effort was successful, and the first assembly saw only a handful of committed Reformers elected from Canada West. Though a significant group of Patriotes was elected in Canada East, the heir to Papineau's mantle, Lafontaine, was defeated. In the end, the governor had an assembly he felt he could work with — a moderate majority of around fifty to sixty members, with a strong but not unmanageable Patriote/Reform opposition on the left and a rump group of hard Tories carping on the right.

With a relatively tame assembly, the Québécois nation again contained, and a sort of half-way house to responsible government in place, the resurrection of the old mercantile dream seemed plausible, even irresistible. Prosperity returned, and the future seemed to hold prospects unlimited for the élite, which, though somewhat transformed and a bit subdued, had survived the worst fear of élites everywhere — a popular insurrection. The St. Lawrence trade route would dominate the heart of the continent — British and American — carrying raw or partly finished staples to Europe and bringing British manufactured goods back. Both trips would fill merchant and forwarding pockets. Settlers would rush in. An imperial loan on good terms and a doubling of the revenue tariff assured the new colony's fiscal recovery, making it possible to complete the St. Lawrence canal system. Alas, for the élite, the golden future was not to be; the house of cards began to collapse.

To the dismay of Canadian merchants and Tories, Britain began to dismantle its worldwide mercantile system and move to free trade. This process began in 1842 with measures that reduced the preference for Canadian wheat and timber; next, the Corn Laws and Timber and Sugar Duties were repealed, and, finally, in 1849 the protection given by *The Navigation Acts* ended. These moves swept away the foundation of Canada's commercial system, which relied on imperial preference and protection for its exports and upon *The Navigation Acts* for its shipping industry. Furthermore, to emphasize London's conviction that British colonies had to find their own niche in the world economy and become responsible for themselves, in 1842 Canada was granted *de facto* responsible government, followed by formal and final measures in 1847. In an irony of history, what the Reformers and Patriotes had failed to win in 1837–38 was granted by the imperial Parliament: economic self-determination and responsible government. The ideological descendants of 1837–38, now more moderate, came to ascendancy; the old Tory bloc was more or less excluded from power; the French language returned to official status in 1848; and a complex and comprehensive reform program was carried out.

Britain's moves to free trade precipitated an economic disaster in Canada. Exports of wheat and flour collapsed, property values declined, bankruptcies accelerated. Even with the changes following on responsible government, Canada's new political and economic élite had no alternative economic strategy for recovery, and consequently the government lurched from crisis to crisis. Eventually Canada's choices became clear, even to the old Tories. The alternatives were not attractive; they were all through perilous uncharted waters, and none included the old secure special mercantilist bond with Britain.

The cruelly orphaned colony could move to a policy of economic protection, keeping the home market for local manufacturers and encouraging industrialization. It could adopt free trade, carving out an economic niche in a world already dominated by

European industrial powers. It could embrace annexation and throw its lot into a continental American empire. It could seek reciprocity with the United States in an effort to exchange benefit for benefit in the hopes of ultimate prosperity. Or, the colony could adopt a mixture of such policies. This last prudent course was adopted, as Canada's élite opted for a judicious application of protection and reciprocity, but with considerable energy also devoted to maintaining a special relationship with Great Britain. The shadow blueprint for Confederation began to be drawn.

The first step to Confederation was the Intercolonial Reciprocity Agreement of 1850 between Canada, New Brunswick, Nova Scotia, and Prince Edward Island, which provided for preferential duties for each colony's products in the others. This worked so well for Canada West that pecuniary enthusiasm for Confederation increased rapidly. In 1854 the Reciprocity Treaty with the United States was signed. Again, Canada West did very well, particularly as the growth in markets began to stimulate Canada's small manufacturing base. There was a brief period of prosperity until the 1857 depression. It resulted in another fiscal crisis, spurring a further strategic innovation, as Minister of Finance Alexander Galt proposed his famous "fiscal tariff with incidental protection." With one bold stroke more revenue was generated at the same time as the government responded to demands from Canada's emerging industrialists for targeted protection of the home market. Growing discontent with the Reciprocity Treaty in Canada, especially among farmers, fishermen, and lumbermen, who were becoming unhappy with the free flow of natural products, was now joined by annoyance from the Americans at these moves to protection. The victory of the protectionist North in the American Civil War in 1865 and the subsequent abrogation of the treaty by the U.S. government simply confirmed the wisdom of the already well-prepared underpinnings of Confederation: westward expansion, an east–west transcontinental railway, and industrialization through protection.

This colonial project, though largely conceived in London, received its strongest support in Canada West, soon to be Ontario. London's interests were clear: to preserve a British North America from sea to sea. To realize it, London had to beg, cajole, and threaten the elites of Britain's North American possessions, except in Ontario. There Confederation, particularly the economic prospects of a vast westward expansion, captured the imagination. Canada, as a transcontinental national economy, was to be Ontario's. More importantly the West was to be Ontario's frontier. What of Canada East, soon again to be Quebec? In the period leading to Confederation, Québécois nationalism had divided between the conservative *Bleus* and the more radical *Rouges*. The *Bleus* entered into a pact and shared power with the English moderates of Canada West. Radical nationalism ebbed and became more and more isolated. Anti-clericalism and freethinking became increasingly unacceptable, and the Church enjoyed a renewed status in the society, joining the governing coalition. The pact, quite simply, was to accept the defeat of the Québécois nation in 1837–38 and to attempt to salvage the essence of the nation — its language, religion, and culture — through accommodation and compromise with the dominant English. And, though the *Act of Union* imposed strict limits on the Québécois nation, significant concessions had been secured.

As the Confederation scheme unfolded, supported by the *Bleus* in Canada East, a promise was held out to the Québécois nation. Canada would be divided into two provinces, Ontario and Quebec. Thus, the Québécois would again be granted a political and constitutional home in which they would enjoy a certain hegemony within the considerable constitutional limits of Confederation. The French language and civil law would prevail in Quebec, and significant powers would be granted to all provinces — education, health, local government, property, resources, civil rights, a large say in agriculture — powers sufficient to defend the cultural and linguistic foundation of the Québécois nation. The powerful English minority in Quebec would be reassured by Article 80 of the *British North America Act*, which established seventeen protected English provincial constituencies in the Eastern Townships, the Ottawa Valley, and northwestern Quebec. These constituencies were to remain protected until a majority of the seventeen sitting members agreed otherwise. And, for the first time since 1837, the Québécois nation would be able to express its democratic political will, however circumscribed by the *British North America Act*, through a National Assembly.

For the British-dominated Canada West, the dangers inherent in defying Durham's advice never again to allow the Québécois domination in an elected assembly were offset by being rid of the burden of having constantly to reconcile the divergent interests of the united Canada. The establishment of Ontario as the biggest, richest, and most dynamic and powerful province, freed of all the messy history of the old colony, would allow the province's élite to get on with nation-building and westward expansion — British nation-building and westward expansion. With the Québécois nation safely secured in a separate province under a strong central government dominated by Ontario, the élite of Ontario could turn its mind to other more important matters.

Yet the Québécois in their new province could pose a threat. With its large population, economic base, and strategic location on the St. Lawrence, Quebec was the only province that could present itself if not as an alternative leader of Confederation, then at least as a serious counterweight to Ontario. This might prove a serious problem if the Québécois nation decided to play a significant role in westward expansion through settlement. This was unlikely to happen since Québécois nationalism was obsessively rooted in Quebec soil. Nevertheless, it could occur if opportunities arose for those with a broader vision of the role that the Québécois nation could play in Confederation, a vision that might include the co-development of the West to include a significant French population. After all, the Québécois had not been reluctant to move in droves to the United States to seek their fortunes. Why would they not move in large numbers to a West that was welcoming and congenial to them? It was one thing to lock up the Québécois nation in the province of Quebec, but it also had to be isolated and confined there, and the rest of Canada, especially Ontario's frontier in the West, quarantined from the French fact. The vision of Canada as a British nation from sea to sea — except for Quebec — could not be realized if the West were to become a series of New Brunswicks. And it was indeed in the West that any emerging aspirations of the Québécois nation to play a significant role in building Canada outside Quebec were firmly thwarted.

In March 1992, the House of Commons honoured Louis Riel by adopting a resolution recognizing his "unique and historic role" in founding the province of Manitoba and in defending the rights of the Métis. Riel has long been viewed by western Canadians as a hero in the West's battle against Central Canadian domination. And it goes without saying that he has been held in deeper reverence by both Indian and Métis.

Louis Riel led two rebellions resisting the terms of incorporation of the Prairie West into Confederation — one in 1869–70 in Red River, the other in 1885 in the Saskatchewan region. In 1670 the Prairie region and most of the vast northern territory had been granted by the British Crown to the Hudson Bay Company, which for two hundred years exercised relatively complete economic and political control over the region and its inhabitants. In 1867–68 Canada negotiated the purchase of the entire region from the Company for 300,000 pounds sterling, retention of one-twentieth of the "fertile belt" in the region (about seven million acres), and further land grants around the Company's many trading posts. In 1869, Canada dispatched a governor to take control of the entire region as a colonial possession of Ottawa. At no time were the Red River inhabitants consulted. Sixteen hundred white settlers, fifty-seven hundred French-speaking and four thousand English-speaking Métis lived in the region. (The entire area — including what is now Manitoba, Saskatchewan, Alberta, parts of western Ontario, and the Northwest Territories — in 1871 boasted a meagre total of just seventy-three thousand inhabitants, including the native nations.)

The local people responded with something less than enthusiasm to their annexation by Canada. The French-speaking and Catholic Métis feared for their language, education, and religious rights. White settlers and the Métis as a whole shared a concern that their rights, particularly land rights, would be overridden without prior guarantees. Both groups wanted some form of responsible government and full provincial status and rejected the prospect of exchanging the dictatorship by the Company for one by Ottawa. When the Canadian governor, William McDougall, declared his authority over the region, the overwhelming majority of white settlers and Métis united under the leadership of Riel, proclaimed a provisional government, issued a list of rights and demanded negotiations with Ottawa. Ottawa agreed to negotiate, and as a result the province of Manitoba was established in 1870. The French and English languages were both granted official status, local control of education was assured, the recognition of the rights to tenure on existing farms was promised, and 1.4 million acres of land were designated for the settlement of outstanding Métis land claims. This was a significant victory, though it was somewhat offset by Ottawa's decision to constrict Manitoba's size to just ten thousand square miles around what is now Winnipeg and to deny the new province control of its lands and resources.

The grievances in Saskatchewan in 1885 were similar, again uniting white and Métis. This time there was also significant support from the native nations, which faced starvation and were angered at the failure of Ottawa to live up to treaties. The 1885 "Bill of Rights" demanded more just treatment for Indians, a redress of Métis land grievances, and guarantees of security of tenure on existing farms for whites and Métis alike. Additionally, the demands included responsible government, representation in the House of Commons and the cabinet, control of lands and natural resources, improvements in the homestead laws, vote by ballot, improvements in rail transportation, and tariff reductions. The central political demand was again full provincial status and involved a threat of separatism — "we may settle up with the East and form a separate federation of our own in direct connection with the Crown."

When the Red River Rebellion occurred, Québécois opinion insisted that the Canadian government negotiate Riel's Bill of Rights, which included education and language equality for French and English. Ontario opinion wanted to send an army to crush this affront to Canadian law and sovereignty. In Quebec, Riel was celebrated as a Québécois hero battling against British arrogance. In Ontario, Riel was viewed as a rebel and, after the execution of Thomas Scott, a villainous murderer. British refugees from Red River wanted nothing less than a war of conquest, followed by the imposition of a stern regime until British immigration could increase the loyal population sufficiently to outvote the French in the colony. Ontarians largely shared that view.

Prime Minister John A. Macdonald initially tried to appease both sides. He agreed to negotiate Riel's Bill of Rights, but he also agreed to send a military expedition. In an effort to reassure Quebec, Macdonald promised that the military expedition would not be punitive and let it appear that he agreed that an amnesty would be granted to the rebels. This amnesty was widely understood in Quebec, and among the rebels, to be a general one, including Riel. When some twelve hundred troops were raised for the expedition, an effort was made to include Québécois. But the Québécois proved reluctant, and the Quebec battalion that finally went west included mostly British volunteers. In Ontario, there was no problem recruiting for this *cause célèbre*, since many did see the main object of the expedition as avenging the executed Scott. Given the mood, an amnesty was simply unthinkable in Ontario.

Increasingly, the debate about Riel and Red River became a more fundamental one about the character of Confederation in the West. The Québécois hoped to assert that the West was not the private possession of Ontario and the Orange Order. Ontario was determined to claim just that: the West did belong to Ontario, and Quebec ought not to meddle.

In the end, the Québécois felt betrayed. Riel did not get amnesty and fled into exile, where he lingered despite his continuing popularity in both Quebec and Red River. In 1873 and 1874, he was elected to the House of Commons *in absentia*. The military expedition turned out to be sufficiently punitive to drive many Métis westward. The land settlement the Métis gained was more or less annulled through deliberate administrative delays and harassment and the issue of scrip negotiable for cash. But the defeat was not complete by any means. The province of Manitoba was established, both French and English were established as official languages, and two school systems were guaranteed. The French fact had an official and legally equal foothold in the West.

The script was more or less replayed in the North-West Rebellion in 1885. Riel was called back by his people, Métis and white, French and English, to lead the region's campaign for settlement of its grievances. Riel had, after all, despite his personal banishment, been successful in winning the establishment of Manitoba. But English Ontario immediately vilified him as a rebel, a murderer, and a traitor. Again, the Québécois praised Riel as a patriot, almost equal to the 1837 leader Papineau, fighting the good national cause against English domination and injustice. Opinions were somewhat harder and more polarized this time. Many in Ontario saw the Rebellion as a determined effort to impose the French language and culture on what should be English Canada's western preserve. Facing overwhelming odds, including eight thousand men, artillery, and machine-guns, Riel's forces were easily defeated at Batoche. This time there was no pretence that the military expedition was not punitive. Métis communities and farms were looted and burned, and the population was dispersed westward and northward. Riel surrendered, was taken to Regina, tried before an English and Protestant jury, found guilty of high treason and condemned to death despite the jury's recommendation for mercy.

With the death sentence pronounced, the national debate between Orange and English Ontario and French and Catholic Quebec became intense and bitter. Many Québécois now saw Riel as a potential martyr on an equal footing perhaps with Joan of Arc, certainly with the Patriotes of 1837–38 who went to the scaffold. The Québécois demanded virtually with one voice that Riel be pardoned. English Ontario saw him as a twice-over traitor who must not be allowed to escape the noose again.

Macdonald played his usual double game, but in the end he had to make a decision amid a great deal of political pressure and turmoil, some of which had spilled from the editorial pages and the meeting halls onto the streets in minor riots. If Macdonald agreed to allow Riel to hang, he risked his loyal Conservative base in Quebec. On the other hand, given the intensity of passions aroused in Ontario, if Macdonald agreed to pardon Riel he risked his base in Ontario and perhaps in the rest of English Canada. Reasoning that he had survived the 1869 Red River controversy and that nationalist passions in Quebec usually died down with time, Macdonald decided to yield to Ontario. There is no doubt that Macdonald personally preferred that course. His preference was revealed in a remark that has echoed through the pages of Canadian history ever since: "He shall hang though every dog in Quebec bark in his favour." And so, on 16 November 1885 Riel was hanged. Macdonald seriously miscalculated this time, for the bark of Québécois nationalism turned out to have a serious bite indeed. The hanging of Riel, and the bitter division between Québécois and English Canadians created by that sorry event, resulted in the rise of a Québécois nationalism strong enough both to defeat the Conservative provincial government in Quebec, and, ultimately, to ruin the federal Conservative party in Quebec for almost a hundred years.

The message to Quebec was obvious. The Québécois nation could play no significant role in westward expansion. The West belonged to English Canada. The Québécois had earlier made some symbolic, even practical, gains, thanks to the apparent victory at Red River. French and English were made official languages in Manitoba in 1870, and in the North-West Territory in 1875. In the aftermath of the 1885 Rebellion and Riel's execution, these gains were quickly and unconstitutionally erased. In 1890 the Manitoba legislature declared that French was no longer an official language, and in 1892 the North-West Territory legislature followed suit. In 1912, French was eliminated from public education in Ontario. In 1916, after a series of crises and unsatisfactory compromises, Manitoba abolished French, or any language other than English, in that province's schools.

From the defeat of Riel in 1885 until the Quiet Revolution of the 1960s, enormous impediments were thus put in the way of those francophones in English Canada who wished to retain their language and to educate their children in French. It was in this period that the incredible and moving stories of the Québécois diaspora outside Quebec emerged, stories of assimilation, ridicule, prejudice, and discrimination — even of training children to hide their French texts when the education inspectors came to town. In Quebec, by contrast, the English minority enjoyed enormous privileges. The message that the Québécois were unwelcome in Confederation if they ventured outside of Quebec was taken to heart by the Québécois. At the turn of the century, just over 7,000 francophones resided in Saskatchewan and Alberta, which had a total population of 165,000. Another 16,000 could be found among Manitoba's population of 255,000 and 5,000 among B.C.'s population of 179,000. In other words, from the western border of Ontario to the Pacific, at the height of the western settlement boom, there were fewer than 30,000 francophones in a total population of approximately 600,000. Among those deciding to seek their futures outside of Quebec, few came to the western frontier where they were obviously not wanted, while more than 500,000 immigrated to the U.S. Had this population remained in Canada, Canada would today have in excess of six million more francophones. One cannot help wondering how different Canada might have been today had this tidal wave of Québécois come west. There is no doubt that Canada would have become an entirely different country. But that, of course, is the point. English-Canadian opinion in Ontario was determined that Canada could never be allowed to become such a place.

It should be understood clearly that the Québécois nation backed down from the immediate confrontation over the 1885 Rebellion and Riel's fate. Many historians express admiration for this statesmanlike behaviour, as well as for Québécois reasonableness over the subsequent suppression of French-language rights outside Quebec. Had Québécois political leaders pushed the issue further, the very foundations of Confederation might have broken asunder just before success began with the 1896 Wheat Boom. It was clear to the Québécois that English Ontario had no intention of backing down. But was their behaviour an act of statesmanship, or was it a frank recognition of yet another defeat? Conquered in 1759, reconquered in 1837–38, having had the apparent Red River victory turned into defeat, and then having been defeated by proxy in 1885, the Québécois nation again retreated into a degree of passivity.

Ontario had carried the day. The Confederation project, including the development of the cherished western frontier, would proceed on Ontario's terms without any significant compromise. Though the national pride and sensibilities of the Québécois had again been wounded and a more aggressive nationalism had briefly stirred, the Québécois nation remained locked up in Quebec, deliberately isolated from Confederation's western realization. Across English Canada the mocking stereotypes of the Québécois held sway, and within Quebec the population played the passive role of captive market and source of cheap labour, overseen by English-Canadian economic masters, as wave upon wave of British and then Eastern European immigrants passed through the Québécois national enclave on the St. Lawrence. Yet, it was also self-evident that the Québécois nation had to be handled with care. If the events of 1837–38, 1869–70, and 1885 proved anything, they proved that there were limits to the endurance of the Québécois, limits that English Canada transgressed at the peril of keeping Confederation intact. During the conscription crises of World Wars I and II, the limits of that endurance were again tested significantly by English Canada. By far the most serious crisis of the two was that of World War I.

When Great Britain declared war on Germany in August 1914, Canada, as a loyal dominion in the British Empire, was automatically at war as well. It may seem incredible that a nation could go to war without a decision of its people or their representative institutions, but the war was completely, even enthusiastically, accepted by English Canada. Among the Québécois, there was no such enthusiasm. Nationalists in Quebec had long attacked British imperialism and warned that Canada would be dragged into distant wars Canada had no tangible reason to fight. Ever since the Boer War, Québécois nationalists had taken the position that the Québécois should eagerly share the burden in dollars and blood of defending Canada but absolutely oppose fighting British wars of imperialism. Rather than enthusiasm, then, the Québécois accepted Canada's role in World War I with resignation, insisting that fighting in the war remain voluntary and that Canada not jeopardize the national treasury. Resigned to their isolation and exclusion, yet still annoyed over the loss of French education in Ontario, and even more annoyed by Manitoba's English-only education decision in 1916, the Québécois made it clear that military service by conscription could not be imposed on the Québécois and that if it were attempted, it would not be tolerated.

The glorious "war to end all wars," which many expected to be over by spring of 1915, dragged on and on into a bloody stalemate, and the new industrial techniques of mass war combined with the military tradition of fighting from fixed positions to produce staggering casualties. The demand for fresh troops to be fed into the European meat-grinder could not be met by voluntary recruitment, despite the government's information campaign, which combined censorship to hide the truth of what was happening with a duplicitous propaganda effort. From the beginning, the Québécois had not been eager to enlist, and that resistance grew as the war continued. Even in English Canada, where early efforts at voluntary recruitment had been quite successful, eagerness subsided, especially as the truth trickled home from the trenches to families of men undergoing the horror. Criticism of the war was not then limited to Quebec. Québécois voices of dissent were joined by those from farm and labour movements in English Canada, especially in the West. Though English Canada was divided, the loudest clamour still came from those supporting the war, and they increasingly began to point an accusing finger at Quebec for not carrying its fair share.

In this context, Prime Minister Robert Borden approached what he viewed as the need for conscription gingerly, aware that the Tory government could go down to defeat on the issue. He therefore first tried to make the recruitment effort more effective, but he declared that he would move to conscription if necessary in order to raise sufficient troops to fulfil Canada's commitments. In 1917, after voluntary recruitment had failed to reach acceptable levels, Borden decided to institute conscription. Acutely aware of the anger his action would provoke in Quebec, Borden approached Wilfrid Laurier to join a coalition government in order to prosecute the war effort. Laurier refused and Borden then approached members of the English-Canadian wing of the Liberal Party, most of whom joined him in the Union government. Though Parliament passed the conscription measure, serious implementation awaited an election on the issue. Deeply uncertain of victory, given both Québécois and growing English-Canadian opposition, the Union government passed *The Military Voter's Act* and *The War Time Elections Act* just before calling the 1917 election.

The first law gave the vote to all those in the armed forces, including women (who as a group did not yet have the vote), without any residency or citizenship requirements. Leaving nothing to chance, the military ballots were cast simply for or against the Union government and not for candidates. Furthermore, if the military voter did not designate his or her home constituency, the vote was assigned by the elections officer. The second law gave the vote to all female relatives of persons in the armed services, including wives, mothers, daughters, and sisters. Even Borden did not dare include grandmothers, female cousins, sisters-in-law, and mothers-in-law. Furthermore, the law took the vote away from conscientious war objectors and all immigrants from enemy countries who had come to Canada since 1902. As the election campaign came to a close, Borden was still worried about continuing farmer opposition. Just two weeks before the vote, the cabinet issued an order-in-council exempting farmers' sons from conscription. Taken together, these efforts were probably the most comprehensive (and perfectly legal) attempt to fix or steal an election in Canadian history.

It worked. The Union government won an overwhelming victory, 153 seats to 82 with a popular vote of 57 per cent. English Canada delivered massively: 12 of 16 seats in Nova Scotia; 7 of 11 in New Brunswick; 74 of 82 in Ontario; 14 of 15 in Manitoba; all 16 in Saskatchewan; and all 13 in British Columbia. In Quebec the results were quite different. The Québécois gave 62 of 65 seats to Laurier with 73 per cent of the vote, and the 3 seats that went to Borden were English-speaking. But the actual vote was closer than it appears. Just under 320,000 votes separated the Union government and Laurier's anti-conscription Liberals. Of this victory margin, 200,000 came from the military vote and only 100,000 from the civilian vote. Had *The Military Voters Act*, *The Wartime Elections Act*, and the last-minute exemption of farmers' sons (which was withdrawn the following spring) not been put in place, the Union government might well have either gone down to defeat or achieved such a narrow majority that Borden could not have proceeded the way he did without risking losing the confidence of the House of Commons.

The Union government's efforts to impose conscription on the Québécois were a monumental disaster. The mood of the Québécois had been made clear when the bill was first introduced and passed: virtually the entire Québécois press opposed the measure; opponents carried out a massive lobby effort; protest rallies were held; the home of the pro-conscription owner of the Montreal *Star* was bombed; and serious rioting occurred in Montreal. And in January 1918, on the heels of the Union victory, a

Québécois member of Quebec's National Assembly introduced a motion offering to separate from Canada if English Canada found Quebec's presence distasteful. The motion was short and blunt: "That this House is of the opinion that the province of Quebec would be disposed to accept the breaking of the Confederation Pact of 1867, if in the other provinces it is believed that she is an obstacle to the unity, progress and development of Canada." The motion provoked a lively debate and received a lot of headlines, but it was withdrawn before a vote was taken. Clearly, the purpose of the motion was to warn English Canada just how serious the situation had become.

The Union government failed to heed the warning and proceeded to implement the law. In defiant response, the Québécois engaged in a mass resistance to it. Local boards granted wholesale exemptions. Draft dodging and aiding draft dodgers became nearly universal. Deserters fled to the United States. Even the Quebec legal system could not be counted on for systematic enforcement. The situation became an ugly confrontation between an English-Canadian government with no Québécois representation, a government that furthermore appeared to have rigged an election and that therefore had little democratic or moral legitimacy, and the Québécois nation. Never had the divisions been so deep since 1837. The Union government, under relentless pressure from English Canada, was determined to impose the law of the land upon the Québécois. The Québécois were just as determined to defy it.

Matters came to a head in Quebec City on Easter weekend, 1918. On the evening of 29 March, Dominion Police officers detained a Québécois on the street, and when he could not produce his draft exemption papers, briefly arrested him and took him to his home, where the proper papers were produced. However, his public arrest was the spark for bloody rioting, which lasted until 2 April. The crowds burned a police station, vandalized a newspaper, and stormed and burned the office of the registrar of *The Military Service Act*. The police asked for military help. Martial law was declared. In an act of abysmal stupidity, or of deliberate provocation, a battalion of English-Canadian soldiers from Toronto was sent to relieve the civil authorities. Their clumsy and brutal efforts to contain the crowds — including bayonet charges and mounted attacks using axe handles as clubs — were completely unsuccessful and served only further to enrage the local population. On the evening of 1 April, the military authorities claimed that the troops had been fired on by snipers, and they responded with rifle and machine-gun fire. Others claim the troops fired on an unarmed crowd. In all, five civilians were killed, a great many were wounded, and scores were placed under military arrest without bail. The authorities produced four wounded soldiers, which suggests that the snipers, if there had indeed been any, were remarkably bad shots. At an inquiry, a local jury laid the entire blame for the incident at the feet of the authorities.

The situation was reduced to a stalemate after the Easter riot. The Union government refrained from enforcing the law too vigorously, and the Québécois continued their passive resistance. When all special exemptions from the draft were withdrawn later that month, rioting and draft resistance became significant in English Canada. Then refraining from a zealous enforcement of the law seemed an even wiser course for the government to pursue. Furthermore, as the war began to turn in the Allies' favour and the end came in sight, the only effect of enforcing conscription would have been to create an even deeper cleavage between Quebec and English Canada. By the end of the war, English Canada could only claim a partial victory over Québécois war resistance. About the same number of Québécois — nineteen thousand — submitted to conscription as resisted it. The Québécois nation had a chance to pass judgement on conscription in the 1919 provincial election when the Quebec Tories won only five seats with less than 24 per cent of the vote, the lowest *Bleu* vote since Confederation. And in the 1921 federal election, the Québécois gave all sixty-five seats and over 70 per cent of the vote to the Liberals, entirely shutting out the Tories.

The World War II conscription crisis was much less serious, but it again revealed the deep chasm between English Canada and Quebec. When Canada's Parliament declared war, Prime Minster Mackenzie King, remembering Quebec and World War I, made an early promise that no Canadian would be conscripted for the war effort and that Canada would focus on supplying war material and equipment rather than cannon fodder. This promise mollified Quebec, and the provincial Liberals actually defeated the Union Nationale when Duplessis called an election to criticize Canada's involvement in the war. But King's position did not please English Canada — or Canada's allies. As the war continued to go badly, with victory after victory by Germany, and particularly after Japan entered the war with stunning success at Pearl Harbor, pressure for conscription mounted. In fact, English

Canada clamoured for conscription. But the Québécois made equally clear their determination to resist it. The King government tried to extricate itself by holding a plebiscite asking the Canadian electorate to release the government from its no conscription promise. English Canada said "yes" with a resounding 80 per cent. Quebec said "no" with an equally resounding 73 per cent. The stage was again set for an ugly confrontation. King, however, adroitly implemented his "conscription if necessary, but not necessarily conscription" compromise. There would be conscription, he said, but no one who did not volunteer would be sent overseas to combat. Those who were conscripted for home defence and refused to volunteer for overseas service became know as "zombies," a term that did not sit well with the Québécois. Even though the King government later reneged and repealed the measure limiting overseas service to volunteers, the practice of sending only volunteers overseas largely continued. Nevertheless, the holding of the plebiscite and the breaking of the no conscription vow, led directly to the re-election of Duplessis and the Union Nationale in the 1944 Quebec election. Only military victory in 1945 and the fact that the federal Tories were now totally unpalatable to the Québécois saved King from a similar fate in the federal election of 1945.

By the end of the era of the world wars, Québécois nationalism had changed considerably, but it remained largely divided between two great ideological streams. One stream, which adhered more or less to the Liberal Party, argued that Quebec should seek to affect the Canadian identity in ways that pulled it away from the British Tory tradition in order to achieve a more significant place for the Québécois in Canadian national life through the positive use of the Québécois presence in federal institutions. At the same time, this group held, the Québécois should sustain and develop their unique cultural and linguistic identity as a small nation within the larger one. The larger nation of Canada, which included both Québécois and British traditions, should develop a unique Canadian nationalism, simultaneously incorporating both traditions and accommodating the inevitable divergences when they occurred. This stream, though federalist, could still be fiercely and assertively nationalist when confronted by threats to the Québécois nation and its cultural and linguistic life.

The other stream of Québécois nationalism remained largely turned inward on itself and its political enclave in Quebec. It was more intensely nationalistic and viewed the Québécois role in Canadian federal institutions merely as one of protecting Quebec from encroachments by English Canada. In a sense, federal institutions were seen as agencies that could be used when necessary, but not as ones to be embraced positively. There was no commitment to an effort to build a unique Canadian nationalism blending British and Québécois traditions. Such a project was seen either as an illusory fool's paradise or as a dangerous trap that would lead to assimilation. The proper nationalist project was to defend and sustain the Québécois nation and to take every opportunity to empower it further. This stream was further divided into a variety of smaller tendencies, ranging all the way from a right-wing, ultra-religious nationalist tradition to varieties of progressive and anti-clerical nationalism. The conservative stream tended toward a defensive strategy, rooted largely in fond remembrances of the past, reacting aggressively only to attacks and outrages on national sensibilities. The more progressive stream tended toward a more assertive and aggressive nationalism, advocating programs of modernization and sometimes of radical social change.

Despite the obvious and often bitter divisions, there was a basic core of beliefs that united the entire Québécois nation, whether federalist/nationalist or nationalist. The Québécois people were a nation whose political and constitutional home was Quebec. That nation had experienced forms of oppression at the hands of the English-Canadian nation, and such oppression had to be resisted. Above all, the Québécois nation had to survive and its institutions, if they were changed, had to be changed according to the Québécois' own desires. Changes could never be imposed by English Canada. And, however federal institutions were used, they should never be used to violate the integrity of the Québécois nation. The Québécois presence in federal institutions had to be used to prevent violations from happening. Typically, the Québécois supported the strongly nationalist stream in provincial elections and the federalist/nationalist option in federal elections, a shrewdly effective hedging of bets.

English Canada was also changing. The British Tory traditions were dying, slowly, perhaps too slowly, as the old generations died off, and many of the traditional British myths died with them. Furthermore, many English Canadians reacted defensively to longstanding Québécois nationalist claims that the Québécois nation was the only true Canadian nation firmly and uniquely rooted in Canada and that English-Canadian nationalism, such as it was, was overly devoted to the British connection and sustained itself too often by anti-Quebec posturing. Finally, as non-Anglo-Saxon immigrants streamed into Canada, especially into the West, the British flavour of English Canada was increasingly diluted as subtle, sometimes even dramatic, modifications of the "Canadian identity" began to occur.

Whether it was the demand for a separate seat at Versailles after World War I, or the winning of a separate seat at the League of Nations, or the establishment of an independent foreign policy after 1922, or the achievement of true legislative independence with the *Statute of Westminster*, or the independent declaration of war in 1939, or the attraction to the Red Ensign over the Union Jack, English Canada was evolving — slowly and reluctantly from the point of view of the Québécois — toward a sense of identity incrementally separate from its British roots. In the past, English-Canadian nationalism had shown only brief episodes of an intense sense of unity of purpose, usually as a negative reaction, sometimes against a real or perceived external American threat, more often against a perceived and exaggerated Québécois threat. That negative feature of English-Canadian nationalism was slowly disappearing and being replaced more and more by an open, frank, even naive search for a new sense of national purpose. As a result, when the Québécois nation once again asserted itself, English Canada's reaction was more ambivalent than before, swinging from openness and sympathy, on some occasions, to the old hostility and anger, on others, but always in the context of a willingness to accommodate Québécois nationalism to an extent unthinkable in the past.

4

The Quiet Revolution

From 1936 to 1939 and 1944 to 1959, conservative Union Nationale premier Maurice Duplessis governed Quebec through a close alliance with the English business establishment and the Catholic Church. It was a period in Quebec's history marked by patronage, corruption, and the manipulation of anti-communist hysteria to justify the repression of trade unions, movements for reform, and progressive ideas. Consequently, in Quebec, the period became known as *La Grande Noirceur* — the Great Darkness. The end of the darkness and the beginning of *La Révolution Tranquille* — the Quiet Revolution — is marked by the death of Duplessis in 1959 and the election of Liberal premier Jean Lesage in 1960. These events, however, were merely external confirmations of long developing social and economic changes that would have inevitably burst through. While conservative Québécois nationalism had continued to dominate the province's politics under Duplessis, it was a doomed domination based on resisting disquieting changes the ideology could neither understand nor ultimately control. In fact, the 1960 victory of Jean Lesage, and of his leading minister René Lévesque, merely accelerated the long overdue transformation of Quebec.

Between Confederation and World War I investors were primarily attracted to Quebec by its copious supply of cheap labour and its large market. Consequently, much of Quebec's industrial development was labour intensive and heavily dependent on low wage costs. This relatively narrow industrial sector co-existed with a large and backward rural economy rooted in a small-holding, inefficient agriculture. After World War I Quebec was suddenly thrust into the modern era by a rapid industrialization based on the discovery of important new resources — copper, pulp, iron, asbestos, chemicals — and the development of an apparently endless supply of cheap hydro-electric power. These developments were less dependent on cheap labour, more on cheaply available natural resources. Indeed, the modern industrial sector tended to be capital intensive, using advanced technologies that required skilled rather than unskilled labour. The speed of change was breathtaking with, for example, industrial employment during the single decade of World War II growing by the same amount as it had during the previous century.

After World War II the dual trends of industrialization and urbanization totally transformed Quebec, laying the material basis for the Quiet Revolution. The rural farm population that had comprised 41 per cent of all Québécois in 1941, plummeted to 13 per cent in 1961, while urban dwellers went from 55 to 71 per cent. This dramatic change, coupled with very large natural population increases during the 1940s and 1950s, resulted in the rapid emergence of an entirely new way of life for the Québécois nation. Conservative Québécois nationalism still faced firmly backwards, nostalgically regretting a disappearing past, and remained rooted in a rural way of life remote from the concrete experience of a whole new generation.

One of the consequences of rapid urbanization was the reconquest of Montreal by the Québécois. After the Conquest in 1759, Montreal became the centre of the English minority, and for a time in the nineteenth century the English even outnumbered the Québécois in the city. Even in the 1950s, almost one in four Montrealers was English, and the centre of the great city, dominated by English cultural and business institutions, remained essentially English-Canadian. By the 1960s, with the rapid urbanization of the Québécois, the English share of Montreal's population had declined to under one in five, and it was continuing to fall. Nevertheless, the tendency to Québécois cultural dominance, including accepting French as the language of city life, was still successfully resisted by the English minority. It is not, therefore, surprising that Montreal became and remains the focus of the contest between the new assertive nationalism of the Québécois and English-Canadian resistance. The English-Canadian minority of Montreal was, if you like, English Canada's cultural and economic garrison in the heart of a conquered Quebec. And that garrison became increasingly beleaguered, first materially, then intellectually and culturally and, finally, politically.

Initially, however, it was among the Québécois themselves in Montreal that the soil was tilled for the Quiet Revolution. Since Montreal was the emerging centre of gravity of the new Quebec, the intellectual ferment there was greater than elsewhere, if only because of the ever-present weight of the English fact. But the ferment reached out and touched the Québécois everywhere, even those in the diaspora. In one sense, it was a replay of an old scenario, whose issues remained the common themes of Québécois nationalism since Papineau and before. How shall the nation be preserved as an island in a continental sea of English speakers? How shall the nation affirm itself, grow, and change to meet the new challenges of modernization? How shall the nation best deal with English Canada and Ottawa: confrontation? accommodation?

Increasingly, this intellectual ferment achieved a certain uneasy but clear consensus. The Duplessis mixture of manipulative, right-wing, and paranoid nationalism, relying on patronage, corruption, and the cultivated ignorance of the masses, had to be swept away. The new trade unions, locked in a fierce battle with English and/or American bosses backed by the Duplessis regime, had to be supported in their bitter struggle. The Catholic Church, which held a central position in the conservative power bloc and which intruded heavily on daily life, had to be trimmed, tamed, set aside, and directed to focus on spiritual concerns, leaving worldly power and administration to democratic and secular forces. Quebec had to catch up quickly if the Québécois nation was to determine its future effectively. Beyond that, there was much disagreement.

At first, the debate was between the new nationalism, reflected in *Le Devoir*, and the new liberalism, reflected in *Cité Libre*. Though they shared a common political foe in Duplessis and conservative nationalism and a common project in bringing Quebec society into the modern era, they disagreed deeply on ideology, methods, and ultimate objectives. The new nationalism argued that Quebec had to be secularized, modernized, and democratized but that the objective of the reform program also had to be to win and consolidate Québécois power in Quebec, to make French the working language of life in all public spheres in Quebec, and to shape the provincial state into a modern political and constitutional tool for the Québécois nation. The new liberalism opposed nationalism, whether in its backward Duplessis guise or in its modern, enlightened guise. In the process of modernization, secularization, and democratization, liberalism argued, Quebec must abandon and reject the nationalist project and substitute concepts of individual and social rights for those of national collective rights.

Both nationalists and liberals wanted to construct and use an interventionist and technocratic provincial state. But the nationalists insisted that the state must always serve the nation in the task of progress and nation-building. The two streams also divided deeply on the correct approach to federalism and Quebec's place in Confederation. The new nationalism argued that the Quebec provincial government apparatus had to be used, as nationalists had always maintained, as an instrument to protect and to enhance the place of the Québécois in the federal system. Thus, they insisted that, given its unique role as the political and constitutional home and political instrument of the Québécois nation, Quebec had to strive to win increased powers from Ottawa, particularly fiscal, social, and cultural powers. The new liberalism did not see the need for new or enhanced powers and appeared content to argue that existing arrangements, coupled with a flexible and reasonable government in Ottawa, were sufficient for Quebec's assured future.

These, of course, were the polar streams, and many tried to bridge the gap, wanting to serve both masters. Indeed, Jean Lesage and the Quebec Liberal Party made an effort to do so. In fact, in its first phase, the Quiet Revolution was very much a successful effort to create a hybrid of liberalism and nationalism, a hybrid that took much more from the new nationalism than from the new liberalism. As events unfolded these two dominant streams divided into three, each represented by one of the leading politicians of the era. René Lévesque became the most prominent advocate of the new nationalism. In the face of an unyielding federalism, he believed that some form of sovereignty was essential for the Québécois nation. Robert Bourassa became the leading advocate of Quebec liberalism. He sought special status and significantly increased powers for Quebec within the federal system. Pierre Trudeau became the symbol of an uncompromising federalism determined to block the inevitable secessionary tendencies of the newly aroused and progressive Québécois nationalism. The three men began their careers as friends and colleagues who met together in intense face-to-face debates in countless kitchens and living rooms during the early phase of the Quiet Revolution. At the end of the process, they had become bitter political foes.

In 1960 Lesage and the Liberal Party campaigned on the slogan *"C'est le temps que ça change!"* There were few across Canada who did not applaud his victory in 1960 — the Duplessis regime had come to epitomize corruption and extreme reaction; it was an embarrassing relic from the past. Indeed, many English Canadians were smug about the Duplessis era. That the Québécois would tolerate and continue to elect such a government could be cited not only as evidence of the backwardness of the entire population but also as further confirmation of the dangers of Québécois nationalism. What Lesage appeared to propose seemed self-evidently good and necessary — reform, modernization, catch-up, the integration of Quebec into the mainstream of modern Canada. What followed, however, was less reassuring.

During its first brief term from 1960 to 1962, the Lesage government took the obvious reform steps, many of which had begun during Paul Sauvé's Union Nationale government. Most of the program amounted simply to beginning to provide in Quebec what were considered normal government services across English Canada in areas like health, education, labour law, social welfare. Then, in 1962, under the influence of nationalists like René Lévesque, who was minister of natural resources, and Paul Gérin-Lajoie, who was attorney-general, Lesage successfully sought a new and stronger mandate, using the more dramatic slogan, *"Maîtres chez nous!"* This slogan, and the palpable quickening of the Quiet Revolution, were more disturbing to English Canada. For the Québécois to want obviously needed changes to catch up to the rest of the country was one thing, but for them to want to be masters in their own home, whatever that meant, was quite another.

Gérin-Lajoie pushed a more aggressive line for Quebec in constitutional matters, seeking what was in effect "special status" in a variety of areas as well as the right to enjoy international recognition and representation, particularly in areas of exclusive provincial jurisdiction. Lévesque ardently pushed the need for the Quebec state to become more interventionist on behalf of the Québécois nation, advocating the nationalization of the Quebec power industry and the establishment of Hydro-Québec as a crown corporation. This proposal in fact became the central issue in the 1962 election. Furious and enraged at the paternalistic attitude of the many English Canadians who believed that the Québécois lacked the necessary skills and qualifications to do the top jobs, Lévesque was determined to use Hydro-Québec as a model of what the Québécois could accomplish if they had the necessary powers. Lévesque also pressed the idea of special status for Quebec, going so far as to propose that Quebec be granted the status of "associate state" in Confederation. There was no doubt that the decisive 1962 victory of the Lesage Liberals confirmed an overwhelming desire among the Québécois both to get on with, and to speed up, the Quiet Revolution.

"Maîtres chez nous!" enjoyed a variety of meanings in Quebec. At a minimum, the slogan called for a cultural and linguistic revolution to bring the Québécois a real sense of cultural and linguistic domination in the daily life of the province. This was reflected in an enormous proliferation of the arts and letters, cinema and drama, and a push to make French the language of work and common usage. This cultural and linguistic revolution had a couple of false starts during the Duplessis regime. Back in 1937, Duplessis' Union Nationale government passed a law officially making French the pre-eminent language in the province's legislation and administration. In 1938, under pressure from the English lobby, he backed off. Though they were fearful that the move might be misinterpreted as secessionary in English Canada, the Union Nationale also adopted the *fleur-de-lis* as the official flag of Quebec, a nice gesture. But Duplessis had not been a true friend of Québécois culture, certainly not in its progressive and secular manifestation. In contrast, during the Quiet Revolution, the Lesage administration supported the flowering of Québécois culture as no regime ever had, and the provincial government's efforts to make French the language of business and government, as well as of cultural life, resulted in a surprisingly aggressive assertion of the French reality in Quebec.

But the meaning and implications of the slogan quickly began to expand. Lévesque and other nationalists in the Lesage government interpreted the slogan as meaning that Québécois mastery in Quebec had to extend beyond culture and language into both the economy and Quebec's place in the federal system. The state had to become an instrument to build Québécois economic power and influence from the bottom to the top. It had to be used as an instrument to achieve social and economic justice for the Québécois, which meant inevitably that the state had to be used to attack and dismantle the two-hundred-year-old structure of English privilege in Quebec. Furthermore, the state had to be used to defend Quebec from unwarranted intrusions of federal power into the national life of the Québécois. This expanded meaning of *"Maîtres chez nous,"* more and more shared among the Québécois, was enormously disquieting to the English establishment, both within and outside Quebec.

It is not surprising that the speed of change and the growing dominance of Québécois nationalism led to an explosion of expectations among the Québécois. By 1964, in terms of the modernization of the programs and infrastructures in health, education, and social policy, Quebec had more or less caught up with English Canada. But the Québécois had not caught up economically. The new labour law, the most progressive and pro-labour in Canada, extended the right to strike to the public sector and provided an important means for catching up. During the period from 1964 to 1966, Quebec was hit by an astonishing wave of labour militancy. Strikes by taxi drivers, police, postal workers, engineers at Hydro-Québec, teachers, hospital workers, and civil servants rocked the province. For example, in 1964 just over four hundred thousand person days were lost as a result of strikes. In 1966 this figure approached two million. Everywhere the demands were the same — income parity with English-speaking equivalents in Canada (usually in Ontario). In the case of the taxi strike, the demand was that the airport monopoly be taken away from the English firm, Murray Hill. For more and more among the Québécois, *"Maîtres chez nous"* meant nothing less than economic equality with English Canadians and an end to the system of English privilege in Quebec.

Nationalists frequently evoked the image of Quebec as a colony of English Canada. And reality suggested the image was apt. The Québécois nation was confined in a federal system that prevented self-determination and imposed constraints according to the will of English Canada. The system treated the Québécois as second-class citizens economically and gave them fewer opportunities and lower incomes than English Canadians. The Québécois language and culture were confined, suppressed, and marginalized. Most telling, of course, was that in Quebec itself a small, powerful English minority enjoyed enormous privileges — economic, political, and cultural — while the Quebécois majority languished at the bottom of the heap. It was not surprising that Québécois nationalists often compared Quebec to Rhodesia, where a tiny English white minority ruled an overwhelming majority of blacks. Nor was it surprising that leading Front de Libération du Québec (FLQ) intellectual Pierre Vallières wrote a best-seller entitled *Nègres blancs d'Amérique.*

The emergence of the Front de Libération du Québec further provoked growing English-Canadian anxiety. In 1963, the FLQ commenced a terrorist campaign of bank robberies (called "voluntary taxes"), armoury raids, and bombings. The campaign began in 1963 with the bombing of the Wolfe monument in Quebec City and stretched over six or seven years. The targets were carefully selected symbols of English privilege, English political and/or economic power, and the federal presence in Quebec. Westmount, a wealthy English residential neighbourhood, and McGill and Loyola, English universities, were targeted because they represented privilege. Eaton's and the Montreal Stock Exchange were selected as bastions of English economic power. Federal targets included various military and paramilitary headquarters (the buildings housing the Army recruiting office, the RCMP, the Black Watch Regiment, the Canadian Army office, the Ministry of Defence), and other symbols of Ottawa's power (the National Revenue building and CNR headquarters). In addition to the Wolfe monument, a monument to Queen Victoria and the office of the Queen's Printer were also hit. Though the objective of the bombings was clearly symbolic, six lives were tragically lost during the campaign. These events increased the tensions caused by the wave of strikes and the almost routine occurrence of large and small demonstrations. Taken together, they profoundly disturbed English Canada. To many it appeared that changes they had warmly supported in 1960 were getting out of control, heading in unforeseen and undesirable directions.

Nevertheless, the reaction in English Canada remained ambivalent, and feelings often cleaved along generational lines. Among the younger generation, particularly those touched by the growing radicalism of the 1960s, there was a great deal of openness and support for what was happening in Quebec. Increasingly critical of the establishment, its old ways and outdated attitudes and symbols, many young English Canadians enthusiastically endorsed Quebec's right to special status and ultimately to self-determination. Within the older generation, especially among those supportive of tradition and the establishment, there was confusion. For many, their old hatred of the Québécois was rekindled. Yet many of the strongest voices defending Quebec were English. English Canada, therefore, from the outset of the Quiet Revolution was seriously split. Gone were the days when English Canada spoke to Quebec with a unified and implacable voice. Rather, Quebec received mixed messages.

Prime Minister John Diefenbaker seemed to have won the forgiveness of the Québécois for past Tory sins when he swept the country in 1958. In some ways, the Quiet Revolution was initially seen merely as the Quebec reflection of the mood for change igniting the entire country. In Quebec, the Diefenbaker landslide included fifty of the seventy-five seats with 50 per cent of the popular vote. This was a remarkable achievement compared to the dismal Tory showings in the five previous elections, which ranged from one seat and 20 per cent of the vote in 1940, up to a meagre nine seats and 31 per cent of the vote in 1957. But Diefenbaker neither understood nor responded effectively to the Quiet Revolution. Some of his well-intentioned gestures only exacerbated the situation and made the Québécois angrier. In 1958, for example, his government introduced simultaneous translation in the House of Commons, a sensible and long overdue measure. But this was hardly *un beau geste*, since it called attention to the fact that for almost a hundred years the two solitudes of Canada had made speeches to each other that neither understood. Most members of Parliament on both sides of the language barrier were unilingual, and it seemed bizarre that no federal government had ever set up translation services. Quebec saw it as a reaffirmation of a basic truth — Quebec's voice, on most national issues, was irrelevant when English Canada's Parliament made decisions. The 1962 decision to issue all federal cheques in both languages was again perceived as more of an insult than anything else in Quebec — as if bilingual cheques addressed the issues raised by the Quiet Revolution!

While Diefenbaker was preoccupied with his "Northern Vision," events in Quebec were showing that Canada would be made or unmade there and not in the north. Diefenbaker never understood this at the time — or during the rest of his political life, when he continued to rage and fume from the Opposition benches. And it was the Québécois, who had embraced him so warmly in 1958, who sent him firmly into Opposition in 1963. He never forgave Quebec, constantly attacking the aspirations of the Québécois, in a vendetta that shredded his own party when he fought the "two nations" concept without compromise. In 1958 Quebec — and the rest of Canada — had given Diefenbaker a great opportunity to move the nation forward in new ways by bestowing on him the greatest measure of trust ever given to a prime minister. Sadly, Diefenbaker squandered this opportunity. Even more sadly, he never realized that such an opportunity had been thrust into his hands. He went to his grave without remorse, without regret, without any doubt, firm in his conviction that he had stayed the course for the cause, deluded that the masses loved him deeply, unaware that in Quebec he had become a laughing stock.

Liberal prime minister Lester Pearson, in contrast to Diefenbaker, was well aware of the depth of the crisis Canada had entered as a result of developments in Quebec. Having won his first minority government in 1963 thanks largely to Quebec, Pearson knew that both his future as prime minister and Canada's future as an intact federation depended on more effectively winning the hearts and minds of the Québécois. His regime took steps to deal with Quebec that were denounced on both sides at the time — in Quebec as much too little and much too late and in English Canada as much too soft. As a result, these measures took considerable political courage. But the overwhelming *raisons d'état* always weighed heavily on Pearson — if Ottawa did not do something and only replaced Diefenbaker's policy of hostile indecision with one of friendly indecision, then events in Quebec could spiral out of control. Above all, if Canada were to survive, the federal state had to act decisively, or at least appear to act decisively. And any such actions had to be sufficient to produce two almost contradictory results: to begin to win over English Canada to the need for accommodation and a willingness to yield and to convince the Québécois that real change and accommodation were possible within Confederation.

In 1963 the Pearson government established the Royal Commission on Bilingualism and Biculturalism (the B and B Commission), whose interim report in 1965 asserted that Canada was in the midst of "the greatest crisis in its history." The basic premise of the inquiry was politically courageous and will endure as a major feature of Pearson's legacy. The commission was directed to base its recommendations on the controversial doctrine of Confederation as "an equal partnership between the two founding races." For the Pearson government this move not only provided needed temporary breathing space but also ensured that the eventual recommendations would focus on seeking a significant accommodation with the Québécois. Convinced that pro-federalist elements in the new Quebec had to be co-opted into national leadership to replace the traditional old Liberal guard in Quebec, Pearson persuaded three leading Quebec personalities to join his government: the intellectuals Pierre Trudeau and Gérard Pelletier and the prominent labour leader Jean Marchand. Then, as a significant linguistic concession, in 1964 the Pearson regime directed the federal civil service to launch an ambitious French- and English-language training program. Further gestures were made to Quebec. It was allowed to opt out of the 1964 Canada Pension Plan, retaining control of pension funds as part of the Quiet Revolution's strategy of economic development and empowerment. (By 1996 the resulting Caisse de dépôt et placement du Québec controlled a $51-billion pool of capital.) The decision was also taken to drop the Red Ensign in favour of the present flag.

Armed with these moves — some substantial, others symbolic — and amid a growing uneasiness and anger among traditional English Canadians, Pearson, more desperate than hopeful that he would receive a majority, called an election in 1965. The "three wise men" from Quebec agreed to run and were promised cabinet posts. Pearson asked Canadians to give him the majority mandate he needed to finish the tasks he had begun, both in the reform and expansion of social programs and in resolving the Quebec problem. The Quebec electorate responded, giving him 56 of 75 seats. But the response was not enthusiastic — the Liberal popular vote in Quebec remained unchanged at 46 per cent. It was clear that in Quebec Pearson was regarded as the lesser of two evils, not as a reformer. In English Canada the results were much less gratifying; Pearson won only 75 of the 190 remaining seats, 51 of them in Ontario, and he faced almost a total shutout in the West (only 9 of 70 seats). So while Pearson had the lukewarm support of Central and Atlantic Canada — 107 of 160 seats in Quebec and Ontario; 20 of 33 seats in Atlantic Canada — the largest of the two great English-Canadian peripheries had refused to embrace him.

Undaunted, the Pearson government continued completing the construction of the welfare state — under prodding from the NDP — by proceeding to a national medicare program and announcing a war on poverty. Further concessions were made to Quebec with Pearson's 1966 policy of equality of treatment for francophone and anglophone applicants for jobs in the federal bureaucracy, supplemented by a bilingualism bonus for those in the lower levels of the civil service who worked in both languages. This was the carrot. The stick was the new justice minister, Pierre Trudeau, who began a sustained ideological offensive against Québécois nationalism, particularly its tendencies toward separatism. In the 1966 Quebec provincial election, this separatist tendency in Québécois nationalism became explicit for the first time.

The 1966 defeat of the Lesage government and the re-election of the Union Nationale were largely attributed at the time to a feeling among the Québécois that things were going too quickly and that it was time to slow down and return to the safe embrace of conservative nationalism. A close examination of the results, however, suggests otherwise. Two separatist parties ran candidates in the election. The right-wing Ralliement National (RN), which favoured associate state status for Quebec, won about 4 per cent of the Québécois vote (3.1 per cent overall). On the left, the socialist and separatist Rassemblement pour l'Indépendance Nationale (RIN) won about 7 per cent of the Québécois vote (5.6 per cent overall). The RIN vote hurt the Liberals badly and helped defeat the Lesage government. The RIN ran in just over two-thirds of the seats, focusing on metropolitan Montreal and other major urban centres. They won about 11 per cent of the Québécois vote in metropolitan Montreal and between 8 and 12 per cent in places like Trois-Rivières, St. Jérôme, Hull, and Shawinigan. More significant, perhaps, was the fact that the RIN attracted very strong support among Québécois between the ages eighteen and twenty-five where the party presented candidates. At the time, the spectacular and unexpected defeat of the Lesage government overshadowed this much more significant development. The separatist option in Quebec had sufficient electoral support that it now had to be taken seriously, even if only because it could act as a spoiler. Only six seats separated the victorious Union Nationale from the defeated Liberals, and thirteen of the Union Nationale victories had occurred because the RIN had pulled sufficient votes from the Liberals. The real message of the election then was not to slow down the process of change, but to speed it up — not to return to the old quiet nationalism, but to become more assertive in advancing the claims of the Québécois nation.

If the size of the separatist vote was disturbing, the demographics were doubly so. The size of the vote suggested that the left-wing RIN had broken out of the student and New Left ghetto where it had got its start six brief years before. The separatist option received its strongest support among young people. In addition, intellectuals in cultural areas — teachers and professors, artists, actors, writers, musicians — were tilting more and more to independence as were the new generation of Quebec professionals, white- and blue-collar workers, and small-business people, who were all rankling at the system of English privilege. Significant inroads were made in working-class districts, particularly among young workers. These demographics could only be interpreted to mean that the electoral future of the separatist option in Quebec was one of growth, particularly if a party presented itself in which the electorate had confidence. Though the RIN was clearly not yet that party, the support it had won on a shoestring budget, with a chaotic organization, and in spite of the excessive abuse heaped upon it suggested the political situation was ripening for independence. If nothing else, the 1966 election made separatism, in a non-terrorist and democratic expression, a coin of common political currency, a choice in the accepted political discourse, an option to be debated and voted on, rather than simply an option to be discussed on the intellectual sidelines and political fringes of Québécois nationalism. The lid of Pandora's box was off, and it has remained off.

Events in Quebec accelerated incredibly between 1966 and 1970, and many thought that the trajectory was toward separation. René Lévesque, who more than any other single figure embodied the ultimate aspirations of the Quiet Revolution, appealed to the Quebec Liberal Party in 1967 to adopt his idea of "sovereignty association." The idea was seductively simple. Quebec would become a sovereign nation but maintain a close economic association with Canada. Indeed, the associative bonds could be extended into other areas, as long as Quebec's sovereignty and equality as a nation were the first premise of negotiations and agreements.

Lévesque's proposal was soundly rejected, as everyone expected, whereupon he split from the Liberals and founded Le Mouvement souveraineté-association (MSA). Within months, buoyed by the support he found everywhere in Quebec and the surprisingly high levels of sympathy he galvanized in English Canada, Lévesque was confidently predicting Quebec's independence in two to five years. French president General Charles de Gaulle had lent considerable credence to the separatist option with his provocative declaration in July 1967 from the balcony of Montreal's Hôtel de Ville, "Vive le Québec Libre!" — a call that palpably electrified the huge listening crowd and created a major diplomatic furore that resulted in de Gaulle's premature departure from Canada. The French government heaped insult on Canadian injury by providing quasi-official welcomes for visiting separatists from Quebec, like RIN leader Pierre Bourgault and

MSA leader Lévesque, that gave considerable international legitimacy to the movement.

Unity negotiations between the RIN, MSA, and RN led in 1968 to the founding of the Parti Québécois, under Lévesque's charismatic leadership. It had the declared and prescient intent of winning at least one in four Quebec votes in the next provincial election, expected in 1970. The major Quebec trade union federations moved toward the explicit endorsation of independence, as did the nationalist, popular mass organization, La Société Saint-Jean-Baptiste. All of these events were sharply punctuated by the FLQ's apparently unstoppable symbolic bombing campaign.

While René Lévesque was rising to political leadership of the Québécois nation on this wave of separatist sentiment, Pierre Trudeau was rising in the federal system on the inevitable countervailing wave of anti-separatist sentiment both in English Canada and among the still powerful federalists in Quebec. Trudeau was the perfect foil for English Canada in general, and Quebec federalists in particular, in the struggle against Québécois nationalism and separatism. Urbane, witty, highly educated, independently wealthy, and unsullied by past associations with the old Liberal Party, Trudeau was seen as a fresh force in national politics. Despite his previous lack of involvement in electoral politics, he had strong, if unusual, political credentials. He had fought Duplessis and supported the unions during their darker days. He had flirted with the NDP but never embraced the party. He had publicly denounced the Liberals for accepting U.S. nuclear weapons on Canadian soil. More importantly, Trudeau was a firm and dedicated opponent of Québécois nationalism and had been throughout his adult life. The son of a wealthy French-English marriage, he was fluently bilingual. For many he embodied the ideal of the new Canada — at ease in both languages and cultures but emotionally committed to neither. He presented himself as the rational, sophisticated, bilingual model of the new unhyphenated Canadian. Given his roots in Quebec, Trudeau was able to denounce Québécois nationalism and, even more severely, separatism with a contempt and arrogance that would have provoked mass indignation among Québécois had his statements come from an English-Canadian politician. Having failed in four elections, Pearson decided to step down. His invitation to Trudeau and the other two wise men from Quebec to join his government, and Trudeau's immediate elevation to the role of justice minister amounted to a "laying on of hands." Trudeau was clearly the leadership choice of the prime minister and most in the Liberal establishment.

The increasing popular support for independence in Quebec made Trudeau, a recognized foe of nationalism, a logical successor to Pearson. Pearson's decision to give Trudeau primacy of place, second only to his own, at the key federal-provincial constitutional conference in February 1968 immediately buoyed Trudeau's chances for success in the coming April leadership convention. Trudeau boldly faced down Union Nationale premier Daniel Johnson, refusing to recognize Quebec's special status as a province containing one of the two founding nations. Rather, Trudeau laid out the doctrine that would more or less guide his years in power: a binding national Charter of Rights; the constitutional equality of provinces in a co-operative federal system orchestrated by the senior government at Ottawa; the determination of the character of any new federalism not by negotiation between English Canada, represented by Ottawa, and Quebec, but by negotiations between all eleven governments. At root, of course, was Trudeau's conception of a dominating unhyphenated Canadian nationalism, nourished and sustained at the federal level. His vision was in fact not much different from Diefenbaker's, and it was no less offensive to Québécois nationalists.

Perceived as the one candidate who would not only stand up for Canada but could also effectively keep Quebec in line, Trudeau easily won the leadership. Immediately thereafter, on 20 April 1968, he was sworn in as prime minister. Three days later he dissolved Parliament and called an election for 25 June. The campaign was dominated by the Quebec question. The choice was clear: who could deal best with Quebec? The accommodating Robert Stanfield, willing to take seriously the two-nations concept, or Pierre Trudeau, who would make no such accommodation with Québécois nationalism?

Trudeau's victory was sealed on 24 June 1968 during the Saint-Jean-Baptiste Day parade in Montreal. Separatists chose the occasion to demonstrate against Trudeau, denouncing him as a traitor. Riot police moved in, and the scene beneath Trudeau's reviewing stand became an ugly and violent confrontation, as police bludgeoned and arrested demonstrators, who responded with bottles, bricks, and attacks on police vehicles. A few of the missiles were hurled in Trudeau's direction. The prime minister's bodyguard tried to convince him to leave the stand for his safety. Trudeau refused and even physically resisted his protectors' efforts to pull him from the stand. All this occurred in front of television cameras and was instantly broadcast across the nation. The next day, as Canadians went to the polls, the news coverage on radio and television and the laudatory front-page stories in daily newspapers across the country left no doubt that this was a prime minister who would face down the separatists. Lost amid the waves of adulation was any doubt about whether a wise and mature prime minister ought to engage in such bravado. The electorate had few doubts. Trudeau won a convincing victory, the first for a prime minister in a decade, taking 154 of 264 seats, including 7 of 32 Atlantic seats, 56 of 74 Quebec seats, 63 of 88 Ontario seats, 27 of 68 Western seats, and the seat for the Yukon and the Northwest Territories.

During this same period, the B and B Commission continued its quiet work. The preliminary report in 1965 had warned of the crisis. Volume I of the report, *The Official Languages*, released in 1967, had concluded that the Québécois constituted a "distinct society" with control over key features of their collective life. This reality, the report suggested, should be confirmed at the federal level through the legal adoption of French and English as equal official languages of Canada and the appointment of a regulatory mechanism to enforce the language law. Provincial governments were similarly called upon to adopt the two official languages. Volume II, *Education*, was issued the next year. It sought to placate the fearful by suggesting that parents be allowed to educate their children in the official language of their choice and that educational choice be provided across the country for speakers of the minority official language. One of the first acts of the Trudeau government was to accept the recommendations of Volume I by introducing the 1969 *Official Languages Act*, which granted equal status to French and English in federal institutions, guaranteed federal services in both languages across the country, and established the Office of the Commissioner of Official Languages to police implementation.

Under the constitution, the Volume II proposals on education required provincial action. The language of education was a key issue in Quebec. The English minority in Quebec had long enjoyed access to their own cultural institutions, including most importantly a well-funded school system from kindergarten to university (including the internationally prestigious McGill). Meanwhile, francophone minorities in English Canada enjoyed no such special consideration, even when numbers made it feasi-

ble. Indeed, what few rights to French-language use and education francophones had possessed had been unconstitutionally
snatched from them. Only in locales in English Canada where
there were large concentrations of French speakers — St.
Boniface in Manitoba, Gravelbourg in Saskatchewan, major portions of
New Brunswick — had francophones managed to maintain a toe-
hold against hostility and pressure, often having to create an
elaborate community conspiracy to circumvent provincial laws
designed to suppress the French language. Though long since resigned to the obliteration of French in English Canada for all practical purposes, a key feature of the Québécois nationalist
consensus was that French had to be well protected in Quebec. A
combination of assertive self-confidence deriving from the Quiet
Revolution and the growing demographic changes led inevitably
to confrontation on the language question. As the Québécois birth
rate fell and as immigration into Quebec increased, the Québécois
share of Quebec's population declined slightly. In the Montreal
area, this decline was quite sharp. Assuring the future of the
Québécois meant ensuring the integration of immigrants to the
French-speaking majority rather than to the English minority. Yet
immigrants realized that the gateway to success in Quebec and to
easy mobility across the rest of Canada was integration with the
English minority and the adoption of English as the language of
education and work. This meant that, where possible, immigrants
wanted to educate their children in the English school system.

Matters came to a head on 27 June 1968, just two days after
Trudeau's election. The local school board in the Montreal suburb
of St. Léonard moved to limit the language of instruction in all
grade one classes in the coming school year to French. That this
action was aimed primarily at families of Italian origin who persisted in their preference for English language instruction, there
was no doubt. That this was a step towards imposing French as
the sole official language of the province, there was no doubt.
There was even less doubt that this was an attack on the English
minority; it struck at one of the most important roots of any cultural community's self-perpetuation and social reproduction —
schooling in that culture's language. And there was no doubt that
this was potentially a first step in dismantling the English minority's structure of privilege in Quebec. That is certainly how it was
seen across English Canada, both within and outside Quebec, and
those who had never shed a tear for the generations of franco-

phone victims of forced integration wept many public tears for the oppressed children of the Italian families of St. Léonard.

The St. Léonard board was in fact doing nothing different from what had been done to the French minority elsewhere from the Conquest on. Receiving a taste of its own medicine, English Canada reacted with indignation, demanding rights for itself in Quebec that it had refused to give to French speakers in the rest of Canada — preferred language protection, including the right to education in English at the state's expense. The St. Léonard crisis, involving demonstrations, counter-demonstrations, and even violence and rioting, rocked the nation.

Again, English Canada, and most importantly the English minority in Quebec, won the confrontation. In 1969 the Union Nationale government, in a spirit of concession to the B and B Commission's recommendations and reeling from the intensity of the language conflict, introduced and finally adopted Bill 63, *An Act to promote the French language in Quebec*. This outraged Québécois nationalists. They saw it as a profound humiliation, as a sign of defeat by and surrender to English power and influence. Where was the legislation to promote English in Ontario or Saskatchewan? More than that, despite the bill's small but significant efforts to enhance French and to assure some knowledge of French by all, it in fact caved in to the pro-English lobby both by giving all parents the freedom to choose the language of instruction for their children and by obliging school boards to establish and fund programs of instruction according to those choices. The bill was a total capitulation to English Canada. It provoked mass protests in Quebec that involved tens of thousands as well as serious rioting during a strike by Montreal police — troops had to be called in to maintain order and protect property. As a concession to this popular opposition, and in an effort to defuse it, the Union Nationale government established the Gendron Commission to make a full inquiry into the language issue.

The St. Léonard crisis and Bill 63's passage presented English Canada with a perfect opportunity to make amends for the past and work toward a more amicable future by imitating the generosity of Quebec's Bill 63, by in fact and spirit heeding the call of the B and B Commission. Two actions on the part of the English-Canadian provinces would have indicated good faith — guaranteeing the right of French-speaking minorities to educate their children in French and declaring French and English to be equal official languages in each province. In other words, measures were required to give to francophones across Canada what English Canada was determined the English minority should have in Quebec. English Canada missed another opportunity.

Only New Brunswick, with its large Acadian minority, responded by adopting French and English as official languages of equal status. No other English-Canadian province followed suit. Some small concessions were made: amendments to education legislation to allow the use of French as a language of instruction under highly controlled and limited conditions; promises to provide some provincial services in French where numbers warranted and when feasible; the Ontario legislature agreed to permit a member to speak on the record in either language; and so on. These gestures were not enough. Indeed, they were so slight that they seemed more like insults. Québécois nationalists — who had long since abandoned francophone minorities across English Canada — used the gestures to full advantage to expose English-Canadian hypocrisy, bad faith, and lack of generosity. For federalists in Quebec — and in Ottawa — the sheer stinginess of English Canada's response was a profound embarrassment. As a result, Quebec continued on its march toward declaring French the sole official language of Quebec, though that move took another five years.

The B and B Commission lobbed a further bombshell with the 1969 publication of Volume III, *The Work World*. This report documented the yawning economic chasm between the Québécois majority and the English minority in Quebec. It was common knowledge that the English minority enjoyed considerable economic privileges, but they had never been so thoroughly revealed. Nor had the gap between French and English ever been so clearly set out. When the cultural and linguistic privileges enjoyed by the English minority were combined with their considerable economic benefits, the political impact was incendiary.

The B and B Report was relentless and microscopic. The average English male in the labour force earned just under 50 per cent more than the average Québécois male. The commission's researchers controlled for all factors relevant to income earning ability and found that about 80 per cent of the difference could be explained only by the Québécois / English ethnic difference. But it was more than just income inequality; it was everything else. The English were over-represented, and the Québécois under-represented, in the better occupations; while the reverse was true in the unskilled labour categories. The upper management of most firms was English, while the Québécois took the lower and poorer-paid jobs. Large business concerns tended to be English; the small ones tended to be Québécois. Even the skilled and better-paid working-class occupations were dominated by English workers. English engineers, architects, lawyers, and physicians earned more than their Québécois counterparts. The most privileged group in all of Canada was located in Quebec: unilingual anglophone males. The aptness of the colonial analogy struck a now deeper chord — you did not even have to speak the language of the majority to hold, enjoy, and retain your privileges. And the very real economic reasons why immigrants to Quebec yearned to integrate to the English minority rather than the French majority were made crystal clear by the B and B data. Italians in Quebec did much better than those in Ontario. The only place in all of Canada where a salary earner of Ukrainian origin exceeded the national average income was in Quebec, again ahead of the Québécois average. The B and B report also detailed that English was not only the language of work but also of promotion and career opportunity. To be successful a Québécois had to be fluent in English, slamming the door of opportunity on the overwhelming majority of Québécois who were unilingual. Furthermore, the report noted that the economic status of the Québécois, compared to the English minority, had actually worsened since 1930.

Needless to say, this volume of the B and B Report was considerably more popular among Québécois nationalists than others because it lent all the weight of a federal royal commission to their claims that Quebec languished in a colonial situation. Lévesque and Bourgault never tired of quoting from *The Work World*. Journalists pored over the data and generated countless articles in the popular press, while scholars crunched and re-crunched the numbers, which, ironically, though generated by a royal commission to save Canada, appeared to contradict the arguments about the economic benefits of Confederation for the Québécois. Any new deal for Quebec in Confederation was going to have to address the touchy issues of making French the language of work and of closing the economic gap between the Québécois and the English minority. Behind the language issue, therefore, lurked the deeper structural issue of the transfer of real economic power, opportunity, and privilege. If English Canada and the English minority in Quebec had shown themselves not to be very generous on language and education issues, on the economic issue Québécois nationalists expected even fewer concessions.

In such circumstances, the election of 29 April 1970 was a significant test of the mood of the Québécois. Was Lévesque's prediction of a 25 per cent vote for sovereignty correct? Was the Trudeau formula — bilingualism, French power in Ottawa, greater economic opportunities for the Québécois, all in a context of hard-nosed federalism — winning favour? A Gallup poll in 1968, using a toughly worded question on support for separation in Quebec, found 11 per cent in favour, 71 per cent opposed, and 18 per cent undecided. Yet, in 1969, when Gallup asked people in Quebec about the breakup of Confederation, 47 per cent thought a breakup would occur, 25 per cent thought not, while 28 per cent remained undecided. With Lévesque asking for support for something non-threatening and vague like "sovereignty-association," all bets were off, and English Canadians, especially in Quebec and Ottawa, became increasingly worried about the outcome, especially when Lévesque's Parti Québécois campaign seemed to catch fire.

The Union Nationale government was thoroughly discredited as a result of the Bill 63 fiasco. The Liberal Party, now led by Robert Bourassa, had just come through a divisive leadership race. The Créditistes decided to shift from their exclusive focus on the federal arena to run provincially. In such a four-way fight, the outcome was highly uncertain, and many in English Canada and in federalist circles feared that the charismatic Lévesque could conceivably win. So the dirty tricks and fear campaign began. What Lévesque referred to at the time as a propaganda campaign of "economic terrorism" started. Federalists in Quebec and Ottawa claimed that the Québécois would experience an overnight drop in their standard of living of 35 per cent if Lévesque and the PQ were elected. Plants would shut down, unemployment would spiral, savings and investments would be put at risk. Potential investors would panic and refuse to risk their capital. Worse, there would be a massive flight of capital out of the province.

This point of view seemed confirmed by events that occurred early on Sunday 27 April, two days before the election. That morning, nine Brinks armoured trucks pulled up to the front door of the Royal Trust building on Dorchester Boulevard. This in itself was unusual, not only because it was Sunday morning but also because Brinks typically used the garage entrance for obvious security reasons. Despite the early morning hour, photographers from the Montreal *Gazette* were on hand to get some front-page pictures. The trucks were ostentatiously loaded with boxes of "fleeing capital" in the form of what were claimed to be "securities" and were driven toward the Ontario border. Their route conveniently took them past waiting television camera crews, who duly recorded this tangible evidence of a "flight of capital," which was then broadcast and rebroadcast for the next two days to counterpoint the newspaper pictures and headlines and hysterical interviews with representatives of the business lobby and responsible Quebec politicians, like premier-in-waiting Bourassa. The event had been elaborately staged, requiring the co-operation of the media, Royal Trust, and the Brinks Company. It was just one more incident in a campaign of hysteria and fear.

Lévesque and the PQ were temporarily stopped on 29 April 1970. The PQ won 24 per cent of the vote but took only 7 of 108 seats in the National Assembly. The Liberals took 72 seats with 44 per cent of the vote, winning a comfortable majority government. The Union Nationale won 18 seats with 20 per cent, while the Créditistes took 12 seats with 11 per cent. The English minority voted en bloc for the Liberal Party, while the Québécois were deeply divided. But a close analysis of the results was deeply disquieting for the federalist victors. About one Québécois in three had voted for the PQ. Again, like the RIN before it, the PQ did best among the groups that owned the future: the young, the educated, and cultural workers. When one also considers that the conservative nationalists in the Union Nationale (UN) won 20 per cent of the vote, the political message was not reassuring. Though Lévesque personally went down to defeat and it retained the status of official Opposition, there was little doubt that the UN was in its death throes and that the real opposition and the real alternative in Quebec had become the PQ. For this reason the PQ election-night rally had all the characteristics of a victory party, and one can understand why Lévesque's statement "this is a defeat which feels like a victory" brought the PQ partisans to their feet, cheering. A PQ victory appeared as close as the next election if the Quiet Revolution continued to unfold as it had since 1960. For the first time since 1837 a sovereign future for the Québécois seemed a real possibility. The events of October 1970 were, however, to result in a brief but painful delay.

On 5 October 1970 the Quiet Revolution ended, the gloves came off, and the apparently irresistible democratic trajectory of the Québécois toward some form of sovereignty was derailed by political violence — the illegal political violence of the FLQ and the legal state violence of Ottawa. Early that morning, the FLQ escalated its terrorist tactics by kidnapping the British trade commissioner in Montreal, James Cross. Threatening to kill Cross, the FLQ gave authorities forty-eight hours to meet seven demands: the cessation of police actions to find the abductors and Cross; the broadcast of the FLQ manifesto on prime-time television over the CBC and its affiliates across Quebec and its front-page publication in the major Quebec newspapers; the "liberation" of twenty-three "political prisoners," twenty of whom were in prison, while three others were on bail; the provision of a plane to take the freed FLQ cadres to Algeria or Cuba; the re-employment of the "Lapalme boys" by Canada Post; the payment of "a voluntary tax of $500,000 in gold bullion" to be placed on the plane; and the release of the name and picture of the latest police informer in the FLQ.

Not unexpectedly, the Quebec and Ottawa governments initially refused all the demands and took considerable pains to reject the FLQ's allegations about the twenty-three "political prisoners." These were FLQ activists convicted of terrorist actions: mainly armed robbery and bombings. A few had also been convicted of murder when deaths had occurred during the commission of the offences. They had, of course, been convicted of violations of the Criminal Code. Yet everyone understood that, however misguided, their motives were political. Their crimes were politically motivated by the romantic vision of the terrorist hero who courageously confronts the state and, by example, hopes to inspire more and more among the population to do likewise. The FLQ had also begun to win some public sympathy because of their treatment by the criminal justice system: two had been held for over three years with neither bail nor trial; those convicted, often first offenders and certainly not criminals in the normal sense, received sentences unprecedented in length; FLQ members who were charged were routinely denied bail; one of the prisoners had been sentenced to 126 terms of perpetual confinement; many of the twenty-three claimed to have been beaten and tortured. Under the circumstances, it appeared that FLQ activists, when convicted, were treated much more harshly precisely because their crimes were politically motivated. This issue of the "political prisoners" became the source of a temporary split between Trudeau in Ottawa and Bourassa in Quebec.

In retrospect, Ottawa and Quebec then made a serious political miscalculation. Having initially rejected all seven demands, the authorities relented and, as an act of good faith, agreed to the broadcast and publication of the FLQ manifesto. The 1970 manifesto was a much better polemic than the more tedious academic version of 1964. It was full of the immediacy of recent political events, made free use of the vernacular, reiterated many widely held grievances, and was salted with irreverence and contempt for key authority figures ("Drapeau the dog, Bourassa the Simard sidekick, Trudeau the queer, the sub-ape Robert Shaw"). It made good use of the distortions of the earlier election, especially the electoral maldistribution that gave the PQ less than 7 per cent of the seats despite their winning 24 per cent of the vote and what it called "the Brinks show."

It is not clear why the decision was taken to permit the broadcast. Perhaps it was seen as the most innocuous of the demands, involving no compromises of the state's authority. Perhaps the authorities believed that the tone and content of the manifesto would alienate ordinary Québécois, that the excessive political rhetoric would leave them unmoved. Perhaps they just hoped to buy a few days' time, during which the police effort would successfully uncover the location of Cross and his abductors. Whatever the official reasoning behind the decision, the impact of the manifesto on the Québécois population was entirely unexpected. Everywhere people from all walks of life — priests from the Gaspé, students and professors, trade unionists, randomly selected "person in the street" TV interviewees — began to draw a clear and sophisticated distinction that was very unsettling to the authorities. They liked the FLQ's analysis and political message but disliked their terrorist tactics. There followed a flowering not only of an intense media discussion and debate of the issues but arguments and discussions on street corners, in taverns, in classrooms. Background articles on Québécois grievances appeared in newspapers both in Quebec and across English Canada. Though the authorities had bought some time with the broadcast, that time was taking events in an unexpected political direction and appeared only to make the climate of opinion increasingly favourable to the FLQ. The public reaction — "I like what you say, but not what you are doing" — was not what the authorities had had in mind. Indeed, the political debates were deflecting attention away from the central issue from the perspective of the governments in Ottawa and Quebec — the kidnapping and threatened "execution" of Cross. Public fear began to ebb over the next few days, as the FLQ kept cancelling and reissuing new execution deadlines, while demanding negotiations. Increasingly the view was that the FLQ were not really serious about the threat to kill Cross. On the sixth day, 10 October, Quebec Justice Minister Choquette issued a joint declaration on behalf of the governments of Ottawa and Quebec declaring that the broadcast was it — there would be no deals and no further concessions on the seven demands.

No one expected the FLQ's reply, perhaps anticipating only another ultimatum. Instead, later that same day the FLQ kidnapped Quebec labour minister Pierre Laporte, a further escalation of the confrontation and a stunning blow to the hard-liners in government circles. The stakes were immediately higher. It was one thing to kidnap a foreign diplomat, a symbol of the British tradition. It was a more serious matter directly to attack the state by abducting and threatening the "execution" of a cabinet minister. Jean Drapeau, the mayor of Montreal, continued to take a hard line, rejecting any idea of concessions to or negotiation with the FLQ. However, the former unity of position that had characterized the Ottawa, Quebec, and Montreal governments finally cracked and then collapsed completely under a growing demand that negotiations be opened with the FLQ in order to save the lives of Cross and Laporte.

The day after Laporte's abduction, Premier Bourassa broke ranks, partly as a result of a sad and disturbing letter from Laporte begging that he and Cross be exchanged for the FLQ "political prisoners." In his statement, Bourassa did not hesitate to use the term "political prisoners," and he offered to open official negotiations with the FLQ regarding what amounted to an exchange of Cross and Laporte for the liberation of imprisoned FLQ members. The Quebec government appointed lawyer Robert Demers, and the FLQ named Robert Lemieux, who had represented FLQ members in the courts. In an effort to encourage Bourassa in his decision to open negotiations, sixteen prominent Québécois leaders, including Lévesque, the leaders of the major trade union federations, the leader of the Catholic Farmers' Union, and the editor of Le Devoir, issued a statement declaring that this crisis was a Quebec crisis to be solved by Québécois, concluding "we most urgently recommend negotiations to exchange the two hostages for political prisoners — these negotiations must be made in the teeth of all objections from those outside Quebec." Meanwhile, junior college and university student activists were organizing meetings to discuss the FLQ manifesto, where proposals for a student strike in support of the document's program were considered. This process culminated in a huge and boisterous rally of students on 15 October in Montreal's Paul Sauvé Arena at which the crowd demonstrated its wholehearted support for the FLQ's manifesto. During the rally the Quebec government announced its final offer: the release of five of the FLQ prisoners in exchange for Cross and Laporte.

Two days earlier Trudeau had made clear his opposition to Bourassa's decision to negotiate with the FLQ and to accept the term "political prisoners"; for him, the FLQers were in fact and in law nothing more than "criminals," "bandits," and "outlaws." During a famous confrontation with TV journalist Tim Ralfe on the steps of Parliament, Trudeau justified his initial deployment of troops in Ottawa and Montreal to guard public buildings and public officials with repeated references to the threat posed by a "parallel power." He said, "Society must take means to prevent the emergence of a parallel power which defies the elected power," even if such harsh measures offended the "bleeding hearts" and "weak-kneed." As far as Trudeau was concerned, such people could "go on and bleed." When asked by Ralfe how far he would go, his answer left no room for doubt: "Just watch me...I think that goes to any distance." Trudeau was clearly convinced that any concessions to the FLQ would amount to a total capitulation to an illegal power derived from the kidnappings and execution threats. But his comment was also directed at the group of sixteen who were presenting themselves as advisers to Bourassa in the midst of crisis and instability. His greatest fury, however, was reserved for Bourassa's capitulation, which he saw as the first step in what could be the collapse of the Bourassa government's resolve to stand firm. Such a collapse, particularly in the context of growing popular support for the aims of the FLQ, could set the stage for the onset of a more general political crisis.

Furthermore, Bourassa's decision to break with Ottawa and the declaration of the sixteen essentially telling Ottawa not to meddle amounted to a demand that Ottawa cease acting as an effective federal government with the overriding constitutional power to ensure "peace, order and good government" in Canada. Trudeau had no doubt that such a course would accelerate Quebec's path toward separation and transform Lévesque from premier-in-waiting to *de facto* premier. However one assesses Trudeau's subsequent actions, his political analysis of the crisis the federal government faced was brutally sound. Had he not acted decisively, Trudeau's worst fears might well have been quickly realized given the tempo of events in Quebec. That he went much further than was necessary in the circumstances is without question. Trudeau was never one to take half or quarter measures when it came to exploiting an opportunity to squash or to humble Québécois nationalism, for which he had nothing but contempt.

On 14 October troops were sent into Ottawa. On 15 October troops began to be positioned in Quebec, especially in Montreal. At 4 a.m. on 16 October the *War Measures Act* (WMA) was invoked by Trudeau and his cabinet, making Canada the only western democracy to use war powers during peacetime. Indeed, Ireland and Canada were alone among democracies having such powers at a cabinet's fingertips, without reference to Parliament. Ottawa declared that a state of "apprehended insurrection" existed in Quebec, citing letters from Premier Bourassa, Mayor Drapeau, and the Montreal police chief. Over five thousand troops were deployed in Quebec. The FLQ was outlawed, and membership became a retroactive crime, without an opportunity to recant, punishable by five years in prison. Even having associated with a member of the FLQ became a crime, as did giving assistance to the FLQ or to a member or making any statements that appeared to advocate the aims of the FLQ, all similarly punishable by a prison term of five years. Again, quite unlike previous invocations of the law during wartime, no opportunity was provided to anyone suspected to renounce association with the FLQ. All civil rights and liberties across Canada were technically suspended: a person could be arrested without charge, held incommunicado and without bail for twenty-one days, and without trial for ninety days. Since it was a federal statute, the proclamation, though focused on Quebec, extended to all of Canada. The WMA gave the government dictatorial powers over virtually every aspect of Canadian life. The immediate public reaction, particularly in English Canada, was massive support for Trudeau: a poll days after the proclamation found that 87 per cent of Canadians supported the move. Three days after proclamation the government asked for the support of the House of Commons. NDP leader Tommy Douglas, in what was his finest hour in federal politics, stood alone, together with fifteen members of his caucus, to oppose the government, likening the invocation of the WMA to using "a sledgehammer to smash a peanut."

As soon as the WMA was proclaimed, the arrests in Quebec began. Before the sun came up 242 people had been arrested, fifty of whom had run for the PQ in the April election and two of whom were candidates opposed to Mayor Drapeau's Civic Party in the coming 25 October Montreal municipal election. Those arrested, besides the core leadership of local PQ associations, included not only those suspected of FLQ sympathy, very broadly defined, but also labour leaders, community activists and organizers, separatists of all types, and those known for effective opposition to any of the three levels of government. By the end of the arrests some days later, 465 had been arrested, their homes and offices ransacked and searched, their families and neighbours terrorized. Of these, 403 were eventually freed without charge. Most were not even subjected to any kind of interrogation. Of the remaining sixty-two, thirty-two were charged, but the government decided not to prosecute. At the end of the day, only eighteen were convicted of minor offences, like complicity, or of being accessories after the fact. Leaders of the police units trying to crack the case later revealed that the invocation of the WMA provided no help in the investigations that finally solved the case. Indeed, not a single FLQ member involved was caught in the WMA arrest net (ten members were directly involved in the actual abductions, and twenty-five members acted as a courier and support group). Nor did the WMA and the 5,000 troops provide any help in finding the hostages. The case was finally solved using normal painstaking police investigative procedures. The people arrested were victims of state violence: often arrested in the dead of night; not allowed to inform family, friends, or employers about what had happened; held without charges or bail. Some lost jobs; others claim to have been verbally and/or physically abused by police and prison guards; all experienced terror, degradation, and humiliation. And that appears to have been the only reason most of them were arrested in the first place — a settling of political accounts and a warning of the possible costs associated with their political convictions and actions.

But the person who paid the highest price was Pierre Laporte. The day after the proclamation of the WMA Laporte's body was found in the trunk of a car in the parking lot of a small military airfield on the outskirts of Montreal. The FLQ communiqué announcing Laporte's "execution" suggested the act was a cold-blooded response to the harsh actions of the authorities. The condition of the body (many cuts and bruises), the results of the autopsy, and various statements by officials and the accused, in subsequent interviews and at trials, suggest the murder of Laporte was not coldly calculated.

The best reconstruction of the death appears to have been as follows. The FLQ cell holding Laporte panicked when the WMA was proclaimed. Laporte, already in a very fragile emotional state as revealed in his earlier letter to the premier, also understandably panicked, fearing that his abductors might carry out their threats. While temporarily left alone in the bedroom where he was held, Laporte either freed himself from any bonds restraining his wrists or made his escape attempt despite the bonds and threw himself through a window. His abductors, hearing the noise, raced into the room, saw Laporte part-way out the window, and pulled him back inside. In the ensuing struggle, Laporte was strangled by the chain holding the religious medal he wore around his neck. If it happened that way, it was certainly murder. But was it a cold-blooded, deliberate execution? Or was it the action of frightened, violent, and fanatical young men who suddenly realized the enormity of the consequences of what they had done? Many questions remain. Did they really intend to murder Laporte? If so, why did the FLQ cell holding Cross not follow suit? Though Laporte was the victim of FLQ political violence, in another sense he was the inadvertent victim of state violence. The unanswered question that will always plague reflections on the October Crisis remains: Had Ottawa not proclaimed the WMA and sent in the troops, would Laporte, like Cross, be alive today? There is no doubt about the criminal responsibility for Laporte's death, and those responsible were tried, found guilty, and sentenced. But a large share of the moral and political responsibility for Laporte's death must be assigned to Trudeau, Bourassa, Drapeau, and all those Canadians who cheered and applauded the harsh meas-ures. Laporte's life was sacrificed for reasons of state — to protect the integrity of state power. The state wanted more, however. His family, against their inclinations, were pressured into allowing of-ficials to put on an elaborate state funeral at which Trudeau, Drapeau, and Bourassa sought public justification for their ac-tions. It was one of the most grotesque and maudlin events in Ca-nadian history.

But Laporte's kidnappers were not the only ones to react with fear and panic. Fear, panic, and hysteria became general, affecting the whole country, touching down here and there with sometimes comic, other times malevolent, results. Much of this mood resulted from a deliberately orchestrated campaign by the governments involved to justify their actions. The really serious fear campaign began with the imposition of the WMA and intensified with Laporte's death. Claims were made that the FLQ had infiltrated all key institutions of Quebec, that three thousand armed FLQ terrorists were ready to begin an insurrection, that the FLQ had a "hit list" of two hundred Quebec leaders marked for assassination, that the kidnappings were just the first step in a revolutionary plan — next, there would be mass meetings, then a massive bombing campaign, then a bloodbath of executions, all followed by the installation of a provisional government. No scenario was too fantastic, no tactic too bizarre, to be blurted out by one prominent politician or another. The media, which had been somewhat balanced though sensationalist before the imposition of the WMA, got clearly on the government's side after the proclamation, reporting as fact every wild exaggeration and every fantastic notion.

English Canada was not left unscathed by the hysteria and fear. The B.C. cabinet passed an order-in-council requiring the instant dismissal of teachers or professors who, in the opinion of the police, advocated the policies of the FLQ. Seven members of the Vancouver Liberation Front, a student-based radical group, were arrested without charge and held over a weekend by Vancouver police. The mayor of Vancouver threatened to use WMA powers to clean his city of hippies and transients. A student at Carleton University had his home searched in the first hour; nothing was found but he was taken to jail and held incommunicado for six days. A student at Ottawa University was arrested and held for four days because he happened to be called Bernard Lortie, the name of a known member of the FLQ. The editors of several university newspapers across Canada were visited by police and threatened because of their intention to print the FLQ manifesto. The Regina police chief expressed a desire to use the powers to clean out what he called "undesirable elements" — he had a notorious antipathy for hippies, student activists, indeed, for all young people with long hair. A man from Maple Creek, Saskatchewan, arrested for failing to produce a registration form and for having an unpaid 1967 parking ticket, was held in jail for three days. Former brigadier and then Regina Chamber of Commerce president Keehr advocated strengthening the militia by giving employees time off with pay for training so that Canada could better defend itself against a "bunch of kooks who think they can actually take over this country."

Then there was the extensive self-censorship by the media, often more vigorous than any government-appointed censor would have dared. Toronto's CHAN Television abruptly stopped a 60-minute taped interview show when it realized that the guest was a prominent Quebec labour leader who had been arrested in the first hours of the WMA. National CBC radio cancelled the broadcast of a Max Ferguson skit satirizing the WMA with a routine where Trudeau has been mistakenly arrested and held incommunicado. The CBC sent out a directive to all producers and directors ordering them to get on side with the government during the crisis. Government censors in Alberta banned the film *Red*, which featured a Métis who goes to Montreal. The airing of a TV documentary on Lenin, the Russian revolutionary leader, was cancelled. Mayor Drapeau told Quebec film censors to order the withdrawal of the film *Quiet Days in Clichy* from two Montreal theatres, or he would have the theatres raided and arrest everyone seeing the film, as well as the censors themselves. (The film was pulled.) Virtually every journalist and commentator active at the time in Quebec, as well as elsewhere in Canada, is full of stories of how censorship was imposed on his or her work during the crisis.

The fearsome icing on this cake of hysteria for all of Canada was Créditiste leader Réal Caouette's 18 October 1970 call for the summary execution by firing squad of all FLQ leaders. Despite continuing support for Trudeau's actions, enthusiasm waned, and doubts about the wisdom and necessity of the state's measures increased. Even Trudeau himself had warned of the inherent dangers of such an authoritarian approach when he proclaimed the act. The situation was salvaged when the crisis more or less ended with the arrests of those responsible for Laporte's kidnapping and murder in November, followed quickly by the discovery on 3 December of the location where Cross was held. Negotiations resulted in Cross's release in exchange for safe passage to Cuba for his kidnappers.

The immediate political effect of the October Crisis no doubt fulfilled many of the expectations and intentions of Ottawa. The FLQ was utterly destroyed. The confusion and vacillation of the Bourassa government was abruptly halted. The popular mobilization — meetings, demonstrations, student strikes — was stopped dead, and we will never know what might have been the final outcome. Mayor Drapeau won a 92 per cent victory in the Montreal civic election, and his left opposition was crushed. The WMA clearly played no role in the final resolution of the kidnappings and the murder of Laporte, and the trials and convictions went forward through the criminal justice system. And that system, to its credit, did not reflect the hysterical mood at the height of the crisis. All those convicted were out of prison, either on parole or with sentences completed, in eleven years or fewer and have since "gone straight." A few have written books about their experiences. Most have remained politically inactive and silent about the October events, often as a condition of parole. Efforts to get the full story have been unsuccessful — the Quebec Keable Commission to inquire into police wrongdoing in Quebec was stopped by Ottawa's refusal to co-operate and finally by court injunction. The 1980 McDonald Royal Commission on the Security Service examined a great deal of the evidence, but key parts of the report have been kept secret.

Despite this veil of official secrecy around the October events, enough has leaked out over the years to suggest that at least some aspects of the crisis were deliberately orchestrated by authorities in an effort to provoke polarization, perhaps as part of a campaign to discredit the democratic separatist option by linking it in the public mind with extremism and terrorism. At the public political level, this was very clear at the time — there was no "apprehended insurrection," no uprising of three thousand armed FLQers, no systematic assassinations, no widespread and focused bombing campaign. Nor did the authorities find any physical evidence of such plans as a result of the searches and arrests under the WMA. But there was also a great deal going on at the level of the clandestine state. Prior to the kidnappings, both the Montreal police and the RCMP security service knew a great deal about the FLQ, as did many journalists who covered FLQ activities and the trials of FLQers. An hour after the Cross kidnapping, *La Presse* correctly named one of those involved. The fingerprint of another prominent and well-known FLQer was found on a FLQ communiqué after Laporte's kidnapping. Most of the FLQ militants involved in the kidnappings — thirty-five of them — were routinely followed by undercover police long before the October events. Some were even followed during the crisis! The police actually had photos of FLQ members stalking Cross in the days before his abduction. One of the kidnappers had been linked earlier that year to FLQ kidnap plans. He had been arrested in February

1970 in a panel truck on his way to kidnap the Israeli consul. In the truck police found a sawed-off shotgun, a ransom note, and a wicker basket large enough to hold a man. He was merely charged with possession of the illegal shotgun and released on bail. In June 1970 a police raid on an FLQ safehouse in the Laurentians scotched a plan to kidnap the U.S. consul. In that raid the police found weapons and 250 copies of the manifesto that was later read over the air. In the circumstances, why did the authorities claim they knew nothing and were completely baffled by the October kidnappings? One of the kidnappers complained in 1985 that he now feels that he was manipulated and that the authorities could have prevented the whole thing, given the extent of their knowledge at the time. He is convinced that for some reason the authorities wanted the plans to go ahead.

When these scattered facts are put together with later admissions of illegal and provocative activities by members of the RCMP security service, the scenario gets shadowy. RCMP security service agents have admitted to stealing dynamite; setting off bombs; writing FLQ communiqués; breaking into a left-wing news agency's office; breaking into the PQ office to steal membership lists and financial information; opening mail; routinely gaining access to confidential medical files; committing arson to destabilize the FLQ; using kidnapping, unlawful confinement, and threats of violence to frighten FLQ members and associates to become informants. Suddenly, some FLQ claims that they didn't set off all the bombs or write all the political communiqués attributed to them in the 1960s become more believable. The claim by former FLQ intellectual Pierre Vallières that the communiqué written announcing Laporte's murder was not written by a Québécois no longer seems just paranoid fantasy. One obvious possibility is that the security forces sought to get maximum public impact from the panic slaying of Laporte and put the car there themselves. The FLQ allegedly left Laporte's body in a car parked in the parking lot of a military airfield, adjacent to the military's Mobile Command headquarters. Therefore, by some means, the FLQ killers, well known and sought by every military and law enforcement agency in the province, managed to drive a car carrying Laporte's body in the trunk through a series of two or three roadblocks in broad daylight in order to reach a risky parking lot. This is difficult to believe.

Some have suggested that the RCMP security agents acted on their own in an excess of zeal. That is unbelievable. Security agents do not engage in such domestic activities without clearance and orders from the highest political level. The hints and pieces of the October puzzle are tantalizing and suggestive but incomplete. Too many gaps have to be filled by conjecture and hypothesis. But we do know that the politicians in power and the clandestine security forces joined together to obscure the facts and to manipulate the Canadian people in October 1970. And only some of those responsible — those directly involved — have been brought to justice. The veil of secrecy must be lifted so that the full facts can be disclosed and those responsible can be called to the bar, if not of justice, then at least of history and public opinion. Until that happens, the 1970 October Crisis remains unfinished business.

In English Canada support for Trudeau's use of the WMA was very high, in some quarters almost obscenely enthusiastic. Many in English Canada believed that the October events marked the effective end of Lévesque and the PQ — that on sober reflection of the implications of separation, the Québécois would wake up to the folly of that option. Indeed, many in English Canada believed that merely advocating separation by democratic means amounted to treason and ought to be treated as such. For those, the whole repressive episode, as long as it remained confined to Quebec, was a necessary and long overdue tonic to shock ordinary Québécois and to deflect them from the separatist course. Many, many in English Canada shared the view that the events had hopelessly compromised Lévesque and the PQ and that political support for separatism in Quebec would begin to melt away.

If it is true that one of the long-range political goals of the authorities in using the WMA was to link terrorism and the PQ's democratic separatist option, thereby discrediting the latter, the effort was a failure. Lévesque emerged from the crisis looking good. He had tried to save lives by calling for negotiations. He had denounced Bourassa's weakness and vacillation *vis-à-vis* Ottawa. He had warned Trudeau not to try to turn Quebec into a prison by imposing collective repression. He declared that he and the PQ would fight if Trudeau tried "to tie up Quebec in impotence." And he had movingly and repeatedly denounced terrorism at every turn.

Perhaps the October events slowed down the PQ's momentum to some extent, but there was no fundamental reversal. In the February 1971 by-election to fill Laporte's seat, the PQ vote held at the level of April 1970. And in the provincial election of 1973 the PQ vote grew to 30 per cent, though it still only won 6 of 110 seats. Though the PQ was now the official Opposition, Lévesque, who again failed to win personal election, and the PQ had believed they would win. There is little doubt that residual fear from October 1970 played a role in postponing the PQ's victory. In fact, the electoral fall-out from October 1970 seemed also to hurt Trudeau. In the 1972 federal election Trudeau was humbled by the English Canada he had served so well. In Quebec, support for Trudeau faltered only slightly, falling by 4.5 per cent but still delivering 56 of 74 seats. But in English Canada Trudeau only won 53 of 190 seats with 34.5 per cent of the vote. It appeared that though English Canadians had cheered him in 1970, they had very serious reservations about the concessions he continued to insist on making to Quebec.

Indeed, that was the nub of the problem. The WMA and the troops, though provoking temporary fear and hesitation, could not hope, in the long run, to win the hearts and minds of the Québécois. And English Canada yearned for a final settlement. At the end of the Quiet Revolution, the choices for the Québécois were clarified, and they were now reflected in the National Assembly: they could either remain in a Canada that accorded Quebec a place of cultural security and dignity or adopt some variation on the theme of independence. For English Canada that meant recognizing that there could be no going back to the good old days of English-Canadian certainties. In fact, concessions would have to be made; the structures of English privilege in Quebec would either have to be greatly modified or be made to disappear altogether. Even in the midst of the October Crisis, on 18 October 1970, the National Assembly voted unanimously to abolish Article 80 of the *BNA Act*, which guaranteed the boundaries of what were originally seventeen English provincial constituencies. The boundaries of these protected constituencies could not have been changed without the consent of a majority of the MNAs occupying them. Though most of the constituencies had become largely Québécois, it was the end of yet another piece of the elaborate structure of English privilege in Quebec. To win and keep Quebec for Canada, many more concessions would be necessary.

The Quiet Revolution, ending so dramatically and abruptly with the October Crisis, had permanently transformed politics in Quebec and, by extension, in Canada. A political process was begun in Quebec that posed sharp questions that could not and cannot be avoided. Nor can the process be reversed. The trajectory was set and the choices for the Québécois were clear: continue in a satisfactorily reformed Canadian federation or embark on the path to sovereignty. The former path requires structural concessions from English Canada sufficient to satisfy the Québécois nation's sense of injustice from the past and anxieties about the future. The latter path requires the consent of a majority of Québécois, a consent they have been reluctant to grant. Still, support for sovereignty among the Québécois has continued, despite ebbs and flows, to grow.

5

Lévesque, the Referendum,
and Patriation

On 15 November 1976, René Lévesque and the Parti Québécois won a convincing victory: 71 of 110 seats with 42 per cent of the popular vote. Lévesque had not expected to win, anticipating only a significant breakthrough, including personal victory for himself and a very strong PQ Opposition. He certainly never expected the opportunity to govern with a comfortable majority. The Liberal collapse was so thorough that even Premier Bourassa was defeated, ironically at the hands of poet and journalist Gérald Godin, who had been arrested under the *War Measures Act* in 1970. The Québécois — at least the PQ supporters — were jubilant and began an exhilarating all-night celebration in the streets of Montreal that took some of them to Westmount where their celebrations rubbed salt into English wounds.

English Canada's initial reaction was one of shock, anger, incredulity. Many had forgotten that old axiom of the British parliamentary system: once you become Her Majesty's official Opposition, it only takes one election to become Her Majesty's government. Despite the concessions, despite the October Crisis and the troops, despite yet more concessions, the Québécois weren't satisfied. Their demands were endless and unreasonable went the dominant English-Canadian view. With an avowedly separatist party now in power in Quebec, what had been a perceived but distant threat of the breakup of Canada suddenly became real and palpable. English Canada, therefore, braced itself for the beginning of a process that might well have ended with the separation of Quebec. And nothing that English Canada had done to placate Quebec had been sufficient to postpone this awful final moment of decision.

Indeed, from the point of view of English Canada, great strides had been taken since October 1970 in order to accommodate Québécois aspirations. Constitutional renewal, including patriation, a language charter, an amending formula, and an opting-out provision, were offered at Victoria in 1971. At first, Premier Bourassa agreed to this Victoria Charter, but after a brief sampling of opinion back home, alive with negative opinions, fears, and reservations about the deal, Bourassa withdrew his agreement with a great deal of egg on his face. The charter had failed to come to grips with the constitutional bottom line of Québécois nationalism — special status for Quebec, a new division of powers, and a guaranteed Quebec veto. Meanwhile, Trudeau pursued his strategy of federal bilingualism and French power in Ottawa, while he flatly rejected any notion of special status for Quebec. Furthermore, Trudeau turned up the heat on Québécois nationalism. He instituted an aggressive multiculturalism policy, partly in an effort to reduce the centrality of the French/English polarization, and insisted on the constitutional doctrine of the equality of provinces, in an effort to forestall Québécois insistence that the matter ought to be resolved through bilateral negotiations between Ottawa and Quebec.

Federal bilingualism and French power in Ottawa — though they created many career and business opportunities for a significant number of Québécois — did nothing to relieve the language tensions in Quebec. In Quebec, the language issue remained a matter of making French the language not only of day-to-day life and work but also of economic decision-making and career opportunity. The Gendron Commission, appointed by the Union Nationale government in 1969 to defuse the St. Léonard crisis, issued its report in 1972. The report included extensive research studies on the language of work and economic opportunity and again confirmed, in more detail, the dramatic economic disadvantages experienced by the Québécois compelled to use English as the language of work, especially as they moved up the occupational hierarchy. Comparisons with the past again indicated that the Québécois were not progressing very rapidly in closing the gap with English Canadians in Quebec. The evidence showed that language was the key to dismantling English privilege and unlocking economic opportunity for the Québécois.

As a result, the Gendron Commission recommended that French become Quebec's official language, though English would continue to enjoy the status of a national language in the province. Under growing pressure, in 1974 the Bourassa government introduced and passed Bill 22, *The Official Languages Act*, which declared French the province's official language in all key areas: business, labour, education, selected professions, public administration, and so on. Further, a program of implementation and a system of regulation were put in place to enforce the new law. An important escape hatch was left open, however. Those who wished to educate their children in English could choose to submit their children to testing to ensure their knowledge of English. If they failed to demonstrate such knowledge, they would be enrolled in the French-language system.

Predictably, English Canadians were not happy with this development. While English Canada was reluctantly embracing official federal bilingualism, Quebec was apparently bloody-mindedly marching towards French unilingualism. Though this sentiment overlooked the fact that all provinces but New Brunswick continued to embrace English unilingualism, English Canada's capacity for upholding a linguistic double standard remained unchallenged.

Bill 22 particularly angered the English minority in Quebec. The law compelled them to make profound linguistic adjustments in all spheres of life. Furthermore, the language test for education inevitably began to divert immigrant enrolments from the English to the French school system. Yet the Québécois nationalists were not satisfied. The law did not go far enough or fast enough in making Quebec a thoroughly French-speaking province. The language test still allowed access to the English school system to those willing to go to the expense and effort of tutoring their children. At the end of the day, Bill 22 was a political disaster for Bourassa; it won the premier no friends and created new enemies, particularly among the English minority and immigrants.

Any political good that bilingualism may have done among the Québécois during the early 1970s was at least temporarily wiped out by the dispute over the language of air traffic control at Quebec airports. Québécois pilots and air traffic controllers resented being compelled to use English, even at Quebec airports. English-Canadian pilots and controllers insisted that English was the language of international aviation, and that, for safety reasons, it ought to continue to be the uniform language in Quebec.

In 1973 Ottawa created a task force to look into the matter, and in 1975 its report recommended that both French and English be allowed at five Quebec airports.

English-Canadian air traffic controllers went on strike to express their opposition, and English-Canadian pilots supported them, creating major national disruptions in air service. Meanwhile, Québécois air traffic controllers and pilots split off to form their own organization, Les Gens de l'Air, to press the case for bilingualism in air traffic control. When Ottawa caved in to the English air traffic controllers and settled the strike by allowing them a veto over the use of bilingualism in the air, there were angry convulsions in Quebec. Although the crisis was finally resolved in stages by a commission of inquiry between 1976 and 1979 and the final result was that bilingualism was extended to all airports in Quebec, the immediate political damage in Quebec was considerable.

To the Québécois, English Canada appeared unyielding and arrogant, willing to permit only a restricted use of French, a sort of bilingualism by English permission. At the same time, English Canadians took the view that the Québécois were again being hypersensitive and unreasonable in pressing the language issue in ways that jeopardized air safety. In retrospect, it was another unnecessary and gratuitous language dispute provoked by English Canada. But it struck at the very heart of the language issue in Quebec. If French was to become the language of work, it had to be the language of work in all spheres, not just in those conceded by English Canada. And if Canada truly embraced official bilingualism in the federal sphere, then it had to be nothing less than a real, day-to-day bilingualism, not a bilingualism based on English-Canadian sufferance.

Despite these continuing confrontations, the Québécois remained ambivalent about the stark choices before them, which explains why the same electorate could strongly support the implacable federalism of Trudeau in 1974 and yet elect the separatist Lévesque in 1976. The Québécois had indeed made significant gains since the Quiet Revolution. French was gradually becoming the dominant language in Quebec; federal politicians and senior civil servants from Quebec played leading roles at the highest levels in Ottawa; the system of English privilege in Quebec was either being actively dismantled step-by-step or was under serious seige. In 1961, an English male in the Quebec labour force earned, on average, just under 50 per cent more than his

Québécois counterpart. By 1970 this income lead had been narrowed to about 33 per cent. In 1961 unilingual English males in Quebec comprised the most privileged group in Canada. By the mid-1970s, the most privileged group was made up of bilingual English males in Quebec. Still, the upper ranges of the occupational hierarchy remained beyond the reach of most Québécois. The English minority was still heavily over-represented at the top. For English Canadians, however, the change was sufficient evidence that real structural transformation was indeed occurring and would continue. For the Québécois, it was happening much too slowly, and their impatience was growing.

Clearly, this mood of exasperation had finally grown sufficiently to express itself electorally in Lévesque's victory. Fearing the worst, English Canada made great efforts to remind the PQ government of the limits of its mandate. Editorialists and commentators in English Canada, and Trudeau himself, pointed out that the PQ had no mandate to move towards sovereignty. Only 42 per cent of the electorate had given Lévesque his majority. Just two years previously 54 per cent of the same electorate had supported Trudeau and the federalist Liberals. The Quebec electorate had simply voted out a bad government in the hopes that Lévesque and the PQ would bring good government. The Québécois had perhaps voted for change. But they had not voted for independence. Further evidence of this position was provided by a Gallup poll held just a few months after Lévesque's victory. Only 22 per cent in Quebec favoured the hard separatist option. While this figure was certainly ominous — it had doubled since 1968, and the question was on separation not sovereignty-association — it revealed no mandate in Quebec public opinion to pursue separation.

English Canada began to relax as the intentions of the PQ government became clearer. Though many in English Canada did not realize it at the time, Lévesque and the PQ had long before separated the election of the PQ to provincial power from the achievement of Quebec sovereignty. Even if a PQ government were elected, there would be a separate referendum on sovereignty. This commitment had been made in the 1973 election, and it had been made even more clearly in the 1976 campaign. The moderate architects of this strategy contended that without promising a separate referendum on sovereignty, the PQ could never hope to win election. Their position seemed to be confirmed by the 1976 results. Yet, had the PQ government wished to, it could have made building toward a referendum a central thrust of the work of both party and government from the outset. But it did not, since the PQ had also promised to move to a referendum only after making an effort to achieve a negotiated settlement with Ottawa. As a result, both sovereignty and the referendum were, for all practical political purposes, put on the back burner during the PQ's first three years in power.

Lévesque's careful, non-inflammatory approach to the sovereignty issue was indicated in his decision regarding the Bourassa government's Centre d'Archives et de Documentation (CAD). CAD, composed of bureaucrats at the highest level in the Premier's Office, was established in 1971 in the aftermath of the October Crisis, and it was assigned the task of collecting clandestine political information in co-operation with federal and provincial police agencies as well as the Privy Council Office in Ottawa. When Lévesque took over as premier in 1976, CAD had assembled confidential files on thirty thousand people and six thousand organizations in the province. Lévesque chose not to expose the situation by establishing a commission of inquiry to uncover just how far the political spying had gone. It would have been particularly significant to reveal whether laws had been broken and civil rights violated, whether the active infiltration of organizations had been carried out, and whether efforts to destabilize organizations and discredit selected activists had been undertaken. Lévesque simply disbanded CAD and ordered the files destroyed. In the context of the dirty tricks of 1970 and after, a thorough public exposure of CAD and its activities might have proven a potentially potent weapon in mobilizing the population more quickly in the direction of sovereignty. Lévesque chose not to do so, an act of statesmanship. It may also have been a serious error in political judgement, as later events were to suggest.

But the PQ's moderation extended beyond its approach to sovereignty. Given the key role the Quebec state had played in the Quiet Revolution and given the view of the PQ, held since its founding, that the provincial state had to be used aggressively to empower the Québécois nation in its march toward self-determination, there was a general expectation that under the PQ the provincial government would become more intrusive in the economy and act as a more aggressive instrument for attacking both English privilege within the province and English Canada's external influence. Except in the areas of auto insurance and asbestos, this did not occur. The PQ government was careful and prudent. It made no large, dramatic strides in expanding the role of the state. This was the source of some comfort in English Canada, since the doctrines of the new Québécois nationalism pointed strongly in the direction of an expanded and more powerful provincial state.

The PQ government did move, however, on a series of social measures in accord with its social democratic program, making it the most progressive provincial government in Canada, far ahead of Allan Blakeney's NDP regime in Saskatchewan. Anti-scab legislation was passed, restricting the use of "replacement workers" during a strike to essential activities and property protection. The regressive sales tax on shoes, clothing, and furniture was removed, a benefit to those with lower incomes. The minimum wage became the highest in Canada and was indexed to the cost of living. More generous income supports were provided to the poor. Quebec became the national leader in programs designed to support the family and working women. Income tax rates were indexed to the cost of living for those earning less than $30,000 annually, a real boon to ordinary wage and salary earners. Children under sixteen got free dental care, while senior citizens got free prescription drugs. And there were many other such measures, few of which received attention in English Canada.

Overall the PQ approach was one of *étapisme* — a gradual step-by-step approach to ultimate sovereignty. Having unexpectedly won power, the PQ, the argument went, must first prove that it was a competent, prudent, and responsible government. Above all, the government must not rush off in too many directions and initiate drastic changes that might worry the population, arouse the business lobby, or fail abysmally. Reforms must be carried out, but only those the people strongly supported and only those the PQ government could be certain would have positive outcomes. Most important, the PQ must reassure internal and external investors by proceeding cautiously in the sensitive area of the economy. Lévesque did not need to be reminded about how well-orchestrated economic fear campaigns had been used against the PQ from the outset. The issue of sovereignty was to be postponed while the PQ government carried out this program of reassurance. No hasty moves would be taken; no abrupt changes in the course of the government would occur. Except for the PQ's ultimate commitment to sovereignty, which for English Canada hung ominously in the air, Canadian political life went on much as before, and the initial fears provoked by the PQ victory ebbed among English Canadians.

Though many in English Canada were pleasantly surprised by the PQ's moderation, close watchers of the PQ were not. In fact, Lévesque and Claude Morin, his minister of intergovernmental affairs, had fought the *étapisme* strategy through the structures of the PQ only with great difficulty, opposed at every step by party activists and significant elements of the top leadership. Lévesque, it must not be forgotten, had been a late and reluctant recruit to sovereignty. He was never committed to independence in its fullest sense, and he was uncomfortable with and suspicious of those, like the RIN, who were. Lévesque was a bit of an anglophile — he did not want to sever links with English Canada, hence his concept of sovereignty-association, and he was a vigorous champion within his party and his government of the rights of the English minority in Quebec. In retrospect, if there ever was a Quebec separatist leader with whom English Canada could have made an excellent, workable deal, Lévesque was that leader. From the founding of the PQ, which at Lévesque's insistence had only officially included the MSA and the right-wing RN (the RIN dissolved itself and advised its members to join the PQ), the marriage between Lévesque and determined separatists was uneasy. Lévesque needed the talent and energy of the *indépendantiste* movement, and the movement needed Lévesque's popularity and credibility. Though they agreed sufficiently to work for sovereignty, there were constant sharp disagreements on strategy and tactics. Lévesque and his MSA group refused to conceive of a sovereign Quebec in the absence of an economic association with Canada, while the *indépendantistes* saw sovereignty as the priority, untied to any conditions about association.

Lévesque was aided immeasurably in his battle for a moderate, *étapiste* approach to sovereignty by Claude Morin, whose decision to join the PQ in 1972 had been a major coup for the party. His decision came as a surprise to many, since Morin was widely known for his self-interested caution, particularly when it came to career decisions. Morin had been a central figure in the Lesage government — Lesage's key economic adviser from 1961 to 1963, then his first deputy minister of intergovernmental affairs, a post Morin held, despite changes in government, until resigning in 1971. He was widely recognized as the most significant adviser during both the Liberal and UN periods in office. After his resignation he wrote a book, *Le pouvoir québécois...en négociation*, lamenting the fact that Quebec always lost out in federal-provincial negotiations, something the PQ liked to hear from a man of his experience.

It was not therefore unexpected when Lévesque catapulted Morin into a leadership role second only to his own. Morin became the key architect and engineer of the PQ's *étapiste* referendum strategy. Prior to the 1973 election, PQ policy called for a referendum solely to accept or to reject a proposed constitution for an independent Quebec. During the 1973 election campaign, the PQ promised that independence would only result after a separate referendum on the issue. This arbitrary policy change in the heat of an election was later confirmed as party policy. But Morin also added a further twist. Such a referendum would only occur after efforts to negotiate sovereignty-association with Ottawa had failed. After the 1976 victory, Morin added a further modification to the referendum commitment — that the PQ government would begin to negotiate sovereignty-association for Quebec only *after* winning a referendum. Morin also played a central role in successfully advocating another significant modification to the PQ's sovereignty strategy: as long as Quebec remained in Confederation, a PQ government would participate fully in federal-provincial negotiations in order to win more concessions for Quebec within the federal system.

An additional feature of PQ policy had to do with the concept of "sovereignty-association" itself. Was the emphasis to be first on winning sovereignty, then on negotiating association? Or was there a hyphen between the two words? With a hyphen, the concept "sovereignty-association" was a package, the one went with the other, winning sovereignty depended on winning association. Morin came down heavily on the side of the hyphen. This may sound like a petty, pedantic issue, merely a question of quibbling about punctuation. But it was absolutely central to the PQ's approach. Clearly the strategy for winning sovereignty first and then negotiating some form of association would differ markedly from that used to win sovereignty and association at the same time. What if Ottawa and the other provinces spoke loudly with one voice saying there can never be any form of economic association between an independent Quebec and the rest of Canada? The debate raged in the party until October 1978, when Lévesque, speaking in the National Assembly as premier, clearly placed the hyphen in the phrase and said Quebec aspired to sovereignty-association, which would be the basis of any referendum question. Morin proceeded to work on the wording of the future referendum question with a focus on seeking the public's authorization to negotiate sovereignty-association rather then on its support for sovereignty.

The overall impact of the Lévesque–Morin *étapiste* strategy was to defuse the sovereignty issue in the short and medium term by postponing the day of the hard final question into the relatively distant future: first, there would be a referendum seeking permission to try to negotiate sovereignty-association; if the referendum were successful, the PQ government would then enter what might be fairly lengthy negotiations; if those were not successful, then there would be another referendum on some sort of declaration of sovereignty. Furthermore, by focusing on providing a good, moderate, business-like day-to-day provincial government, the PQ administration was increasingly caught up in the detail of running the province and carrying out those reforms constitutionally possible under the *BNA Act*. Finally, by deciding to participate fully in federal-provincial negotiations, the PQ government was drawn into federal-provincial gamesmanship, slipping deeper and deeper into the give-and-take of Canadian federalism. Such an approach had the clear advantage of easing fears and quieting nerves.

But the approach also carried with it serious political risks. First, by defusing the sovereignty issue and postponing the final decision into the distant future, the PQ's central *raison d'être* was compromised. Second, a good, fair, reform-minded provincial government might deliver enough to make leaving Canada less and less attractive to the average Québécois. Third, by seeking to appease investors and the business lobby, especially those from English Canada and the U.S., the PQ inadvertently delivered the message that perhaps there were serious economic risks and sacrifices attached to sovereignty after all. Fourth, an aggressive participation in federal-provincial negotiations might prove sufficiently successful in winning significant constitutional concessions that the need for sovereignty might appear much less urgent to many Québécois. And finally, a soft question that asked only for a mandate to negotiate sovereignty-association might lead many to believe that the PQ, behind its bold façade, really had cold feet about the whole project and was just using the threat as a means to squeeze more out of English Canada. This last opinion was widely held in English Canada and served to stiffen resistance to Quebec's demands.

There was, however, one issue on which the PQ government did not dare to be moderate and compromising — language. And despite Lévesque's hesitations and reservations, the PQ government made rapid irreversible progress on the francization process in Quebec. Bill 101, la Charte de la langue française, was introduced and passed in 1978 and more or less rapidly completed the work started by Bourassa's Bill 22. In effect, French, already the official language of Quebec in most crucial spheres, became the official language in all areas of life. There was no way to avoid it: if you wanted to live and work in Quebec, you had to do so in French. Only those parents who had obtained an English-language education in Quebec could enrol their children in the English school system. All others — immigrants as well as English Canadians from outside Quebec — were compelled to enrol their children in the French system. The testing escape hatch was closed. Companies with fifty or more employees had to embark on a compulsory and regulated francization program. Significantly, as a gesture of goodwill to non-Québécois and to business, the law backed away from compelling a Québécois quota among those employed. The focus remained on language skill in French, regardless of ethnic origin. English Canada was not pleased. Many English Canadians in Quebec, faced with the daunting prospect of achieving fluency in French, chose to leave. Amid much publicity the century-old Sun Life Insurance company announced the move of its head office from Montreal to Toronto as a result of Bill 101. Québécois were bitterly angry at Sun Life, and Ottawa was profoundly embarrassed. Sun Life's departure had been preceded in 1976 by the move of important sections of Prudential's head office operations from Montreal. Subsequently, there was a haemorrhage of head offices of English businesses leaving Quebec in the ensuing years, including, according to a survey by Quebec's organized business lobby, 629 firms between 1979 and 1982 alone.

Bill 101 was a clear declaration to all of Canada. No provincial political party in Quebec would survive if it dared to compromise the essential features of the bill. Many English Canadians outside Quebec were outraged by the law, and provincial politicians in English Canada frequently attacked it to pander to anti-Quebec sentiments. But the wise and the prudent among English Canadians, both within and outside Quebec, knew that the francization process was irreversible and represented the linguistic minimum that the Québécois would accept in the Canadian federation.

Quebec was demanding for itself neither less nor more than English Canada had long since imposed, often unconstitutionally, in the other nine provinces. At least Quebec could point with justified pride to how well it treated its established English-Canadian minority — for those educated in Quebec in English, their children could enjoy the same privilege. Certainly, the English school system could no longer grow as a result of providing education in English to newcomers to the province; indeed, the system went into sharp decline, but the option remained in place.

Despite the initial attention focused by the election of the PQ in 1976, punctuated by the Bill 101 furore, English Canadians understandably were equally if not more preoccupied with other issues that affected them more directly throughout the 1970s. Quebec was not the only crisis afflicting the federation in that eventful decade. Confederation's other problem child, the West, again began demanding redress of its historic grievances. Relatively quiescent since the clashing battles of Alberta's William Aberhart and Saskatchewan's Tommy Douglas in the 1930s and 1940s, the West roused itself to demand an improved place in the federation.

From Riel onwards, the West, particularly the Prairie West, had resented both its economic place in Confederation as resource hinterland and captive market and its lack of real political clout in determining national policies. Though westerners largely joined Ontario in the commitment to keep the West English and Protestant and in articulating a fundamental hostility to Quebec, they resented the region's status as a dependent investment frontier and captive market for Ontario capitalists. The West's agitations had won many concessions. But they won neither additional constitutional powers for the western provinces nor a basic redesign of national economic policies to benefit the West. The concessions were enough to quiet the West during the period of post-war prosperity, and the West was even initially prepared to accept concessions to Quebec during the Pearson and early Trudeau years, particularly when those concessions cost the West nothing and were made in the context of the general expansion of federal spending programs.

But in the late 1960s and early 1970s when prosperity ended and recession struck the entire region, the West began again to express aggressive anger about its place in Confederation. The first obvious evidence of western arousal led to dramatic changes in government in all four western provinces with the common denominator of dissatisfaction with the resource strategies of the 1950s and 1960s. Everyone in the West wanted economic diversification, new development, secure jobs, and prosperity — but they began to question the price. Clearly, resource development by external, largely foreign, capital was not doing the job. Other than expanding the list of resources being extracted, real economic diversification to ease the booms and busts of a resource economy had not occurred. What little industrial development had occurred in the West — in industries related to the natural products of the region, like milling and meat-packing — was closing down as the magic of the market, improvements in transportation, and technological innovation led to increasing centralization closer to the large markets of Central Canada. In different ways, the new western provincial governments all said: The western provinces should control resource development so that westerners would retain more benefits and revenues. The industrial spinoffs of resource extraction, including inputs and value-added processing, should be located in the West. And more and more revenue from the extraction of non-renewable resources for export had to be reinvested in the region to assure its economic future.

The election of the four new regimes marked a new era in the West's struggle for a place in the sun in Confederation and in the national economy. Just as the great social powers conferred on the provinces by the *BNA Act* had allowed earlier Western movements to push for the construction of the welfare state in the era following the Great Depression and World War II, the provinces' control of natural resources could be used to push for a better economic and constitutional deal for the West. The West therefore began to use its resource wealth as a bargaining chip in the constitutional debate. If Quebec could use its hefty political clout to gain constitutional concessions, perhaps the West could use its resource clout in a like manner. More and more, the constitutional debate, formerly seen in the West as an arcane, technical process largely between Quebec and Ottawa, came to be seen as an arena to push for a western breakthrough. What was sauce for the goose could be sauce for the gander — if Quebec needed constitutional concessions to deal with its linguistic and cultural concerns, could not the West make some kind of trade and obtain constitutional concessions to empower the region in the control of resources?

Trudeau's obsession with Quebec nationalism and separatism, his clumsy agricultural policy initiatives in the West, his imposition of a bilingualism that made no sense to many westerners, and his lack of sympathy for western concerns about resource development began the process of western political estrangement that saw the western Liberal Party, federally and provincially, virtually annihilated in a decade. The once-proud Liberal Party in the West, which in 1969 could boast twenty-seven MPs, fifty-six MLAs, and the control of the Saskatchewan government, was reduced, by 1979, to three MPs and one MLA. Trudeau's conviction that a large part of the Quebec problem, indeed of the growing crisis of Confederation, had to do with an excessively weak federal government and his commitment to strengthen it ensured further confrontations with the West. The West was happy enough to see Trudeau flex federal muscles against the Québécois, as he had during the October Crisis, but it did not appreciate a similar flexing against the West on the issue of resources.

Two contradictory forces ensured a confrontation: the growing determination in the West that provincial powers should be used aggressively to maximize provincial benefits from resource development and a growing conviction on the part of the Trudeau regime that federal power, atrophied by lack of use during the Diefenbaker and Pearson years, had to be reasserted. Ottawa found itself fighting on two fronts: to the East, separatism in Quebec, and to the West, the growing assertion of provincial powers over natural resources.

In the early 1970s the world's oil-supplying countries organized themselves into a cartel, the Organization of Petroleum Exporting Countries (OPEC), determined to reap a greater share of revenue from oil for the producing countries. Sporadic pressure to increase the world price continued until 1973, when OPEC began a series of unilateral moves that doubled, tripled, and finally quadrupled world oil prices. The "energy crisis" was upon us, creating a bonanza for the oil-producing countries and for the major international oil companies. The crisis was a disaster for oil-consuming countries. The industrial sectors of the advanced countries, including Canada, deeply dependent on cheap oil, found themselves in a crunch. The costs of home heating and auto fuel cut deeply into the disposable incomes of families, while oil-price-related spiralling inflation and interest rates further contracted incomes and jeopardized industries. In Canada the energy crisis added a new dimension to the crisis of Confederation.

The western energy provinces moved to capture the windfall profits associated with the oil price rise (which also stimulated a rise in the price for natural gas, as consumers and industries rushed to convert from oil). The federal government also moved aggressively. Ottawa imposed an oil price freeze in the fall of 1973, slapped on a federal oil export tax to capture increased revenues, and decided to deny resource companies the right to deduct provincial royalty charges before they computed federal taxes. All these moves markedly diminished the extent to which the energy provinces could capture the windfall. They were supplemented by a 1974 law granting Ottawa the power to fix oil prices. Furthermore, Ottawa threatened to impose a federal tax on natural gas exports and resisted dramatic increases in natural gas prices in Canada.

Alberta and Saskatchewan responded by revising their royalty schedules upward and, in the case of Saskatchewan, by taking into public ownership all non-crown oil and gas rights and imposing a surcharge on oil production (the surcharge was later ruled *ultra vires*). Alberta similarly moved to establish technical public ownership rights over its oil, though it hesitated to go as far as Saskatchewan, by creating a marketing commission mechanism and by declaring that the royalty share of oil going through the marketing commission was publicly owned. These legislative moves, and a host of other technical enactments and regulations, were designed to buttress provincial constitutional control over all aspects of oil and gas development — production, marketing, and pricing. By asserting their ownership rights over oil and gas after they were out of the ground, the provinces were less likely to be seen as interfering with trade and commerce, an area of clear federal constitutional jurisdiction.

By 1975, an impasse was reached with both levels of government sharing the wealth with the industry in an atmosphere of hostility and confrontation. As the 1970s unfolded, Allan Blakeney and Peter Lougheed won renewed and convincing mandates from their electorates by declaring their intention to continue to fight for provincial control of resources against the arrogant intrusions of the federal government. And for his part, Trudeau repeated that he had no intention of letting the western provinces hold the nation to ransom over energy pricing.

The West had a strong case. Resources came under exclusive provincial jurisdiction. Yet when the *BNA Act* was drafted, its authors had in mind such resources as timber, land, and the less significant mining sector. They saw resources as incidental to the great effort of nation-building and the construction of an East-West economy where the wealth to be made chiefly lay in commerce and manufacturing. As the new resource wealth of the West was developed, most of it was for export, and federal powers over trade and commerce easily contained the situation. However, the Western provinces' efforts in the 1970s to extend their control over resources involved aggressive new departures. No longer simply content to sell the rights to exploit resources to investors and then to collect royalties as the resources were extracted and exported, the provinces were now trying to control the whole process in an effort to capture this new wealth as a basis for economic diversification as well for revenues.

Ottawa also had a strong case. The oil crisis had driven up the price for oil to the point where Central and Atlantic Canada were in deep trouble. Forced to pay burgeoning world prices for much of Canada's needs in the East, the federal government tried to soften the impact by enforcing a low domestic price. The difference between the world price paid and the administered domestic price had to be made up, the federal government argued, at least partly by the greatly expanded revenues being earned by western exports of oil and natural gas. By 1975, Canada was in a serious deficit position in the oil trade — its imports of oil at world prices outpaced the revenues from exports of western oil. The resulting dislocation and inflation would be a disaster for the national economy. Furthermore, the rise in oil prices had worsened the growing crisis in Central Canadian industry, which required cheaper than world-price energy sources in order to sustain its competitiveness. Therefore, the federal government argued that it was in the interest of the national economy, in this case the industrial heartland of the nation, to establish energy-pricing policies that would protect Canada's manufacturing sector.

The western provinces largely agreed with such arguments in principle. The debate centred on how much of the bonanza the West ought to give up in the national interest. Westerners complained that it was not fair that they should again be called upon exclusively to bear the full cost of Canadian nationhood. The 1896 Wheat Boom in the West had set the stage for the realization of a viable East-West economy cementing the Dominion. The West had largely paid, through land grants, mineral rights, and a period of monopoly, for the railway that first bound Canada together. The West's tariff-captive market had helped make Central

Canada's industries successful. Now, once again, Canada was calling on the West to give up the profits of the energy boom to help salvage the nation. Many in the West felt that too much had been asked in the past and that too much was being asked again.

After endless negotiations, the federal and provincial governments agreed on a policy of a gradual upward movement of oil prices, though the federal government refused in principle a commitment to a rapid move to world prices. A complex formula for federal–provincial-industry revenue-sharing was negotiated. There was also an agreement providing for federal–provincial-industry involvement in the development of unconventional oil — the tar sands, heavy oil upgraders, the offshore, and the northern frontier. The compromise was completely unsatisfactory to the West, which continued to insist that the region was being asked to surrender too much of the boom to aid the nation. Anger at Ottawa and a pervading sense of bitterness increased in the West.

In the federal election of 27 May 1979, the West got its revenge on Trudeau, with a little help from Ontario, when Joe Clark won the largest bloc of seats in the House of Commons and became the prime minister of a minority Tory government. After the acrimony of the energy wars and Trudeau's heavy federal hand, the West liked Clark's vision of Confederation as a "community of communities," giving him fifty-seven of seventy-seven seats. Atlantic Canada, as usual, hedged its bets, but it still gave Clark the edge — eighteen of thirty-two seats. Though tempered by a dependence on its expensive imported oil, many of the resource concerns of the Western provinces were shared in Atlantic Canada, which looked with hope at the future promise of offshore oil and gas development. Ontario, disturbed by the energy conflict, a developing industrial crisis, and the continuing Quebec problems and deeply aware that eleven years of Trudeau had seemed to deepen the strains on Confederation (which was, after all, originally largely Ontario's creation), reluctantly shifted into the Tory column, fifty-seven of ninety-five seats, ending seventeen years of Liberal hegemony in Ottawa. If the tough federalism of Trudeau had only served to increase separatist support in Quebec and begun to drive the West into another episode of fury, then perhaps Clark's commitment to reason, compromise and decentralization deserved a try.

Quebec, on the other hand, stayed with Trudeau, giving him the strongest support ever — sixty-seven of seventy-five seats and 62 per cent of the popular vote. As a result of this loyalty,

Clark was denied a majority. The irony of Quebec's electorate voting heavily for Trudeau's strong centralist federalism just two-and-a-half years after electing Lévesque was not lost in English Canada, especially among those who were annoyed and uneasy that Clark had won such a tenuous victory. The result was, however, cause for elation in the PQ government; it gave them a window of political opportunity. Fighting a referendum campaign in Quebec just shortly after Trudeau had refreshed a strong mandate for federalism, including incontestable support in Quebec, was an unhappy prospect for Lévesque and the PQ. Now, however, they had the best of all worlds: Trudeau, the champion of Quebec, laid low by English Canada; an English-Canadian prime minister in power with virtually no support in Quebec (Clark won just two seats there with 14 per cent of the vote); and finally, and perhaps best of all, a prime minister committed to decentralization and ideologically disinclined to make heavy-handed use of federal power. Lévesque wasted no time. Just a month after Clark's victory, Lévesque announced that the voting day for the referendum on sovereignty-association would be in the spring of 1980 — later the final date chosen was 20 May. Trudeau's decision to resign from politics in November 1979 seemed to mark the end of one of the most tumultuous eras in Canadian politics, and many greeted the event without regret.

As it turned out, both the West and Lévesque were to be profoundly disappointed by Joe Clark. At first, things went well for the West. In the late 1979 budget, the Clark government gave the West major concessions on energy. A four-dollar-a-barrel increase in oil prices in 1980, something Trudeau had only promised over two years, followed by equally dramatic increases projected into future years. The overall objective was to move by stages but at considerable speed to the world oil price. This represented a potential windfall for the West, especially Alberta. But this measure was received with less than enthusiasm in Ontario and Quebec, both staggering under the blows inflicted by the energy crisis. Atlantic Canada shared these concerns, though Newfoundland's Brian Peckford was placated by Clark's promise that coastal provinces would enjoy substantial control of offshore energy developments, something Trudeau had flatly refused to concede. In other words, Clark had set himself up to become the lightning rod of the deep divisions between energy-consuming and producing provinces — and Tory Ontario and Tory Alberta pulled him in opposite directions. Convinced that the leaderless Liberals would be hesitant to force an election for some time, Clark had also set himself up for a fall by announcing early in his mandate an intention to govern as if he enjoyed a majority, probably one of the most suicidal positions a leader of a minority government could take. Inevitably, Joe Clark's seven-month-old government was defeated in the House of Commons on 13 December 1979. With visions of Diefenbaker's 1957 and 1958 performance dancing in his head, Clark set the election date for 18 February 1980. Three days later, phoenix-like, Trudeau announced he had reconsidered his resignation and would fight the election as Liberal leader.

Clark's defeat was a foregone conclusion. On the energy issue the West was isolated, finding little support or sympathy in Central and Atlantic Canada. The energy-consuming regions wanted lower than world energy prices and generally supported federal initiatives under Trudeau to regulate energy prices and to share out the costs of the crisis on a fair, national basis. Clark was perceived as weak and as having gone far too far in serving the West's sectional interests to the detriment of the general good of the nation. Given the evident elation of the PQ in Quebec upon Clark's election, and the alacrity with which Lévesque had moved on the referendum after Trudeau's defeat, more and more Canadians were concerned about whether Clark could adequately represent the federalist option in the coming referendum debate.

Trudeau won his majority in February 1980, and his victory can be almost solely attributed to his promise to Central and Atlantic Canada that he would resist the West's demands for unreasonable increases in oil prices and for provincial jurisdiction over energy resources unimpeded by federal authority. (About the vigour of his stance against the threat in Quebec there was never any doubt in English Canada.) Trudeau simply wrote off the West. The results confirmed the effectiveness of his strategy: nineteen of thirty-two seats in Atlantic Canada, seventy-four of seventy-five seats in Quebec, and fifty-two of ninety-five seats in Ontario. In the West, the Liberals won only two seats — both in Manitoba. Despite later myths in the West that blamed Quebec for Clark's defeat, what won the election for Trudeau was the shift in Ontario, largely based on Trudeau's energy promise and on the support of Ontario's Tory premier, desperate for cheap energy. Ontario now again favoured a strong central government in which Ontario would play its proper and decisive role, something denied the province by Clark.

Now unimpeded by any obligation to the West, Trudeau proceeded to impose the National Energy Program, taking for Ottawa authority over energy resources by establishing new price and revenue-sharing regimes without western consent. The regulated domestic oil price would never be allowed to go above 85 per cent of the world price. The new revenue-sharing regime more than doubled the amount going to Ottawa, while it sharply cut the shares for the producing provinces and the industry. The program also involved a strong push for the Canadianization of ownership of the energy industry, incentives for nonconventional development and frontier exploration, and a bigger direct federal role in energy development through PetroCan. The reaction in the West, especially in Alberta, was unconcealed fury. It provoked the rise of western separatist sentiment and eventually led Alberta's Lougheed to do the unthinkable by staging in two cuts of 5 per cent each in the flow of oil eastward.

Immediately after his victory, however, the bulk of Trudeau's attention was devoted to the referendum campaign in Quebec, set for 20 May, just three months after his victory. Fresh from his biggest victory ever in Quebec and armed with a series of polls taken by the Clark government, Trudeau was confident that the No side would carry the day, assuming it had an effective campaign, the planning for which was already in high gear on the ground in Quebec.

In retrospect, a number of things stand out in the referendum campaign that have coloured Quebec politics up to the present. One was the incredible economic fear campaign mounted by the No side, not surprising since economic fear had been the trump card used against the PQ and Lévesque from the beginning. Another was Trudeau's sneering contempt for Québécois nationalism, a contempt that had obviously deepened over the years and that he made no effort to conceal. Yet another was the contrasting crowd scenes conveyed on national television after the results were in (60 per cent No; 40 per cent Yes). At the Paul Sauvé Arena in Montreal, there were thousands of Yes supporters singing, hugging and openly crying as Lévesque spoke and promised *"à la prochaine."* At the No headquarters, there were only a few hundred, subdued in their victory, as if they had just participated in something distasteful in which they could take little pride. Was it another defeat for the PQ that had all the taste and appearance of a victory?

More significant were the demographics of the Yes and No votes. The No vote included overwhelming support from the anglophone and the ethnic vote, in the neighbourhood of 90 per cent. The Québécois vote had split down the middle: about half voted No, half Yes. Québécois No voters tended to be older (over 50) and more affluent, those for whom Confederation had not been such a bad deal and who feared change the most. And fear was the biggest part of the No campaign — fear of change, fear of separatism, fear of the future, fear of losing old age pensions and family allowances, fear of a fall in standard of living, and so on. Québécois Yes voters, on the other hand, tended to be younger and somewhat less affluent as a whole. Students, for example, overwhelmingly voted Yes. This was general among the eighteen- to twenty-five-year age group. Even the working class was split between young and old — and, significantly, the major trade union centrals publicly endorsed a Yes vote. Hence the trade union activists were largely pro-Yes. Those working in Québécois cultural areas — journalists, teachers, professors, artists, writers, actors, the human professions, and so on — tended to go with the Yes option. In other words, the demographics of the Yes vote left considerable room for optimism for the future, suggesting the pro-sovereignty forces would grow quickly in the absence of an acceptable renewal of federalism.

In fact, among the militants and activists on the Yes side there was much disappointment, but no sense of a permanent defeat. There was little demoralization. They believed that the future was theirs. Their arguments made some sense. The hysteria of the No campaign had in fact hardened up Yes support just as much as it frightened away the uncertain. The 40 per cent Yes vote was basically, therefore, a bedrock pro-independence vote. Convinced that English Canada could not and would not give Quebec what it wanted and needed to embrace a renewed federalism, they argued that all Lévesque had to do was to go to the conferences and let the English-Canadian premiers and Ottawa fight among themselves. They argued that if a constitutional change package were developed that won the agreement of all, or even a majority, of English-Canadian premiers, it would be so trivial that it would be offensive to the Québécois. In other words, their view was the referendum campaign was just another step towards ultimate independence. In that context, the 40 per cent result was hardly cause for despair. This was advice, however, that Lévesque rejected, a perspective he declined to share.

Of greatest significance for what was to come in the following months and years was Trudeau's promise in his final speech of the campaign, just days before the vote, that a vote for the No side would be taken as a clear mandate "to change the constitution, to renew federalism." This, Trudeau declared, was a "most solemn commitment." The speech was vintage Trudeau. In the context of the referendum campaign, such a promise implied constitutional renewal that would address Quebec's concerns, concerns on which a consensus had developed among the Québécois since the Quiet Revolution: some kind of special status; a provision for opt-ing-out of federal programs with compensation; an acceptable amending formula that included a Quebec veto in some form, at least in highly sensitive areas (e.g., federal institutions, language, culture, immigration, etc.). Trudeau had never believed in yielding such concessions in the past and had no intention of doing so now — it would negate his whole political *raison d'être*. On the other hand, many believed that this vital vote on sovereignty-association, the first test of popular support among the Québécois for federalism, had perhaps shifted the ground beneath Trudeau enough that he might be willing to yield something.

A variation on this same promise — vote No and all of English Canada will work with you for a renewed federalism — was made not only by Quebec federalists but by federal and provincial English-Canadian politicians throughout the campaign. Saskatchewan's Blakeney came to Quebec with a speech making just such a promise. That was the soft side of English Canada's response. The hard side was a declaration that if Quebec moved to sovereignty, it should not expect association. English Canada was not prepared to negotiate sovereignty-association. The message from English Canada to the Québécois was arrogant: this referendum asking for a mandate to negotiate sovereignty-association is a waste of time because we will never enter into such negotiations. But if you vote No, and express this one last time your commitment to federalism, we solemnly promise that a renewed federalism will be the first order of business for all of Canada.

As in the past, however, English Canada proved to have a short memory when it came to promises to Quebec. English Canada interpreted the 60 per cent No victory with a singular lack of grace, exulting in the defeat of Lévesque and sovereignty-association. The fact that 40 per cent of Quebec voters had supported the Yes side — in itself an ominous and riveting fact — was swept under the carpet of English-Canadian consciousness as if it were of no consequence. For many, if not most, in English Canada, the Quebec issue was now more or less dead, finished, and it was back to business as usual.

Trudeau, however, saw it differently. Now having a strong double mandate from Quebec — 68 per cent in the February election; 60 per cent in the referendum — he was in a position to proceed to realize his dream of patriation of the constitution with a Charter of Rights and Freedoms forever enshrining individual rights and defending them from the collective assaults of Québécois nationalism. This would realize the greatest fears of Québécois nationalists of all varieties, sovereigntist and federalist alike — that Trudeau's brand of federalism, so widely supported in English Canada and so deeply hostile to Québécois nationalism, would be entrenched in the constitution with a charter and an amending formula forever immune to Quebec's desire for constitutional change. In Quebec it was widely believed that this would not only forever shackle the Québécois nation but also deprive it of the means to defend itself from gradual assimilation. Lévesque and a majority of Québécois knew that Trudeau's patriation formula would never include those things Quebec had been demanding since the Quiet Revolution — a Quebec veto, an acceptable amending formula, opting-out rights with financial compensation, a new division of powers to give Quebec the tools needed to defend and empower the Québécois nation. Coming so quickly on the heels of his promise during the referendum battle of a renewed federalism that would address Québécois concerns, Trudeau's determination to proceed unilaterally by exercising ultimate federal powers was seen in Quebec as a profound betrayal.

With nothing owed to the West — except for a small debt for a pro-federalist role in the referendum — Trudeau believed that he was in a position to proceed unilaterally and without provincial consent if necessary. If anything, this determination angered the West as much as it angered Quebec; they both viewed it as a blatant attempt to increase federal at the expense of provincial powers. It was a widely held view in the West that the Trudeau government was determined to get through naked power what it couldn't get through negotiation — control of western resources and a growing share of the wealth from those resources. Premiers Lougheed and Blakeney, supported by other provincial premiers, made clear that no formula for patriation and amendment of the constitution that did not both enhance and enshrine provincial control of resources and provide an acceptable amending mechanism could win their support. Lévesque, in an act of singular generosity and eager for allies, leapt to the West's defence, accusing Ottawa of having "ravaged Alberta's resources." Only Ontario and New Brunswick supported Trudeau from the outset. Ontario wanted to preserve a strong central government able and prepared to assert a national will, a will that Ontario had always played a major role in shaping. New Brunswick felt the need to reaffirm its support for Trudeau's bilingualism strategy and, like others among the poorer provinces, worried about the loss of a strong federal government. The other eight provinces disagreed.

Constitutional opinion was divided, but many experts took the view that Trudeau could not hope to gain the patriation and significant amendment of the constitution with the consent of only two of ten provinces. There was no consensus in appeal court decisions on the issue in Quebec, Manitoba, and Newfoundland. Ottawa referred the matter to the Supreme Court, which further confused the issue by ruling that unilateral patriation without provincial consent would violate the federal principle and that "substantial" provincial consent was required by convention but not by law. Therefore, Trudeau could act legally in a unilateral fashion, but such action would be conventionally improper. A committee of the British Parliament, which technically had to approve Trudeau's request, had already recommended that unilateral patriation not be granted. And hiding in the shadows, waiting to ambush Trudeau, was Quebec with its veto. Though never legally tested, on constitutional matters Canada had always accepted the convention that Quebec had veto rights over constitutional changes (later the Supreme Court was to find that Quebec never had a veto in any legal, constitutional sense).

In Quebec, Trudeau's determination to act unilaterally perhaps saved the PQ from electoral defeat. After the referendum defeat, many expected that the PQ, discredited and humbled, would lose the next election and go though a period of reassessment in opposition. Lévesque, not unexpectedly, denounced Trudeau's patriation plan as treachery, as a betrayal of his promises to Quebec. Having promised that sovereignty would not be an issue in the next provincial election and seeking a common front with the seven English-Canadian provinces opposed to unilateral patriation, Lévesque handily won re-election in April 1981 with almost 50 per cent of the vote, proving that Trudeau was not the only political leader capable of rising phoenix-like from the ashes of defeat. The stage was however set for yet another humiliating betrayal, the worst in Lévesque's political life.

Part of Claude Morin's *étapiste* strategy had included the undertaking that as long as Quebec remained in Confederation, the province would participate in the federal-provincial negotiating process. With sovereignty-association defeated and Trudeau determined to patriate the constitution with a charter, Morin became the architect of a further refinement of that strategy to deal with the current crisis, proposing that Lévesque join with the other seven dissenting premiers in a common front against Ottawa, something Morin had always previously opposed. As Morin himself conceded, it was one thing for Quebec simply to participate in federal-provincial meetings; it was quite another to submerge Quebec as one member in an anti-Ottawa coalition of eight provinces, that included seven English-Canadian ones. Not only could Quebec's distinctive position get lost in such a coalition, but also, given the historical record, Quebec had no reason to expect the English provinces would stick with Quebec to the end. Yet the urgency of stopping unilateral patriation seemed to justify an exceptional effort, which might include such risky coalitions.

The agreement binding the Gang of Eight, as they came to be known, was clear. They would support Trudeau's patriation of the constitution if the amending formula for future changes required the agreement of Ottawa and at least seven provinces containing no less than half the population of Canada and if any province could opt out of such future constitutional changes and/or federal programs with equivalent financial compensation. The dissenting premiers also opposed Trudeau's proposal to enshrine a Charter of Rights and Freedoms. In exchange, Lévesque agreed to relinquish Quebec's veto, since the opting-out/financial compensation clause would protect Quebec from future unacceptable changes. This accord was Lévesque's bottom line on agreeing to patriation, a bottom line he believed he now shared with the other seven premiers.

In the meantime, Trudeau hesitated. The Supreme Court decision was a legal victory but a profound political defeat. Trudeau could act legally in a unilateral fashion, but such action would be conventionally improper. In order to obtain patriation and amendment of the constitution without more deeply dividing the nation, Trudeau needed to win some of the eight dissenting premiers over. It would be seriously divisive if all the provinces of one region, like the West, continued in opposition and forced

Ottawa to walk over them. Ottawa looked for a crack in the common front, putting out feelers to Alberta's Lougheed and Saskatchewan's Blakeney and Romanow, urging the isolation of Quebec on the grounds that Lévesque didn't want any kind of deal and was just using the other seven provinces to scuttle the process.

The western premiers, especially Lougheed and Blakeney, were deeply worried about developing western separatist sentiment. A continued impasse followed by Ottawa taking measures to force the issue would only deepen western disaffection, which was beginning to include attacks on the western premiers for being too soft and ineffectual in the battle with Ottawa. Lougheed's Rambo decision to turn down the flow of oil eastward had led him to the precipice: if he continued the shutdown, Ottawa could eventually assert federal constitutional power to stop him, perhaps taking over the regulation of the oil and gas industry entirely on the grounds of defending the national interest from sectional sabotage. Such an event would lose the gains Alberta had made and provide an incredible stimulus to separatist sentiment. Lougheed needed a way out, or he risked disaster. So, too, did Blakeney, who feared the uncertain outcome of a continuing federal-provincial logjam. Therefore, the needs of these two premiers, on the one hand, and the prime minister, on the other, came together, setting the stage for a compromise on energy policy and the constitution, a compromise that both sides could claim as a victory. Trudeau wanted to patriate the constitution, with a Charter and an amending formula, in ways that would give no concessions to Québécois nationalism. The energy-producing premiers, including those with offshore potential such as B.C., Newfoundland, and Nova Scotia, wanted strong constitutional protection of provincial control of resources and an amending formula that would secure the regions' interests in the future. They also wanted a higher price for oil and gas and a better revenue-sharing deal. The premiers were, in fact, for sale. And Ottawa was in the market for as many premiers as it could buy.

A deal was struck. Ottawa would yield to Alberta and the other energy-producing provinces higher oil and gas prices and a larger share of revenues. This part of the deal was concluded in September 1981 and publicly toasted by Lougheed and Trudeau. Furthermore, Ottawa agreed to consider seriously a stronger constitutional provision guaranteeing provincial control of resources and an amending formula similar to that already acceptable to the

Gang of Eight. This formula effectively gave both Western Canada and Atlantic Canada a regional veto — no constitutional change could occur if all four western provinces or all four Atlantic provinces united in opposition. In exchange, the premiers would have to abandon Lévesque by dropping the opting-out and financial compensation elements of the premiers' accord. They would also have to yield on the question of the Charter.

These were the essential elements, with some fine-tuning, of the final agreement reached in November 1981 at the first ministers' meeting in Ottawa. That many informal meetings and consultations had occurred without Lévesque's knowledge in the months before was obvious in the slick way events unfolded. Final wording of the agreement was initiated by Blakeney, then hammered out by Romanow, Ontario's Roy McMurtry, and Ottawa's Chrétien, and finally approved at an all-night meeting of the dissenting English-Canadian premiers, a meeting to which Lévesque was not invited. It was a sordid episode in Canadian constitutional history. The key players — Blakeney, Romanow, McMurtry, and Chrétien — did not just betray Lévesque; they also jeopardized the future of Canada by excluding and isolating Quebec in this cowardly manner.

The premiers sprung their betrayal on Lévesque at a breakfast meeting on 5 November 1981. The package contained a Charter of Rights and Freedoms (but at the insistence of the western premiers allowed a notwithstanding override for certain key sections) and minority-language law, no provision for opting-out and financial compensation, and a mobility clause that might interfere with Quebec's interventions in the labour market. There was not a crumb for Quebec. None of Quebec's concerns had been addressed. Indeed, the opposite was the case — the whole package seemed anti-Quebec. The West and Atlantic Canada, however, got not only a regional veto but also a strong, though still imperfect, resource-control clause. Lévesque was shocked and profoundly humiliated, initially and uncharacteristically at a loss for words. But upon his return to Quebec, he found the words and did not hesitate to use them — "shameful betrayal, deceit, stab in the back, night of the long knives, treachery, political sluts." No word, no phrase was strong enough to convey his harsh anger and cold fury. With some prescience, though he was not to live to see it, he warned English Canada that this betrayal and humiliation of Quebec would have "incalculable consequences." Lévesque always had a better sense of history than his English-Canadian counterparts.

Lévesque's anger and humiliation at the time had another more private dimension. Just the month before the 1981 first ministers' meeting Lévesque had been informed that Claude Morin, his minister of intergovernmental affairs, was an informer for the RCMP Security Service. Loraine Lagacé, the representative of the Quebec government in Ottawa, presented Lévesque with incontrovertible evidence that Morin was a mole. Lévesque confronted Morin, who admitted it was true, and Lévesque demanded his resignation. Though it was agreed that the resignation would be delayed until after the first ministers' meeting and take effect quietly in the new year, Lévesque must have been devastated. In fact, Ms. Lagacé said later that when he was told, Lévesque clutched his stomach or his heart and left the room briefly. Some have suggested perhaps he had one of the four or five minor heart attacks that preceded his death; *Globe and Mail* columnist Lysiane Gagnon has suggested he perhaps left the room simply and appropriately to throw up. In any event, learning that the key architect of virtually the entire PQ strategy had been an RCMP mole from the beginning was a profound personal blow.

It wasn't until 1992 that the whole sordid story came out. The most influential adviser to every premier of Quebec regardless of party since Jean Lesage, deputy minister of intergovernmental affairs from 1963 to 1971, and then PQ minister of intergovernmental affairs from 1976 until his resignation, Morin became an informer for the RCMP in the early 1960s and was paid as much as six thousand dollars a month for his services. He was widely known to have been the central influence in developing the PQ's moderate course, including the referendum strategy, the decision to place the hyphen in "sovereignty-association," the decision to participate fully in federal-provincial meetings, and the fateful decision to join the common front with the seven dissenting English-Canadian premiers. During all this time, he was secretly meeting his RCMP handlers, who had given him the code names "Q1" before the PQ victory and "French Minuet" afterwards.

It is not clear how much Morin admitted to Lévesque in 1981, and even in 1992 Morin only confirmed the essentials of the story, finally denying wrongdoing and protesting his innocence in his book published in 1994. But Lévesque's understandable bitterness about, and hostility to, the anti-PQ tactics of the RCMP Security Service are well known. During the trial of one RCMP agent for illegal activities, Lévesque lost his cool in the National Assembly, saying "The agents of the RCMP are caught in a trial for illegal acts and they are like fish that eject a sticky, dirty liquid to hide themselves." As a result of his outburst, the judge declared a mistrial.

The as-yet unanswered questions about Morin's role as an informer and mole in the PQ cabinet, especially given his power and influence over the government's policy direction, are obvious. Did the RCMP direct Morin to resign his job in 1971, to join the PQ, and to seek prominence in the party? Did Morin's information-gathering mandate include details about the political discussions and the debates about policy options in the cabinet? Was Morin directed by Ottawa to push for the major shifts in PQ policy, shifts that deeply divided the party and that proved so politically disastrous for Lévesque? Clearly, the RCMP Security Service does not pay six thousand dollars a month for casual conversations in Le Concorde hotel in Quebec City merely as a diverting entertainment. Why did Morin, already long an informant for the RCMP, and not at all known as a partisan for sovereignty, suddenly quit his high-ranking post in 1971 and then join the PQ?

The importance a spy agency attaches to a "source" can usually be judged by the rank and ability of those assigned as "handlers." If this is the case, Morin was viewed as a very, very important source indeed. In the June 1992 *Canadian Forum*, Richard Cleroux, a journalist specializing in Canada's secret police, reported that Morin's handlers were the very best the RCMP Security Service had to offer; all of them rose to very high ranks in either the RCMP or, later, the civilian Canadian Security Intelligence Service (CSIS). Morin's handlers included Raymond Parent, later to become the RCMP's assistant commissioner, and Leo Fontaine, later the deputy director general of CSIS in Montreal, directing security operations in Quebec. A third figure, to whom Fontaine reported, was Jean-Louis Gagnon, in 1992 the director of CSIS for Quebec. Gagnon is well known for his political talents and played a role of major importance in the 1980 referendum. Parent was assigned to "D Branch," the RCMP's separatist hunters working on a cabinet order signed by Prime Minister Trudeau that directed the infiltration and destabilization of separatist organizations. He also worked closely with "G Branch," which was assigned dirty tricks and illegal activities, Parent's signature appearing on the order directing the theft of PQ membership lists. In other words, Morin was handled by three top operatives — Cleroux describes Parent as "one of the toughest anti-separatist spy-masters," Fontaine as "a brilliant spy handler," and Gagnon as "a cultured, educated man...the ideal man to plot the moves."

Morin's claims that he gave away nothing and in fact got more information from his handlers than they got from him is simply not believable. Furthermore, evidence presented to the McDonald Commission revealed the high quality of the information obtained by the RCMP from "paid sources in the PQ," including "the annual budget of the PQ, a project for an independent Quebec, a possible Quebec cabinet shuffle, the legislative priorities of the Quebec government, a proposed federal-provincial agreement between a federal and a provincial cabinet minister, and the instructions from a Quebec cabinet minister to Quebec public servants on how they could use federal funds abroad to promote Quebec interests." In the political chess game between Quebec and Ottawa from 1976 to 1980–81, such information, and probably much more besides, would have been vitally useful as Ottawa plotted its moves and countermoves. Even more useful would have been having a key Quebec cabinet minister proposing measures that would weaken the PQ's drive toward sovereignty.

Despite his continuing denials and assertions of innocence, everything Morin touched is now tainted by the probability that, as a paid informer, he was acting under the political direction of Ottawa. The fact that every major shift he advocated not only deeply divided the party but also proved to be a serious miscalculation can only serve to heighten such reasonable suspicions. Indeed, such a possibility may have upset Lévesque as much as hearing that Morin was an informer. It must have created for Lévesque a moment of terrible, sickening self-doubt to have learned that the man who had appeared most closely to share Lévesque's own tactical approach to sovereignty turned out to be the lowest form of political life — an informer for Ottawa's secret police.

Lévesque's subsequent decline can be dated from this double betrayal: the one a public spectacle of humiliation that he could neither forgive nor forget; the other a private assault on his own political judgement in trusting Morin so completely. His behaviour during this last, painful period of his career, until his retirement in September 1985, became erratic and unpredictable, estranging and driving out of the cabinet almost all of his loyal old *indépendantiste* colleagues and raising widespread public speculation about his stability and health. In some of his speeches at public events and in the National Assembly, he became rambling and incoherent, often losing his train of thought and making inappropriate remarks.

Within the party his sudden political shifts created upheaval and division. Immediately after the first ministers' meeting, his anger was so intense, and his passionate defence of independence for Quebec so eloquent, that PQ delegates responded at the December 1981 convention by deleting "association" from the term "sovereignty-association," declaring that the next election would be a straight fight over sovereignty. This declaration seemed to fit with Lévesque's imposition of a total boycott on Quebec's attendance at all federal-provincial conferences announced just days after the November meeting. But Lévesque still opposed the pure sovereignty option, threatened to resign, and forced a plebiscite in the party. And he finally won overwhelming support. But there was a cost associated with this kind of confrontation and uncertainty: PQ membership numbers went into a nosedive from a high of three hundred thousand in 1980 to just over two hundred thousand during the internal plebiscite. At first, Lévesque threatened to take the PQ directly into federal politics, whereupon the PQ council voted to do so in June 1982, but then four months later the council deferred the question because Lévesque did another flip-flop. The next year, despite Lévesque's profound hesitations, the PQ decided to support a new federal party, Le Parti Nationaliste, a farcical paper creation of a small number of PQ activists. Meanwhile, Lévesque busily offended his former friends in the trade union movement by voiding collective agreements, reneging on negotiated increases, legislating strikers back to work, and taking a hard line in collective bargaining. The PQ vote in three 1983 by-elections collapsed by over 80 per cent in one and by over 60 per cent in the other two. The PQ's membership in 1984 fell to one-half the 1980 figure.

By far the biggest crisis was provoked by Lévesque's *beau risque* strategy during the months just prior to his retirement. When Trudeau announced his decision to step down after his famous walk in the snow on 29 February 1984 and was replaced by John Turner in June, Lévesque recognized an excellent opportunity to help defeat the federal Liberals. Joe Clark's replacement by Brian Mulroney as Tory leader had given the Tories a fluently bilingual leader with some hope of success in Quebec. When Prime Minister Turner called the federal election for 4 September 1984,

Lévesque seized the opportunity. Relegating the Parti National-iste to the sidelines, much of the PQ infrastructure, responding to clear signals from Lévesque, threw in with the federal Tories at the local level. PQ members joined the federal Tory party, sought nominations, and put their well-developed electoral machinery into high gear to help Mulroney. When Mulroney promised "a new era of federal-provincial co-operation" and pledged to bring Quebec into the constitutional fold "with honour and enthusi-asm," Lévesque publicly indicated that he endorsed Mulroney, further distancing himself from the Parti Nationaliste.

Mulroney's enormous victory — including fifty-eight of seventy-five Quebec seats with 50 per cent of the vote — pro-vided Lévesque with what he saw as an opening to Ottawa, a chance both to erase the 1981 humiliation and to address at least some of Quebec's lingering constitutional grievances. As a sign of good faith, Lévesque immediately ended Quebec's boycott of fed-eral-provincial meetings. Mulroney, stinging from attacks that he had made a deal with separatism, called upon the PQ to show Canada signs of good faith as a prelude to healing the constitu-tional wounds. In response, Lévesque accelerated the process, un-derway since 1981, of distancing the PQ from its commitment both to sovereignty and to the left-wing social democratic ele-ments of its original program, laying out his proposal to seek a rapprochement with the federal Tory government, a gamble he called *le beau risque.*

If *le beau risque* were accepted, Lévesque proposed, the PQ had to abandon its central commitment to sovereignty and post-pone it into the distant future, though the ultimate commitment to sovereignty would remain in the background as a sort of "in-surance policy." Then the PQ government would seek a deal with Mulroney. Lévesque proceeded to implement this strategy by making a public commitment that the next provincial election would not be fought on the PQ's traditional commitment to sov-ereignty. This unilateral action provoked the resignation of seven prominent cabinet ministers, including Jacques Parizeau, and the convening of a special convention to decide the issue. There was never any doubt that Lévesque would win the debate, as he had always won every debate within the party in the past. Parizeau and others warned that Lévesque's about-face on sovereignty and the increasing conservatization of the party's policy would lead to political decline and ultimate disaster. These warnings fell on deaf ears.

As far as Lévesque and what was left of the PQ parliamentary caucus and party membership were concerned, the decks had been cleared in preparation for a renewal of constitutional talks with Ottawa. Mulroney, however, remained noncommittal regarding a timetable, preferring to mark time until the Quebec provincial election, due in 1985 or 1986. The PQ appeared to be on the ropes, and Bourassa, now reborn as Quebec Liberal leader, could well become the new premier. From Ottawa's point of view, a constitutional deal negotiated with a Bourassa Liberal government rather than the PQ government would be infinitely easier to sell in English Canada. Not only that, but the continuing carping criticism that Mulroney had climbed into bed with the Quebec separatists in order to get elected was so close to the truth that almost any deal struck with the PQ, no matter how modest, would be tainted, a likely candidate for automatic rejection in English Canada.

Lévesque's turn to *le beau risque* deeply damaged the PQ. Unable to deflect him from his course, a course largely determined by a desire to make up for his failure in 1981, and unable to defeat him, the strong *indépendantiste* wing of the PQ withdrew to the sidelines. Pierre-Marc Johnson, the leader of the *le beau risque*/conservative faction of the PQ, increasingly obtained Lévesque's ear, rising to prominence in the vacuum created by the exit of Parizeau and other key figures in the cabinet. But Johnson did not play the role of loyal dauphin to Lévesque. Rather, he was more like Iago, encouraging Lévesque to abandon his principles and turn his back on his old colleagues. The polls continued to suggest that Lévesque faced certain defeat in the next election, and they indicated the PQ would do better under Johnson. Johnson and his faction urged Lévesque to retire rather than face defeat. Finally Lévesque agreed, and on 29 September 1985 he was replaced as premier by Johnson.

As PQ leader and, briefly, as premier, Pierre-Marc Johnson was convinced that a sharper right turn on social and economic issues, the substitution of a vague notion of "national affirmation" for sovereignty-association, and the pursuit of *le beau risque* with Mulroney's brand of federalism would all lead to victory. He therefore called an election for 7 December 1985. He couldn't have been more wrong. The PQ was crushed by Bourassa's Liberals, taking only twenty-three seats with 37 per cent of the vote, while the Liberals took ninety-nine seats with 58 per cent. The Québécois obviously decided that if Quebec were to abandon the sovereignty option and pursue *le beau risque* with Tory Ottawa, they might as well elect a real Québécois federalist party to do it, rather than the sanitized retread of the Union Nationale the PQ was becoming under Johnson.

The defeat of the PQ and Quebec's return to the safe federalist embrace of Bourassa's Liberals seemed to confirm that one of the most tumultuous chapters in Canadian political history had ended with a whimper. Trudeau was gone, or so Canadians thought. Lévesque was gone. Not only was there a new prime minister with a fresh and strong mandate, but there were also new premiers leading most of the provinces. The Quebec separatist threat appeared doubly dead — not only had the PQ under Johnson decisively turned its back on sovereignty-association, but also the party had been badly defeated. English Canadians therefore relaxed about the Quebec question, though it still simmered on the back burner since Quebec remained a non-signatory to the new constitution, itself an irrelevant legal fact but nevertheless a very significant political reality.

6

The Meech Lake Accord

As a result of his *de facto* pact with Québécois nationalism and separatism, Prime Minister Brian Mulroney had pulled off something of a coup in Canadian history. He was the first Tory leader to sweep Quebec since Diefenbaker in 1958 and Sir John A. Macdonald in 1882. Very much aware of how quickly Diefenbaker's support in Quebec had dissipated, Mulroney was driven by the need to deliver something tangible to Quebec on its constitutional grievances quickly if he hoped to win a second mandate in 1988 or 1989. But in order to deliver to Quebec, Mulroney recognized that he had to give something in exchange to gain the support and acquiescence of the other regions. Having been elected on a decentralist, "provincial rights" platform, this proved an easy task.

Soon after Mulroney's election a metamorphosis occurred in federal–provincial relations. Although things got off to a rocky start over the usual divisive issues and Canadians settled into their favourite sport after hockey — watching Ottawa and the provinces fight it out — very soon reason and contentment reigned. Individual premiers would race angrily down to Ottawa to confront Mulroney but come away happy, apparently putty in the new prime minister's hands. Suddenly Canada's ten provincial premiers had become a remarkably tame bunch. No prime minister in modern times had enjoyed such support from Canada's premiers. The premiers had made life hell for Diefenbaker and Pearson, while Trudeau positively enjoyed his years of strife with them. Joe Clark's brief two-hundred-day Camelot left him shredded by Alberta's Lougheed and Ontario's Davis over the energy issue. Yet, harsh words and expressions of angry resolve seemed to evaporate quickly from the premiers' lips after a little private stroking by Mulroney. It appeared that Mulroney actually had delivered on his promise of "a new era of federal-provincial co-operation," and most Canadians agreed. In early September 1987, Gallup found that 53 per cent of Canadians agreed that since the election of the Mulroney government in 1984, Ottawa and the provinces were getting on better than before, including 62 per cent of those in Quebec. Furthermore, Gallup found that almost one-half of Canadians shared the perception that Quebec was now more satisfied with its place in Canada.

It soon became obvious why federal-provincial peace and harmony began to prevail, and it had little to do with Mulroney's political artistry or social skills. As Trudeau had often sarcastically noted, the one sure way for Ottawa to get harmonious support from the premiers was to give them everything they wanted. Mulroney didn't quite give them everything, but he came close — giving away some very important things that increased provincial at the expense of federal powers. To the Atlantic provinces Mulroney gave everything they asked for to increase provincial control of, and benefits from, offshore energy development. While much of the activity was then mothballed as a result of low world oil prices, it was a boom waiting to happen. To the western energy provinces he also gave everything they wanted on oil and gas policy — a free market, de-regulation, unrestricted exports, the world price, and an end to intrusive federal taxation. (When world oil prices rebound, as they inevitably must, the West will enjoy a bonanza.) By promising to build on existing economic strengths in federal economic development policy while not tampering with the market, Mulroney reassured Ontario that its special place as the industrial centre of the nation would not be put at risk by federal initiatives. But the main dish served up at this provincial banquet was the Meech Lake Accord, which promised powers for provinces that no premier had ever dreamed possible. The Accord assured the premiers that they would finally be relieved of their subordinate status, mounting the Canadian political stage as nothing less than associate prime ministers of ten associate states.

The roots of the Meech Lake Accord lay in the five conditions the new Bourassa government established as Quebec's minimum requirements for constitutional reconciliation with the rest of Canada. They included the recognition of Quebec as a "distinct society" in the preamble of the constitution, an equal say on immigration into Quebec, a right to participate in selecting judges from Quebec for appointment to the Supreme Court, limits on the federal spending power requiring provincial consent for spending in areas of provincial jurisdiction, either a general veto for Quebec on all constitutional changes or opting-out and financial compensation rights in cases of transfers of provincial powers to Ottawa, combined with a Quebec veto on changes in federal structures and the creation of new provinces. Compared to what had been demanded since the Quiet Revolution, these were modest demands for Quebec, so modest that the PQ ridiculed them. But the defeat of the PQ and the election of Mulroney had opened a door: Quebec was in a mood to settle for a minimum, and English Canada yearned to put the constitutional battle with Quebec to rest. On the basis of these demands Mulroney was able to convince a 1986 first minsters' meeting to enter into a negotiating process focusing exclusively on Quebec's proposals.

On 30 April 1987 Mulroney met with the ten premiers at Meech Lake in an attempt to win their final approval for constitutional changes designed to overcome Quebec's objections to the 1982 pact. Here and in later meetings in Ottawa, agreement was reached on a series of proposals. Although Bourassa agreed to many changes that seriously weakened Quebec's five conditions in order to secure support from the other premiers, the essentials of the principles remained intact. The most surprising thing about the agreement was that what had been billed as a "Quebec round" of constitutional negotiations, focusing exclusively on Quebec's concerns, had in fact become a radical proposal to transform Canada fundamentally. In an effort to placate the English-Canadian provinces, which continued to insist that all provinces were equal and must be treated the same, Mulroney managed to grant Quebec's minimum demands for signing on to the constitution only by giving the same powers to all other provinces. Quebec was granted a veto, but so was every other province. Quebec was conceded significant powers on immigration matters, but so was every other province. The same held true for the other features of the Meech Accord: opting-out rights, a say on Supreme Court and Senate appointments. The only unique feature of Meech for Quebec was the distinct society clause. In other words, in exchange for allowing Mulroney to slip the distinct society clause into the Accord to win Quebec, the other nine provinces obtained enormous new powers.

Canadians had been told repeatedly since the Quiet Revolution that to give Quebec what it had been demanding — some form of special status with special powers — would weaken Canada's federal system to the point of rendering Ottawa ineffectual as a national government. Suddenly, as a result of a quickly and secretly concluded agreement, Canadians were now being told that national unity was best served by giving all ten provinces special status and special powers, abruptly transforming Canada's federal system into an agreement among increasingly autonomous associate mini-states, more like ten fiefdoms or satrapies held together by the largesse of Ottawa's taxing and spending powers. Even Joe Clark's idea of a decentralized Confederation as a "community of communities," which Trudeau had ridiculed with heavy sarcasm as a federation of shopping malls, had never dared go so far. Mulroney's Meech agreement seemed more inspired by an extension of Lévesque's notion of sovereignty-association to all ten provinces — growing political autonomy for ever more powerful provinces involved in an economic association overseen by Ottawa.

After the agreement at Meech Lake, which was finalized into legalese at a first ministers' conference in early June, there was enormous pressure on all Canadians to get on side. Those who hesitated to provide instant and uncritical support were accused of sabotage, of threatening national unity. It became the *sine qua non* of politically correct thinking in Canada — all reasonable Canadians devoted to keeping the country together were expected to support Meech. Enormous pressure was put on all political parties in the House of Commons and in the provincial legislatures to make the deal unanimous and to refrain from partisan posturing over the Accord, pressure that was largely successful in the House of Commons but unsuccessful in some of the provincial legislatures. Even the PQ was restrained in its criticisms, recognizing that the Meech Accord — which clearly went some modest distance in enhancing Quebec's powers while reducing Ottawa's — could be of use to a future PQ government in a drive for sovereignty.

A three-year deadline for approval commenced when Quebec's National Assembly approved Meech on 23 June 1987, a day short of three weeks after the first ministers approved the final legal text. During 1987 it appeared that the approval of Meech was a foregone conclusion — speedy passage was obtained in the Saskatchewan and Alberta legislatures and in the House of Commons. In early June 1987 Gallup found that 56 per cent of Canadians thought the deal was good thing for Canada, while at the same time 58 per cent admitted they knew little or nothing about it. Regarding the main details of the Accord, however, they were deeply divided, with 25 per cent believing too much power was being turned over to the provinces and 40 per cent expressing disapproval of the distinct society clause. From the outset the deal was, then, on thin ice — winning initial popular acceptance as an act of blind faith in what the premiers and the prime minister had accomplished in secret. Yet on the two central features of Meech — enhanced powers for the provinces and distinct society — there was deep public unease.

The greatest unease, of course, revolved around the distinct society clause, the one thing Meech gave Quebec that it did not give to all provinces. Much of the concern had to do with the meaning and significance of the term and the contrasting meanings given in Quebec and English Canada by politicians. In Quebec, Bourassa and Mulroney insisted the clause was very significant. In English Canada, the premiers and Mulroney insisted the clause was largely symbolic, that English Canada had nothing to worry about. In Quebec, popular unease had to do with whether the clause had as much meaning as they were assured, while in English Canada it had to do with whether the clause was really as innocuous as suggested. And it didn't help to calm matters that constitutional experts were divided on the issue and that each side marshalled expert testimony to buttress its case.

It was during this period that one of those colossal collective misperceptions occurred that sometimes change the course of history. Thinking the Quebec question was now more or less settled, English Canada fell asleep. It became something of a cliché among the press and politicians in English Canada that Québécois nationalism, especially in its separatist expression, was a spent force. Even Québécois nationalists agreed to a degree, though as PQ MNA Godin preferred to put it, Québécois nationalism was only "hibernating." On the surface, there appeared to be sufficient reason to reach this conclusion, particularly in the political realm, including events all the way from the election of Mulroney to Meech Lake. The loss of the referendum and the right turn of the PQ had, of course, dispirited many nationalists.

Many young Québécois took the view that the great nationalist battle since the Quiet Revolution had been more or less both

won and lost. It was won because French had become more secure as the language of life and work in the province. It was won
because Meech had unprecedently secured unanimous approval
from both English Canada and Quebec. It was won since the
"privilege gap" between English Canadians in Quebec and the
Québécois continued to close. (In the 1980s, English-Canadian incomes in Montreal were an average of 14 per cent higher than
Québécois incomes, but by the late 1980s bilingual Québécois had
finally caught up with bilingual English Canadians. Still, a unilingual Québécois earned about 20 per cent less than a unilingual
English Canadian.)

The battle was also lost. The loss of the referendum and the
turn of Lévesque and the PQ away from sovereignty-association
led to the popular abandonment of the dream of an independent
Quebec, at least for the time being. All of this was grist for the
English-Canadian media, which reported avidly and endlessly on
the decline of Québécois nationalism. We were told that the new
Québécois generation was tired of politics, eager to learn English,
determined to get ahead, and largely uninterested in the clash of
great principles.

But close watchers of Quebec noted that some of the old nationalist spirit was still present. The odd small bomb went off and
the odd brick was hurled through plate glass windows over the
language issue. Premier Bourassa's incomprehensible (for English Canadians) unwillingness to make significant concessions to
the English-Canadian minority in Quebec over the issue of per-
mitting bilingual signs, despite the fact that his party policy explicitly promised such a concession, should have been a signal. As
should have been his calm words, heavy with meaning, in justifying his stubbornness, *"Il y a le programme du party, mais tout chef
politique doit tenir compte de la paix sociale."* In other words, despite this apparent wintertime of Québécois nationalism, there remained everywhere the sense that another explosion awaited if
nationalist sensibilities were seriously affronted. It was a measure
of just how fragile the nationalist peace was that even Bourassa
felt the apparently minor slight of bilingual signs could have been
enough to cause an eruption. It may have been winter, and
Québécois nationalism may have been hibernating, but spring
could come quickly, and Québécois nationalism could reawaken
hungry and cranky.

Two major events occurred in the fall of 1987 that should have
shaken English Canada out of its slumber. The first event of that

momentous autumn was the sudden death by heart attack of René Lévesque on 1 November. His death revived, at least briefly, the nationalist yearnings for independence among many Québécois. Over one hundred thousand Québécois in Montreal and Quebec City lined up to weep over his body while it lay in state, over ten thousand attended the funeral in Quebec City, and many hundreds more wept daily at his graveside in subsequent weeks and months in an outpouring of genuine sorrow no English-Canadian politician's death has ever provoked. It was deeply moving, almost unsettling, to witness. One had the impression that a national hero, not just a politician, had died. More, as all flags flew at half-mast and as one witnessed the grand spectacle of a state funeral, the symbolism was obvious: Quebec buried René Lévesque as if he had succeeded in becoming the president of the independent democratic Quebec republic of his dreams. The distasteful memory of his last few years in power and his turn away from sovereignty were forgotten and his actions forgiven. Québécois nationalism no longer appeared quite so dormant. More than that, the belief that somehow the gulf between the two solitudes had disappeared was called into question by the differing reactions to Lévesque's death in the English and French press. The *Globe and Mail* felt it necessary to qualify English Canada's tributes to Lévesque in ways the Québécois found patronizing. The Montreal *Gazette's* main headline on 3 November, "Lévesque had earlier attacks: M.D.," contrasted sharply with those of *Le Devoir*, "*Deuil national au Québec*," and of *Le Soleil*, "*Le Québec en deuil de René Lévesque: Drapeaux en berne et funérailles nationales.*" The two solitudes remained, even in the grief expressed upon the death of René Lévesque.

The second event that should have awakened English Canada was the fall of PQ leader Pierre-Marc Johnson in the wake of Lévesque's death. Many English-Canadian analysts saw a cause-effect relationship — the emotional catharsis and the brief resurgence of separatist sentiment drove Johnson to resign. The truth was more prosaic. Johnson's fate was sealed long before Lévesque's death, and if the death had any effect, it was simply to speed up Johnson's own recognition that he was finished, especially without Lévesque's personal support. The crucial events leading to Johnson's fall all occurred before Lévesque's heart attack: Parizeau's denunciation of Johnson for abandoning the party's twin pillars of independence and social democracy; Godin's brutal attack on Johnson, saying, "under Johnson the party is going nowhere, except perhaps to its death," as he pointed to the fact that the 1987 PQ membership had fallen to sixty thousand; regular meetings of the *indépendantiste* ex-cabinet ministers, led by Parizeau, had been plotting Johnson's fall for many months.

The reason for their move against Johnson was simple and political: he had failed dismally. First, there was the catastrophic defeat of 1985. Then there was Johnson's lacklustre performance in the Assembly against Bourassa. Finally, there was the September 1987 by-election in Notre Dame de Grâce. Though an 80 per cent non-Québécois riding and a Liberal seat since 1939, the results were disturbing. The PQ vote was cut in half, while the provincial NDP tripled its vote, taking second spot away from the PQ. An earlier province-wide poll saw the PQ's support fall to 26 per cent, while the NDP's shot up to 23 per cent. Another poll just weeks later put the NDP one point ahead of the PQ. Other polls showed the PQ regaining lost ground if Johnson were dumped and replaced by Parizeau. When it became clear that the Quebec NDP was seriously threatening to replace the PQ as the alternative to Bourassa, the knives came out.

Certainly the aftermath of Lévesque's death played a role, but only that of convincing Johnson not to resist. Johnson was remembered by PQ stalwarts, perhaps unfairly, as the man whose counsel led to Lévesque's about-face on independence, whose promise of victory led to the 1985 débâcle, and whose continuing leadership promised an even darker future at the hands of the NDP. The death of Lévesque reminded people of Lévesque's inspirational dream, not his post-1981 betrayal of that dream. Johnson, more than any other prominent figure in the PQ, symbolized, not the early audacious dream of Lévesque, but the later sad, even pathetic retreat. Lévesque's death helped crystallize the moment and the decision: Johnson had to go. The PQ had to re-embrace its *raison d'être*, sovereignty. And new leader Jacques Parizeau made it immediately clear: the PQ stands for "sovereignty, first, last and always." Sovereignty was again a political option for the Québécois. In the fall of 1987, Québécois nationalism may have been sleeping, but it was an increasingly restless sleep. The death of Meech was to awaken it sharply.

The Meech Lake Accord simultaneously unravelled at the top and at the bottom, and as a result its demise became inevitable. At the top, in late May 1987 Pierre Trudeau briefly came out of retirement from public life and issued an op-ed article attacking Meech that was featured in newspapers across Canada. Three months later, he reiterated his attack before the Joint Senate–Commons Committee on the Accord. Trudeau's criticism that the Accord disastrously weakened the federal government by enhancing provincial powers struck a popular chord, confirming the fears of many. However, his attack on the distinct society clause, which struck an even deeper chord in English Canada, on the grounds that it would undermine bilingualism was a bit dishonest. The truth was that English Canada had never embraced true bilingualism, and there was no reason to expect that it ever would. Indeed, English Canada's grudging acceptance of Trudeau's forced bilingualism at the federal level was often used as a club to demand bilingualism in Quebec, while at the same time refusing to endorse bilingualism in English-Canadian provinces. However, the impact of Trudeau's intervention was considerable, serving to galvanize general opposition to the Accord in English Canada, while stiffening the backbones of many in the Liberal Party to begin a campaign of resistance. In October 1987 staunch Meech supporter New Brunswick premier Richard Hatfield was swept from office by Liberal Frank McKenna, a critic of the Accord. In the spring of 1988, the Accord suffered additional blows. Reluctant friend of Meech, Manitoba's NDP premier Howard Pawley was defeated and replaced by a Tory minority government led by Gary Filmon. Filmon was a mild supporter of Meech, but he faced a strong opposition led by Liberal Sharon Carstairs, a fierce opponent of the Accord. After holding hearings, the Senate roused itself from its torpor and approved a basketful of amendments and sent the Accord back to the Commons, forcing the Commons to override the Senate. Despite the fact that in 1988 five more provinces — Nova Scotia, Prince Edward Island, Ontario, Newfoundland, and British Columbia — ratified the Accord, leaving only New Brunswick and Manitoba, the Accord was losing support at the top. The final blow occurred the next year when Liberal Clyde Wells, a harsh critic of Meech, became Newfoundland premier. A year later the Newfoundland legislature withdrew its approval of the Accord.

The Meech Accord was also unravelling at the bottom. The initial popular support for the agreement had been rooted in ignorance and trust, a dangerous combination in democratic politics. That support eroded very quickly as anti-Meech popular agitations swept the country. Women's groups complained that the Meech Accord would freeze the *status quo*, preventing future improvements in women's constitutional status with reference to gender equality guarantees. Still bitter about their failure to win constitutional recognition of the rights to aboriginal self-government, aboriginal organizations were particularly critical, resenting the successful constitutional fast-track for Quebec's concerns, while aboriginal concerns had been dismissed so cavalierly. Furthermore, the provisions of Meech would freeze aboriginals out of future changes in the constitution because of the universal provincial veto. Angry that the Meech Accord granted each province a veto on the establishment of new provinces, people in the Yukon and the Northwest Territories were deeply fearful that such a provision foreclosed the possibility of future provinces in the North. Trade unions and various nongovernmental organizations began to complain loudly about the weakening of federal powers and the resulting end to future national social programs characterized by national standards. The charge was made that had Meech been in place, medicare, old age pensions, the Canadian Pension Plan and the unemployment insurance program would never have been adopted. English Canadians began to complain that the distinct society clause gave Quebec too much and made the English-Canadian provinces second-class constitutional creatures. The NDP began a public and divisive debate over the pros and cons of the Accord. Legal and academic experts lined up on both sides of the issue, giving equally learned but completely contradictory interpretations of the meaning of the legal text. It was not surprising, therefore, that popular support for Meech collapsed. In 1987, while admitting ignorance, 56 per cent of Canadians thought Meech was a good thing for Canada. In 1988, still declaring ignorance, only 28 per cent felt the same way, and, despite small blips, support continued to fall until Meech's official death.

In 1988 and 1989, Mulroney was faced with demands both from premiers and from various popular organizations for a reopening of the Accord. He refused, fearing the agreement would unravel and offend Quebec. As opposition grew and as dissenting premiers felt compelled to use hard-ball tactics to get some changes, the Mulroney government at first refused to consider a parallel accord addressing the desire for changes, then suggested the door might be open to a parallel accord after all. Mulroney established a special Commons committee, chaired by Jean Charest, to hold hearings and to make recommendations for add-ons to Meech. The Charest Committee suggested a series of changes and additions designed to defuse opposition in English Canada. These additions angered Quebec, where they were seen as the beginning of another gang-up, a prelude to yet another betrayal. Mulroney's friend and protégé Lucien Bouchard resigned in protest.

The final death scene of Meech occurred in June 1990. It began with a secret first ministers' meeting called to hammer out a way to salvage the Accord. Prior to that meeting Premier Clyde Wells had offered to submit any revised Meech Accord to a referendum in Newfoundland and to abide by the results. When this proved impossible because of time constraints, Wells offered a free vote in the legislature. New Brunswick's Frank McKenna had offered to approve Meech if his concerns were even partially addressed. Manitoba's premier Gary Filmon promised to fast-track approval of Meech if his concerns were met half-way. Bourassa indicated that, though he was prepared to consider reasonable change, he could not participate in any tampering with the distinct society clause. There was, therefore, considerable tense optimism as the first ministers met from 4 to 9 June 1990, when an agreement to a modified Meech was finally reached, hinging only on the conclusion of a fast-track approval process in Manitoba and a referendum or free vote in Newfoundland.

Then certain key players made some astonishing revelations about what had gone on behind the closed doors. Filmon complained that the feds had engaged in electronic eavesdropping on his cellular phone conversations with Opposition leader Carstairs and NDP leader Gary Doer. Wells complained of "nastiness" and "threats," claiming that if the public knew what was being said behind those closed doors, it would be outraged. Then Carstairs declared that "ethics were absent" during the negotiations, that Ottawa "tried to destroy opponents of Meech," and that the "fear of retribution" was the only reason she finally supported Premier Filmon's decision to sign the agreement.

The Accord collapsed when Prime Minister Mulroney bragged about his "roll of the dice," how he had treated the final Meech negotiations just like an election campaign, deliberately delaying convening the premiers in order to put maximum pressure on the dissenters by creating a crisis atmosphere as well as to prevent Wells from holding a referendum in Newfoundland. This roll-of-the-dice confession perfectly echoed the Mulroney of the 1984 election campaign, who bragged openly about his post-election patronage intentions, saying "Ya dance with the lady what brung ya." The spectacle of the occupant of the highest office in the land bragging about his brazen tactics was the last straw, or, as Premier Wells put it, "the final manipulation." Meech was dead, though it took MLA Elijah Harper's refusal to permit fast-tracking through the Manitoba legislature to deliver the final *coup de grâce*. And it was self-evident to everyone but the prime minister that Meech died largely because he had spoken out a few days too soon. According to the prime minister, however, Meech was dead because of Clyde Wells, who was subsequently publicly punished when Ottawa initially refused to sign the Hibernia agreement and who to this day remains Mulroney's preferred scapegoat for the death of Meech.

Brian Mulroney certainly bore the tactical responsibility for the death of Meech, and to some extent the moral responsibility, not only for his manipulative tactics but also for his effort to slip an accommodation of Quebec by English Canadians unnoticed and without their express approval. Yet the more basic historical reasons for the death of Meech were English Canada's continuing hypocrisy about and hostility to the aspirations of Québécois nationalism. Mulroney might have pulled it off if certain events hadn't intervened at just the wrong moment, events that once again polarized English Canada and Quebec and forced Mulroney to fall between the stools of the two solitudes.

In February 1988 the Supreme Court ruled that section 110 of the 1885 *Northwest Territories Act*, which guaranteed francophone rights to trials in French, the publication of French texts of laws, and the status of French as an official language in the legislature did not cease to have validity when Saskatchewan and Alberta were established as provinces in 1905. In other words, French-language rights had been illegally and unconstitutionally extinguished in the two provinces. These provinces were and remained constitutionally committed to official bilingualism. However, the Court further ruled that section 110 was not entrenched in the Canadian constitution; therefore, both Saskatchewan and Alberta had to decide quickly whether they wanted to proceed with what was now a requirement for bilingualism or whether they wished to adopt English unilingualism by statute. Here was a clear opportunity for Alberta and Saskatchewan, both of which had ratified Meech just months before, to live up to its spirit. Both provinces quickly and with a certain meanness of spirit decided not to do so, adopting Draconian legislation annulling French-language rights. Saskatchewan premier Grant Devine was quite frank about the matter: "This has been very hard. Put yourself in the place of a premier of a province where 97 per cent of the people speak English." Indeed, he went on to assert in an interview with *Le Devoir* that the 97 per cent of Saskatchewan population that spoke English opposed the Meech Accord and was against the use of French in the province in any official capacity. For the Québécois, it was just another outrage to add to a long list and left them wondering why a similar justification for French unilingualism in Quebec was unacceptable in English Canada. The Québécois did not get demonstrably angry about this further suppression of French, since the francophone diaspora had been long ago abandoned by the Québécois to its fate in English Canada, but the event did serve to make the passage of Meech seem increasingly vital in Quebec. English Canadians might be speaking soothing words, but their actions on the bottom line of language issues remained the same as always, mean and nasty.

The November 1988 free trade election also served to drive a wedge between English Canada and Quebec, elevating hostility levels among many English Canadians against the Québécois. In one of the most bitterly fought elections in Canadian history, characterized by a huge expenditure of funds by the pro-free trade business lobby, Brian Mulroney won a second term with a comfortable majority. Many in English Canada opposed to free trade irrationally blamed the Québécois for Mulroney's victory and the securing of free trade, pointing to the fact that without his Quebec seats, Mulroney would have failed. It is true that Bourassa strongly and publicly supported the free trade deal. It is also true that Québécois nationalists either supported free trade or refrained from active opposition. Their arguments were subtle and nuanced. Recalling how economic fear had been used against the PQ repeatedly, and most heavily during the referendum, Québécois nationalists suggested that free trade, which would result in the strengthening of north-south and weakening of the east-west trade flows, would remove economic fear as a trump card that English Canada could use in a future referendum. If the Canadian federation ceased to exist as a viable east-west economy, the arguments about the economic advantages of Confederation would be compromised. Furthermore, a future independent Quebec would benefit from strong, pre-existing trade links with the U.S. Finally, English Canada's fear of cultural domination by the U.S. was understandable, particularly given the weakness of indigenous English-Canadian culture. The

Québécois did not, however, share these cultural fears. Québécois culture, they alleged, was vital and, thanks to its linguistic distinctiveness, had nothing to fear from strong American trade links.

Yet those who blamed the Québécois for Mulroney's free trade victory overlooked the anti-free trade agitations carried out by Québécois farmers and workers. It is doubtful that the Québécois voted for Mulroney primarily because of free trade. It is much more likely the Québécois voted for him because of Meech Lake, which Mulroney was trying to salvage from English-Canadian carping. It may have been true that the Québécois supported free trade in exchange for Meech and distinct society, but that was the best deal ever offered by any prime minister in Canadian history. Unfortunately, many of those in English Canada who were opposed to free trade were also initially most sympathetic to the Québécois nation's aspirations. Bitter at the Mulroney victory, many of them turned their backs on Quebec at this crucial time, depriving Quebec of an important lobby in English Canada. "Why should I support Meech as a gesture of reconciliation, when Quebec has stabbed us in the back on free trade?" became a commonly expressed sentiment among many who ordinarily might have supported the distinct society concession to Quebec.

If it had not had such disastrous consequences, if English Canada had not seized upon the issue to berate Quebec, the public signage and commercial advertising decision of the Supreme Court and Bourassa's subsequent actions might have become a ludicrous historical curiosity. Section 58 of Quebec's Bill 101, la Charte de la langue française, required that public signs, including commercial signs, must be rendered in French only. This law had been challenged in Quebec courts in 1985 and finally percolated up through the system to the Supreme Court. On 15 October 1989 the Supreme Court found that the sign law violated Quebec's own human rights charter, pointing to the predominance of French in bilingual signs as a means of avoiding a charter violation. Unhappy with the decision, cognizant of the explosiveness of the language issue, and aware that the Québécois were determined that Montreal remain a French city, yet also sensitive to the English-Canadian minority in Quebec, Bourassa tried to effect a compromise. First, Bourassa introduced Bill 178 to amend Bill 101, requiring that outside signs be in French only, while signs inside businesses could be bilingual if

French predominated. Then he invoked the notwithstanding clause of both the Quebec Charter and the Canadian Charter of Rights and Freedoms in order to protect the law from further court challenges.

The reaction in English Canada to these events was hypocritical and vastly out of proportion to what had in fact occurred. Looking for a way to tap the traditional and now-growing anti-Quebec mood in his province and party, Manitoba premier Filmon used Quebec's actions as an excuse to withdraw the Meech Accord from the legislature. To suggest — as Filmon did — that Canada now faced a constitutional crisis of the first order as a result of Quebec's sign law was a gross exaggeration. It says a great deal about the mood of the time that Filmon would dare make the language of signs a major constitutional crisis. It says even more that the English-Canadian media took it with the utmost seriousness, rather than with the sarcasm and ridicule it deserved.

The notwithstanding clause was originally placed in the Canadian constitution, not at the insistence of Quebec, which after all had nothing to do with the new constitution, but at the insistence of the English-Canadian premiers, especially Saskatchewan's Blakeney. Forgetting all this, the premiers and the prime minister himself demanded that the notwithstanding clause be removed. The clause had been put in the constitution for precisely this kind of situation — when the courts interpret the constitution in ways that defy the democratic political will of the population as expressed through elected legislators. There had been no outcry back in 1982 when the Lévesque government passed a law providing for the blanket application of the notwithstanding clause to all provincial statutes. There had been no outcry when Saskatchewan premier Grant Devine invoked the notwithstanding clause to order public employees who had not yet gone on strike to stop striking and to get back to the work they had not yet stopped doing. Nor had there been a hue and cry when Saskatchewan and Alberta abruptly revoked French-language rights. But for English Canada, the Quebec sign issue became a pretext for letting loose the pent-up anti-Quebec spleen held in check during the first steps of the Meech process. The language of signs in Quebec was so fundamental a principle, for English Canada, that it was worth putting Canada at risk. If it were not so sad, if the subsequent events were not so divisive, the whole episode would be laughable.

The manipulation of the signs issue by some English-Canadian politicians and the anti-Quebec response of some of the English-Canadian media provoked a knee-jerk reaction across the country. A series of Gallup polls in the weeks and months following the eruption of the signage issue revealed an unprecedented level of English-Canadian hostility to Quebec. Meech was dead as far as public opinion was concerned, all that remained was the drawn-out formal execution — fully 59 per cent of English-speaking Canadians disapproved of Meech's distinct society provision, while 58 per cent of French-speaking Canadians approved. When asked to balance the rights of English-speaking Quebekers to have freedom of speech against the right of the Québécois to preserve their culture, 72 per cent of English-speaking Canadians opted for freedom of speech over cultural protection, while 78 per cent of French-speaking Canadians felt the opposite. And while 96 per cent of English-speaking Canadians supported bilingual commercial signs in Quebec, fully 38 per cent of French-speaking Canadians rejected the Supreme Court's suggested compromise. Astonishingly, 30 per cent of English-speaking Canadians actually supported English-only signs in Quebec, while 95 per cent of French-speaking Canadians rejected such a provocative proposition.

In the aftermath of the signs brouhaha, a petition calling for the declaration of official English unilingualism in B.C. signed by ten thousand people in the greater Victoria area was presented to the legislature. The signatures included five of six Esquimault aldermen, one of whom said, "Bilingualism just shouldn't be here. I'm afraid the French lost it on the Plains of Abraham and we're catering to a minority. I'm sick of it." These were extreme words and actions. Like the incident in Brockville, Ontario, when a group of English Canadians expressed their feelings about Quebec's aspirations by wiping their feet on the Quebec flag, like the scores of local governments across English Canada that declared themselves unilingual English and like Preston Manning's "love it or leave it" challenge to Quebec, they reflected a hostility that seemed to be growing.

As the months passed, this English-Canadian anger over the signage issue spilled over to infect their attitudes towards the entire effort to achieve a constitutional reconciliation with Quebec. Another series of Gallup polls made it evident that there could be no deal, the two solitudes were retreating further from any hope of reconciliation. Clear majorities in the English-Canadian regions

— from a low of 50 per cent in Ontario to a high of 64 per cent in the Prairie provinces — had decided that Quebec was asking too much. Not only that, but a clear majority of English Canadians actually believed that Bourassa was deliberately seeking independence or sovereignty-association. This, more than anything else, attested not only to English Canadians' ignorance about Quebec politics but also to a meanness about Québécois aspirations.

The reaction in Quebec in response to the sign controversy and the final death of Meech was electric, catching many English Canadians off-guard. Not unexpectedly, Premier Bourassa withdrew from constitutional negotiations, saying that he would in future engage solely in bilateral negotiations with Ottawa or one-on-one negotiations with each province as necessary. Mulroney's friend and protégé Lucien Bouchard quit over Mulroney's compromise on distinct society in the late-stage efforts to salvage Meech and founded the Bloc Québécois. The Bloc's numbers grew to nine MPs, who declared their intention to work for Quebec's sovereignty in the House of Commons — an unprecedented development. In August, the Bloc won a smashing by-election victory in a Quebec riding.

Separatist sentiment grew dramatically in Quebec. In 1979, the year before the referendum, separatist support stood at only 18 per cent, and this was on Gallup's hard separatist question. From 1989 to 1992, that figure had fluctuated between 30 and 40 per cent. But on the softer sovereignty-association question, Quebec support fluctuated between 50 and 60 per cent. More worrisome, however, there was deep support for sovereignty-association among Québécois business leaders. A 1991 survey of three thousand Québécois business leaders found 72 per cent not only favourable to sovereignty-association but also convinced that sovereignty-association would be a long-term economic benefit to the Quebec economy. Given the key role economic fear and uncertainty played in the 1980 referendum, the fact that important elements of Quebec's business élite were moving to sovereignty-association suggested that the economic tactic was less likely to succeed in future. Quebec's major trade union centrals once again declared their enthusiastic support for sovereignty. This trend was earlier reflected in the 1989 Quebec election, which resulted in the re-election of Bourassa but in a surge in support for the PQ under Parizeau, campaigning openly on sovereignty. Polls after the failure of Meech put the PQ significantly ahead of the Liberals. The failure of Trudeau's bilingualism flagship was duly recorded in the post-Meech polls; 64 per cent of Canadians believed the program had failed completely. It appears that Trudeau, having helped to destroy Meech, had also inadvertently destroyed the credibility of bilingualism as the preferred alternative strategy for English and French living together in the bosom of a single state.

7

The Charlottetown Referendum

After the death of the Meech Lake Accord in June 1990, Canada was locked into a constitutional dance that increasingly appeared out of control. Both Bourassa and Mulroney were unavoidably committed to carrying on the process of constitutional negotiations. In fact, the political survival of both depended on salvaging something from the wreckage. Both Bourassa's own Liberal Party, through the Allaire Report, and Quebec's National Assembly, through the Bélanger-Campeau Commission, committed Quebec to a referendum in October 1992 on either sovereignty or an acceptable offer of a renewed federalism from Ottawa. Though both reports demanded sweeping powers for Quebec that left English Canadians speechless, Bourassa asserted that his government's bottom line was an offer that addressed the five elements of the Meech Accord in a way that was acceptable to Quebec. Bourassa's political future in the next provincial election and the future of a continuing, viable federalist option in Quebec depended on Ottawa making such an offer before the expiry of the referendum deadline. Having signed on to Meech, widely seen in Quebec as a set of minimal conditions, and having been humiliated as deeply as Lévesque had been in 1981, Bourassa could do nothing less. The PQ and Parizeau waited in the wings, eager to accept the challenge of leading Quebec to sovereignty.

Mulroney also had no choice. The two towering accomplishments that helped his re-election in 1988 — Meech Lake and free trade — had come badly unstuck. As a result, Mulroney's popularity had sunk to a low point never before experienced by an incumbent prime minister. Not only had Meech failed, but support for the free trade agreement had collapsed, and the overwhelming majority of Canadians believed that it had harmed the economy. For Mulroney to have even a remote possibility of political survival, he would have to salvage something from the Meech débâcle. If no reasonable offer were made to Quebec, the Bloc Québécois was poised to sweep the Tories from Quebec's electoral map. If, as a native son of Quebec, Mulroney proved unable to show English Canada that he could return Quebec to the fold "with honour and enthusiasm," his political future in English Canada was bleak.

The events following Meech made English Canadians pause and reflect upon the future of the country. A series of Gallup polls in 1992 left some room for hope, if not for unbridled optimism. Though still overwhelmingly opposed to sovereignty-association, 53 per cent of Canadians favoured an economic union if Quebec should separate. Furthermore, though a majority of Canadians were still strongly opposed to giving Quebec more powers than the other provinces, the national approval rate for distinct society recognition for Quebec in the constitution went up to 40 per cent — the highest level in five years. A strong majority in every region, including Quebec, wanted Quebec to stay in Canada, and only one in five believed the country would break up, the fewest since 1989. In Quebec, 35 per cent thought the country would break up, down dramatically from 51 per cent in 1990. Canadians were clearly hedging their bets, backing off from hard positions, and appeared a lot more willing to contemplate unique arrangements than their leaders admitted. Within Quebec, polls revealed the depth of the crisis and the surge toward sovereignty to be the results of the profound humiliation arising from the collapse of Meech. But despite the growth in separatist sentiment, the overwhelming majority of Québécois remained willing, even eager, to give English Canada another chance to heal the wounds.

When constitutional negotiations reopened in 1991, Canadians were assured that the intention was to develop a package that would not simply be a Meech Lake Accord Part II. This round was to be a "Canada Round," an attempt to address all the issues that helped unravel Meech. It was to be a wide-open, democratic, and public process — no more secret deals cobbled together in private. As discussions took place, they indeed appeared to be wide open, and no issue was unwelcome on the table. The process was long, exhausting, and stressful, involving a joint Commons and Senate committee road-show that heard from seven hundred people and was deluged by three thousand written submissions, a series of six televised and carefully staged national conferences from coast to coast, many top-level secret multilateral meetings over countless days, interminable discussions both within and between the delegations representing each key player, and countless private phone calls to Bourassa and his team, who refused to participate. In addition, there was the very profligate public expenditure of more than twenty-two million dollars by the Spicer Commission. The pace of the process was frenetic, sometimes appearing to border on panic, because the urgency of the process was very clearly established by Quebec's absence from the table and the need to make an offer of renewed federalism to Quebec before the referendum deadline. Clearly, the process had to address the two most controversial features of Meech that had led to its failure in popular support: distinct society for Quebec and the weakening of the power of the federal government. Most urgently, Quebec's disaffection and sense of betrayal had to be overcome. Furthermore, the constitutional concerns of Canada's aboriginal people had to have some priority.

On 8 July 1992, the premiers of the nine English-Canadian provinces announced an agreement on constitutional changes after a lengthy and secret meeting. The first draft of the Charlottetown Agreement was produced, having indeed been secretly cobbled together in private. And what the premiers produced was, in fact, a Meech Lake Accord Part II. Like Meech, the Premiers' Accord proposed the irrevocable transformation of the fundamental character of Canada. Provincial powers were to be increased dramatically, while the central government was to be weakened beyond any reasonable capacity to provide coherent national leadership. In addition, the premiers' package included the abolition of all existing unambiguous federal powers to override provincial legislation. The premiers proposed to pick the federal carcass nearly clean, a carcass Joe Clark and Brian Mulroney willingly yielded up to them. And, though Quebec was granted distinct society status in the new proposed "Canada clause," this concession was dramatically offset by commitments to the "equality of provinces" and to Canada's "linguistic duality" in the same clause. Furthermore, the equality of provinces doctrine was given dramatic effect in a proposal for a new, very powerful Triple-E Senate. Finally, the Premiers' Accord proposed to entrench the inherent right of aboriginal self-government in the constitution.

Reactions to the Premiers' Accord were mixed. Prime Minister Mulroney, who had reportedly expected the premiers to fail, initially expressed cautious and uneasy support. This response was not surprising. Since Mulroney's election in 1984, he had reduced the power and effectiveness of the central government, while giving the provinces much of what they demanded. Even Mulroney, however, may not have contemplated stripping Ottawa of so much power. He was particularly concerned about the Senate proposals. In the West and Newfoundland, partisans of the Triple-E Senate were elated at winning such a complete and stunning victory. Although Premier Bourassa typically neither rejected nor accepted the Accord, opinion in Quebec was uniformly negative, uniting federalist and separatist alike. Quebec could never accept losing so much power at the centre in the proposed Senate. Indeed, a survey conducted just days after the Premiers' Accord by the *Journal de Montréal* found 44 per cent of Québécois opposed, 27 per cent in favour, and 28 per cent undecided.

For a time, it appeared that the Premiers' Accord would unravel, forcing Ottawa to act unilaterally through the House of Commons in order to make an offer to Quebec before the October deadline. But a unilateral offer from Ottawa, without the provincial consent needed to effect constitutional changes, would have been a nearly meaningless gesture. And given the enormous pressure on Bourassa to proceed with a referendum on either sovereignty or an offer of renewed federalism, there would have been little opportunity to put together an alternative package in time. Furthermore, the nine English-Canadian premiers, having reached a consensus on a package that delivered so much to the provinces, were eager to see it accepted as well. Aboriginal leaders, having won the unexpected unanimous consent of the nine premiers and Ottawa to the constitutional entrenchment of the right of aboriginal self-government, were also eager to rescue the agreement.

Desperate for some kind of saleable deal, Premier Bourassa agreed to return to the table at a formal first ministers' meeting if Quebec's three major concerns with the premiers' package could be acceptably addressed. First, Quebec could not sanction the reduction in the province's power that would occur if the proposed Triple-E Senate were accepted. Substantial changes would be required in that area. Second, Quebec might accept the constitutional entrenchment of aboriginal self-government as long as such entrenchment could not be used in the courts to extend aboriginal land claims or to establish complete immunity from provincial law. Third, Quebec required some additional movement on the federal-provincial division of powers. Reassured that Ottawa, the premiers of English Canada, and the aboriginal leaders were open to such discussions and possible substantial concessions, Bourassa agreed to return to the table.

Accordingly, following two preliminary meetings at Harrington Lake, a first ministers' meeting from 18 to 22 August 1992 hammered out an agreement. The July Premiers' Accord more or less remained, despite some significant changes to the Senate and the House of Commons. The agreement was fine-tuned at a final first ministers' meeting in Charlottetown on 28 August 1992. (See Appendix.)

After finalizing the text of the Charlottetown Agreement, the first ministers spent most of their time at Charlottetown discussing a formal approval mechanism. Above all, they were determined to avoid a long, drawn-out process, like Meech, during which support for the Agreement could wither and die. Furthermore, as a result of the collapse of Meech, all first ministers had publicly promised that no more constitutional deals would be approved in secret without public, democratic consultation. In fact, some of the premiers owed their elections at least partly to public disgust with their predecessors over Meech. British Columbia and Alberta had passed legislation requiring a referendum on any constitutional amendment. Mulroney had promised "national consultation" in his 1991 Throne Speech. In the October 1991 Saskatchewan election, voters had overwhelmingly endorsed their right to be consulted by plebiscite on future constitutional changes. Both Manitoba and Newfoundland were committed by statute to a rather complicated process of public consultation before they could approve constitutional changes. And, of course, Quebec was irreversibly committed to a referendum.

Anticipating probable failure by the premiers to agree on constitutional changes, the Mulroney government had earlier introduced legislation to allow a national referendum supervised by Ottawa. Above all, the approval process had to deal with Quebec's already-established referendum date of 26 October 1992. Clearly, the wisest course was to agree on one question to be put to all the people of English Canada on the same day, allowing Quebec to pose the same question in French according to rules already established there for the 1980 referendum. There was some debate about whether to put just one question on the ballot in which the public would be asked to accept or reject the entire package as a so-called "seamless web" or, as Newfoundland's premier Clyde Wells wanted, separate questions on each major item in the Agreement. The problem with Wells's proposal was that the electorate could then support only those items that were popular — such as aboriginal self-government — while rejecting the more controversial items — such as the new Senate or distinct society. Mulroney argued strongly against the proposal, suggesting the question should be the simple and stark equivalent of "Are you for this deal or are you for the breakup of Canada?" The first ministers agreed to this course, although Wells remained reluctant. The final wording adopted was: "Do you agree that the Constitution of Canada should be renewed on the basis of the agreement reached on August 28, 1992?"

The first ministers also agreed that a federal referendum would be held by Ottawa in every province but Quebec. Quebec would ask the same question in French, but carry out the referendum under Quebec law. Finally, Quebec's referendum date was accepted — 26 October 1992. Formal public announcement of these decisions was delayed as a courtesy to Bourassa so he could first meet and persuade his caucus in the National Assembly, as well as the delegates at the already-scheduled convention of the Quebec Liberal Party. To have announced these decisions immediately would have left Bourassa open to charges in Quebec of being a prisoner of an agenda and a process imposed by English Canada. Assuming public approval in the referendum, the House of Commons, the Senate and the various provincial and territorial legislatures would then proceed to speed passage of the required formal legal texts. In this way, it was believed that the pitfalls of Meech would be avoided: rather than secret deals, there would be a public campaign culminating in an expression of the popular will by ballot; rather than a painful, lengthy process of squabbling and nit-picking, there would be a rapid and clear popular decision. The public approval process would be over and settled in two months. Although that would not prevent critics of the deal from attacking it in the House of Commons and the legislatures, any future effort to derail legislative approval after a victorious referendum outcome would have little political legitimacy.

Still, in spite of the apparently impeccable logic behind holding a referendum, there was profound unease among the political leaders. Both Mulroney and Clark had serious reservations about the idea, as did most of the premiers. In June 1992, government house leader Harvie Andre had warned, "I hope we don't have a referendum. A referendum will be a terrible bloody thing." The two major referendums of this century had been deeply damaging and inconclusive. Mackenzie King's 1942 vote on conscription had cleaved English Canada and Quebec more deeply than anyone expected. The result was so politically unacceptable, and the passions aroused on both sides so angry and volatile, that King was forced to retreat from a full implementation of conscription. In retrospect, Ottawa would have been wiser not to have held the vote and to have proceeded with more aggressively persuasive voluntary recruitment, especially in Quebec. The 1980 Quebec referendum had created deep and bitter divisions in that province and arguably set in motion the process that led finally to the Meech disaster. In a sense, the first ministers at Charlottetown were in fact reaping what had been sown in the referendum on sovereignty-association. Although 60 per cent were against a mandate to negotiate sovereignty in that referendum, it had settled nothing. In both cases, the referendums made the controversies they were intended to resolve deeper and more damaging. There was no reason to expect that this referendum would be any different. Yet, despite these reservations, the government appeared unavoidably committed.

To allay these fears, strategists pointed out that the juggernaut of support for the Yes side seemed irresistible. In favour were all the premiers and territorial leaders; the prime minister and his entire cabinet, the House of Commons and all federal party leaders; the Senate; the most prominent aboriginal leaders; the top leadership of organized labour and the established business lobby (although it was split in Quebec). How could such unanimity at the top not persuade the public to get on side? Still, the referendum was a huge gamble that, if unsuccessful, could worsen the situation. What if English Canada voted Yes and Quebec voted No? What if two or three western provinces voted No along with Quebec? What if the result was so close as to be politically insignificant one way or the other, merely confirming that the Canadian public was more or less equally polarized? Was it really worth the almost $200 million in costs to the taxpayer — $150 million for the federal referendum and $45 million for the one in Quebec — in order to find that Canadians were split 51 per cent to 49 per cent one way or the other?

In answer to such gloomy questions, eager proponents of the referendum strategy pointed to polls that suggested Canadians were tired of the reform process, wanted the constitutional issue resolved as soon as possible, and would support their leaders. And an early September Angus Reid poll seemed to confirm this view: in English Canada 61 per cent would vote Yes, 20 per cent No, with 18 per cent undecided; in Quebec Yes had the edge at 44 to 42 per cent, with 14 per cent undecided. These numbers suggested a strong Yes in English Canada and a close Yes in Quebec — a more-than-sufficient mandate to adopt the Charlottetown Agreement. Still, nothing could be certain. Up until the moment the referendum writ was dropped, Canada's united political elite more or less controlled the agenda, stage-managed the process, and paced the debate. After the writ was dropped, control would slip from their grasp and anything could happen. And given the political volatility of Canadians over the last decade and their contempt for their political leaders, there was no guarantee that they would give the political elite what it so eagerly wanted — a clear and unequivocal Yes.

As a result, the cards were stacked to give the Yes option the edge. The question itself was carefully constructed to encourage an affirmative response. The use of the word *renewed*, rather than the more neutral words *adopted* or *approved*, was a clear effort to link the question to the promise made by Trudeau and the English-Canadian premiers to the Québécois during the 1980 sovereignty-association referendum. "Renewal" of the constitution had been promised in exchange for an affirmation of federalism, but no renewal had in fact occurred — at least not one with which the Québécois had agreed. In addition, the word *renew* is loaded: it cries out for endorsation. It is hard to be against renewal, unless you are a backward stick-in-the-mud.

The federal referendum law, in marked contrast to that in Quebec, neither established real spending limits nor provided access to government funds to ensure fair balance in the debate between the Yes and No forces. The formidable Yes forces in English Canada could thereby establish as many Yes committees as they wished and put on a massive propaganda effort with no limits on spending — each and every committee could spend up to $7.5 million. This opened the door to an uncontrolled effort to buy a Yes vote through advertising in print and on the airwaves. The No forces in English Canada — disparate, relatively weak, deeply divided ideologically — could never hope to match the spending potential of the Yes side. In addition, the absence of government subsidies virtually ensured that the No side would be shut out of comparable access to the expensive and effective airwaves. The last barrier to unlimited spending in the referendum campaign was removed when the Canadian Radio-television and Telecommunications Commission (CRTC) lifted all advertising restrictions by ruling that partisan referendum advertising would be considered programming rather than political advertising. The effect of the CRTC decision was to allow unlimited partisan spending during the referendum on TV and FM radio. (Restrictions on AM radio had been dropped in 1985.)

In contrast, the Quebec referendum law was much fairer. The referendum was overseen by a panel of judges. The Yes and No sides were required to organize themselves into two umbrella organizations, each chaired by a member of the National Assembly. Each committee could only spend one dollar per voter to a maximum of $4.7 million for each of the two committees. Third-party advertising was strictly forbidden. Each side received the same subsidy from provincial coffers. Bloc Québécois efforts to obtain similar rules to govern the federal referendum were stonewalled in the House of Commons.

To reinforce the Yes side's advantage, Ottawa released a multi-million dollar blizzard of ads celebrating Canada's 125th "birthday" and providing information on the Charlottetown Agreement, all thanks to the taxpayers. These ads called out for a Yes vote, without explicitly saying so, by appealing to our patriotism and by applauding Charlottetown. The advantage of these ads was that not only were they paid for by the Ottawa government, but they could also be played and printed in Quebec, thus getting around Quebec's referendum law. (A similar campaign in 1980 of federally funded Ottawa ads in Quebec had annoyed Lévesque and the Yes Committee.)

Delaying the actual legal text was another tactic the Yes side used. After the Charlottetown Agreement was finalized in August, Canadians were told a full legal text would be available very soon. Then they were told it would be available midway in the referendum campaign. Then they were told by Clark that the public did not really need a legal text to judge the Agreement. Then there were hints that the legal text might not be ready until very close to voting day and perhaps not until after the vote. It was unclear whether the delays represented an honest difficulty in rendering the Agreement into complicated legalese, whether last-minute, behind-the-scenes negotiations were still going on, or whether the Yes side was deliberately delaying, or even denying, access to the text until the vote was over. Whatever the reasons, it was very risky.

One had only to recall that when the Meech Lake Accord was issued in legalese, its decline began. While it was merely vague principles and propositions, Meech supporters could defend it in platitudes and generalities and easily dismiss opponents. But once the legal text was on the table and the experts began to interpret the meaning and implications of the legal language, it soon became clear that there were deep, honest divisions in the opinions of the experts. Ordinary citizens reasoned that if the experts could not agree, how could they be expected to agree? The early debates on Charlottetown suggested that expert opinion on the meaning of the legal text would be similarly divided. Deliberately delaying the legal text, or even denying access until the vote was over, was attractive to Ottawa. By denying the No side something definitive to attack, the Yes side could easily dismiss the opponents of the Agreement. On the other hand, Canadians might feel manipulated or insulted. It would also be unprecedented in democratic tradition to ask an electorate to approve a constitution before the final legal text was a matter of public record. It was not surprising, therefore, that as the campaign heated up, the lack of a legal text became a burning issue not only among the No forces, but also among some in the Yes camp.

The final tactic for ensuring the success of the Agreement was the formation and launching of the Canada Yes Committee. The committee was composed of several prominent, non-partisan Canadians as national co-chairs and boasted the membership of three former premiers, two former national political party leaders, and prominent personalities in law, business, religion, education, science, and the arts and letters. The Charlottetown Agreement was still vulnerable: it had originated in secret meetings among the nine English-Canadian premiers and had been finally approved in further secret meetings with Bourassa and the prime minister. Given the public's suspicion of politicians, it was crucial to present the Charlottetown Agreement as now outside the grimy world of horse-trading, deal-making backroom politics. Given the record of public anger over Meech and its failure, the appeal to Canadians had to come from a more neutral source. Though the Canada Yes Committee received the explicit endorsement of the three federal party leaders, all the premiers and territorial leaders, and the national aboriginal leadership, its makeup was clearly designed to keep active partisan politicians at arm's length. At its kickoff, the Canada Yes Committee told Canadians that a Yes was not merely an approval of constitutional changes, but a vote for everything that was good, prosperous, and hopeful about Canada, including "a promising, certain future for our young people; the acceptance of a good compromise that has been worked out with intelligence and honour; good news for the economy; an affirmation of the values and the diversity of our country." By extension, a No vote was not just a rejection of a proposed constitutional amendment; it was reckless and irresponsible; it jeopardized our children's future, threatened to wreck the economy, and repudiated Canadian values. The gloves were off at the outset.

Prime Minister Mulroney had signalled this tough campaign line earlier when, upon announcing the successful conclusion of the Charlottetown Agreement, he had harshly said, "I know there will be fights...And I know that the enemies of Canada will...be out in full force. They will encounter me and my fellow first ministers...fighting for Canada." Although Mulroney quickly backed off from his explicit "enemies of Canada" line, the basic theme remained that those who opposed the Agreement would help destroy Canada. The referendum was not just about an agreement; it was about Canada. The answer on October 26 was a Yes or a No to Canada.

Another theme favoured by the prime minister was economic fear. Polls had repeatedly revealed that Canadians were deeply anxious and insecure about the economy. Clearly, if economic recovery, stability, and well-being could be linked in the minds of Canadians to approval of the Charlottetown Agreement, the initial Yes lead might be consolidated and increased. The prime minister hammered home this point relentlessly. A No would lead to "political instability...[which] gives rise to economic uncertainty [and]...the loss of economic opportunity...First and foremost, investors flee political uncertainty." A Yes, on the other hand, would "reduce uncertainty, increase stability and re-invigorate the economy," a Yes would bring "good news for the economy." The Yes team across Canada repeated such arguments. With remarkable unanimity, they insisted that a Yes would be an incredible tonic for a beleaguered economy.

Constitutional affairs minister Joe Clark was assigned the task of carrying messages of political instability. In a set speech repeated at meetings across Canada, he warned that Canada, "the peaceable kingdom...kept without civil war...will not survive a

No vote intact," that "if we reject this agreement...this country would begin to crumble." Clark evoked the terrible choices before Canadians: the "peaceable kingdom" affirming itself with a Yes or another Lebanon or Yugoslavia intolerantly snarling a No.

Clark also raised two subordinate themes. One was that the gains made by Quebec, the West, aboriginal people, and the provinces would be lost and never again resurrected if the No side prevailed. Another warning was that if Canadians did not approve Charlottetown, either the constitutional wrangling would go on endlessly, or negotiations would stop and Canada would be locked in a constitutional crisis for the foreseeable future. Again, other members of the Yes team fanned out and repeated these themes across the country.

Almost as soon as the referendum campaign began, popular support for the Yes side started to drop. By the third week of September, an Angus Reid poll reported that, on a national basis, the Yes and No options were tied in popular support at 36 per cent, while the undecided had gone up to 28 per cent. The No option was leading in Quebec by 45 to 38 per cent and in British Columbia and Alberta by 50 to 34 per cent. The Yes lead in Saskatchewan and Manitoba was cut to a dangerous 41 to 40 per cent. Yes was enjoying a comfortable lead only in Ontario and Atlantic Canada. A Léger et Léger poll in Quebec told an even worse story: 41 to 30.5 per cent for No over Yes, with 28.5 per cent undecided. Mulroney and the Yes strategists undoubtedly followed this drop through their internal polling. As a result, in what he later described as a deliberate "tactical counter-attack," the prime minister took a desperate and risky step by escalating his attack on the No side during a speech at Sherbrooke, Quebec, on Monday, 28 September. Indeed, in retrospect, the prime minister's escalation was clearly co-ordinated with a number of events the previous weekend in an effort to increase the level of economic anxiety among Canadians.

On Friday, 25 September, Royal Bank chair Allan Taylor released a forty-seven-page report, "Unity or Disunity: An Economic Analysis of the Benefits and Costs," at a press conference where he strongly endorsed the Yes side. The report was premised on the worst-case scenario of Quebec's separation — no economic association and hostile polarization — but the timing of its release and Taylor's remarks made it clear that, according to the bank, Quebec's separation might follow a No vote. According to the report, economic and population growth in Canada would grind to a halt and then fall sharply, per capita income would collapse by 15 per cent, and thousands would rush to emigrate from Canada to the United States.

On Sunday, 27 September, speaking to the Canadian Chamber of Commerce in Victoria, Al Flood, chair of the Canadian Imperial Bank of Commerce, provoked dramatic headlines across Canada the following day. The Regina *Leader Post's* front page captured the essence of his claims: "Yes side says No is chaos." Clumsily combining the themes of economic and political instability, Flood said, "The slightest hint of instability can send global financial markets into disarray. We have seen these things happen to other countries...and there is no reason why they cannot happen here if the international investment community concludes that we are politically unsound."

On Monday, 28 September, during a speech at Sherbrooke, Quebec, Mulroney dramatically ripped up a copy of the Charlottetown Agreement for the benefit of the television cameras. He went even further than the bankers. Picking up on the warnings of Taylor and Flood, Mulroney declared, "No means a direct contribution to separatism...the second-to-last step before separation [which] would plunge us into the unknown, into political instability and economic insecurity." No, according to the prime minister, amounted to nothing less than "the beginning of the process of dismantling Canada." Premier Bourassa agreed: "A No vote could mean a possible breakup of the federation."

In what was either a rapid self-fulfilling prophecy or a cynical economic manipulation, the Canadian dollar fell over the next few days to its lowest point in four years and the Bank of Canada raised its interest rate by two points, leading to similar rises in the consumer rates charged by chartered banks and ramming the prime rate up to 8.25 per cent. The Bank of Canada's move represented the biggest single jump in rates since the bank's birth in the 1930s. Stock markets reacted nervously. Many Canadians panicked, rushing to lock in their mortgages, fearing a continuing sharp rise in interest rates. All this seemed dramatic confirmation of the Yes side's negative economic forecasts, and the Yes side wasted no time in linking the fall in the dollar and the rise in interest rates to fears of a No victory. *Globe and Mail* columnist Jeffrey Simpson, deeply disappointed at the decline in Yes support, sternly lectured Canadians: "The Yes side's best arguments are not of its own making...The plunging stock market, the declining dollar, the skyrocketing interest rates...send the clearest message of all."

Economic scare tactics had worked well for hard-line federalists against Lévesque and the PQ during the 1970 and 1973 Quebec election campaigns, and even more effectively during the 1980 sovereignty-association referendum. But in those campaigns, the costs of separation were defensible arguments since the independence of Quebec was clearly on the table. Even hard-line separatists and moderate sovereigntists concede that there are economic costs associated with Quebec's independence, although nowhere near as high as federalists allege. Had the 1992 referendum been on Quebec independence, the economic fear campaign would have had a big impact, perhaps even a decisive one. But the referendum was not on separation, and the efforts of the Yes side to emphasize this issue failed utterly. The Canadian people refused to buy the argument, and the Yes team and the business community themselves were deeply divided on the political and economic consequences of a No vote.

Many Yes team members — including Canadian Labour Congress president Bob White, NDP leader Audrey McLaughlin, Newfoundland premier Wells, social activist June Callwood, and others — publicly and firmly rebuked the banks and the prime minister for their scare tactics. Alhough many among the business lobby continued to issue warnings, business opinion was divided. Some business experts cautioned Canadians not to panic but to ride out what was a temporary blip. Many money market brokers, particularly in the U.S. and Japan, predicted that interest rates in Canada would fall after the referendum regardless of the outcome simply because the Canadian economy was too fragile to sustain high interest rates. They contended that Canada's economic difficulties had to do with the economy itself: nearly negligible growth, little prospect for an upturn, and Canada's structural captivity by the weak U.S. economy, Canada's biggest market. With such conflicting messages coming from the business lobby, it is not surprising that the effort to generate economic hysteria in order to extract a Yes vote fizzled quickly. Although the dual themes of the negative political and economic consequences of a No vote remained cornerstones of the Yes campaign, the tone in which the messages were delivered changed quickly from breathless hysteria to persistent moderation.

While it was true that support for Meech had simultaneously unravelled at the top and at the bottom, support for Charlottetown unravelled almost exclusively at the bottom. Thus, though the political, labour, and business elites remained united in favour of the Agreement, the constituencies they hoped to deliver began to march out of control. This move to a No in English Canada was assisted by the interventions of three prominent Canadians, each representing significant if contradictory political tendencies. Former prime minister Trudeau, Judy Rebick of the National Action Committee on the Status of Women (NAC), and Reform Party leader Manning, speaking from very different ideological perspectives, all came down dramatically on the No side. Their support was a blow to the Yes campaign and helped to derail the initial strategy of insisting that a No vote was not only unthinkable but illegitimate. By their very different interventions, and for very different reasons, each gave many Canadians a rationale for voting No. Most important, each gave a No vote public legitimacy.

Manning did not declare his decision to campaign for a No until 10 September 1992, almost two weeks after the finalization of the Charlottetown Agreement. At first, he briefly toyed with supporting the deal or adopting a stance of neutrality. However, his advisors, middle-level leadership, and the Reform rank-and-file made it clear that he had no choice but to come out strongly against Charlottetown.

Manning restricted his No campaign to a few major themes. He argued the Agreement would lead to almost-interminable constitutional negotiations; he complained that it committed Ottawa to heavy social spending, meaning the government would have difficulty balancing the budget; he stated the amending formula would make the deal irreversible, thereby depriving future generations of the means to fix the constitution; and he insisted the Agreement failed to provide "effective regional representation," the closest he came to embracing the explicit role of champion of western alienation. Given the cauldron of anger bubbling among the Reform rank-and-file, his campaign was remarkably low-key. The rest of the No side, which had nothing in common with Manning other than their opposition, was grateful for the restraint.

While Manning's position on the Agreement was perhaps predictable, NAC's active opposition to Charlottetown caught many observers off-guard. They had expected the organization either to sign on to the Yes side, stay silent, or perhaps simply issue a critical press release. Instead, the NAC executive committed the organization and its president, Judy Rebick, to an active campaign for a No vote.

NAC's opposition to Charlottetown was based on three central concerns. First, Rebick declared solidarity with the Native Women's Association of Canada (NWAC), arguing that the aboriginal self-government proposal failed to provide aboriginal women with adequate equality guarantees. Second, she argued that the Canada clause jeopardized the gender equality rights that women had already won in the 1982 constitution. Finally, she warned that the Agreement might jeopardize existing social programs and make it impossible to develop future social programs with national standards. Rebick became a tireless and effective campaigner for the No side, and as the campaign progressed, she increasingly spoke not only for Canada's organized feminist lobby, but also for the rank-and-file trade unionists and New Democrats who felt that they had been abandoned by their own leaderships.

Trudeau had played a significant role in the death of the Meech Accord, and it was universally expected he would pass judgement on the Charlottetown Agreement as well. His intervention in the campaign came in two salvos. The first was a scathing and contemptuous denunciation of Québécois nationalists in the 28 September 1992 issue of *Maclean's*; then he offered a detailed critical analysis of the agreement in a speech on 1 October 1992. In it, he developed five substantive arguments for voting No. First, he attacked the use of political and economic terrorism by the Yes side: "politicians — and politicians in high places, and even bankers in high places — are trying to make us think, make us believe, that a Yes is a yes to Canada, and a No is a no to Canada. This is a lie that must be denounced." Second, he noted that a Yes would not bring constitutional peace but endless bickering — "the blackmail would continue." Third, Trudeau noted that the Charlottetown amending formula ensured the Agreement would be "irreversible." Fourth, he argued that the proposed Canada clause undermined the individual rights enshrined in the Charter, creating a "hierarchy of classes of citizens," thereby threatening minorities, especially official-language minorities. Fifth, the Charlottetown Agreement seriously weakened the federal government and jeopardized social programs, especially those in the poor provinces. In other words, Trudeau declared, the Charlottetown Agreement was a "mess that deserves a big No."

With these two interventions, Trudeau crystallized significant currents of opposition to the Agreement, appealing simultaneously to anti-Quebec bigots in English Canada, official-language minorities in every province, Canadians who cherished the primacy of the Charter's individual rights over collective rights, those who feared the excessive devolution of federal powers, and those who were concerned about the protection of existing social programs and the development of new ones. Perhaps of greatest importance in the heat of the referendum campaign was Trudeau's blunt condemnation of the scare tactics of the Yes side, thereby giving many Canadians the courage to contemplate a No vote. "The question of Yes or No is," Trudeau reminded Canadians, "yes or no, do you want us to reform, or amend, the Constitution on the basis of the so-called consensus of Charlottetown?" Trudeau's pivotal role in stopping the Yes team's scare campaign in its tracks should not be underestimated.

The unravelling of popular support for Charlottetown cannot be explained alone by these interventions by Manning, Rebick, and Trudeau. They simply helped, giving diverse groups of Canadians intellectual and political hooks on which to hang their relatively spontaneous sense of opposition. It appears that the largely ignored Spicer Commission report of June 1991 had been more on the mark than anyone anticipated — the report had warned of the popular "fury in the land" against politicians, that Canadians had "lost faith" in "the political process and their political leaders." While the Reform Party and NAC had a considerable effect, they were no match for the Yes side's potential. And, of course, Trudeau only had influence at an aloof distance. He did not actively campaign, nor did he have an organization with troops to deliver a No vote. Theoretically and on paper, the Yes side had a formidable organization. By the end of the campaign, 191 Yes committees and only thirty-four No committees had been officially registered with Canada's Chief Electoral Officer. The central Yes campaign in English Canada had an estimated media budget of more than five million dollars, and countless local Yes committees had ample funds to put out their message in local media and local daily newspapers. Maclean Hunter registered itself as a Yes committee in order to run legal pro-Yes ads at its own expense in *Maclean's*, *The Financial Post*, and the *Sun* daily newspaper group (in Toronto, Ottawa, Calgary, and Edmonton). Provincial governments were free to spend as well and did so. The editorial consensus of English Canada's daily newspapers was unprecedented, and they did not hesitate to push the Yes message.

The No campaign in English Canada had virtually no money, relying for national mass exposure on its half share of the ninety minutes of free network time provided under referendum campaign regulations. Since this was a campaign that involved convincing, identifying, and delivering the vote, the Yes side theoretically had the enormous advantage of having the support of the entire campaign infrastructures of the three major political parties. The three-party alliance worked reasonably effectively at the top — the three parties' top media and campaign strategists worked for the Yes team — but it was soon discovered they could not deliver the troops on the ground. Efforts to build joint constituency organizations to go door to door, to put up signs, to check off Yes supporters on the voters' list, and to prepare to get out the vote all failed. Not only did the elites of the three parties find that they could not deliver their activist troops to campaign, they found they could not deliver their supporters to vote Yes.

Although the Liberal Party in English Canada was officially in favour of Charlottetown, Jean Chrétien did as little campaigning as possible, and his defence of the Agreement was neither passionate nor convincing. Trudeau's interventions had the biggest impact among Liberals in English Canada and among English-Canadian Liberals in Quebec. In addition, a number of other prominent party members, such as constitutional lawyer Deborah Coyne and Liberal leaders Sharon Carstairs of Manitoba and Gordon Wilson of British Columbia, came out strongly against the agreement.

Except for Mulroney and a few high-profile cabinet ministers, most Tory MPs either ran for cover or did as little unenthusiastic campaigning as they could. Given the low levels of Tory popular support and the profound unpopularity of Mulroney, this approach was understandable. Indeed, too much aggressive campaigning by Tory MPs might have hurt rather than helped the Yes side. Tory premiers hardly threw themselves energetically into the battle, at least not until the very end.

In supporting Charlottetown, the three NDP premiers and the national leader McLaughlin abandoned the central tenets of NDP policy, disillusioning many NDP supporters in the process. First there was their support of the new Senate, probably the most appalling *volte face* in Canadian political history. From its founding in 1935, the CCF/NDP has always favoured the abolition of the

Senate. Second, McLaughlin's participation in such a transparent provincial-rights grab was inexplicable to many party members. Traditionally, the NDP had opposed the devolution of too much power to the provinces. Third, with the deal, the leaders of the NDP relinquished their willingness to concede special status to Quebec, joining the English-Canadian effort to impose a fundamentally unacceptable constitutional solution upon Quebec. Finally, many NDPers were outraged that their leaders had participated in an effort to constitutionalize one of the major items of the neo-conservative agenda of the last decade — to weaken and render impotent the central government. In exchange for a meaningless and toothless Social Charter, the NDP leadership had largely bargained away the most important tool Canadians have had to fight for reform and change — the instrumentality of a strong central government. The NDP leadership, therefore, found that it was not only unable to deliver its electoral base to the Yes side, but also failed to deliver its party membership *en masse*.

The top leadership of the Canadian Labour Congress (CLC), with its 2.3 million members, faced the same problems as the NDP leadership, largely for the same reasons. Despite formal support for the agreement by the CLC's Executive Council, the rank-and-file of the labour movement remained largely unconvinced. Two major national unions — the Canadian Union of Postal Workers and the Public Service Alliance of Canada — publicly broke with the CLC and formally endorsed the No side, largely over the same issues as NAC. And of course the Quebec Federation of Labour was overwhelmingly against Charlottetown, like all other Quebec labour organizations. Ed Finn, a longtime labour activist and retired research director of CUPE, spoke for many in labour when he called the agreement a "legalistic monstrosity...far better consigned to the garbage dump than enshrined in the Constitution."

The English-Canadian business lobby was solidly on the Yes side, particularly at the top corporate level and among the organized Chamber of Commerce sector. But there were some important cracks. Although the influential Canadian Federation of Independent Business came out strongly in favour of Charlottetown, its leadership admitted that a large portion of its membership was against it. The powerful British Columbia Employers' Council faced such division that it decided to stay neutral. Eric Kierans, one of the most respected English-Canadian business leaders, at first declared himself in favour of the Agreement and then announced, as he left for vacation, that he had changed his mind and had voted No in an advance poll. In Quebec, the business lobby was deeply fractured. The most powerful and influential business organization, l'Association des manufacturiers du Québéc, which includes such members as Alcan, Northern Telecom, and IBM Canada, decided to stay neutral while at the same time describing the Agreement as "disappointing." André Bérard, chair of the National Bank of Canada, formerly seen as a loyal federalist, also declared neutrality. Finally, in a significant setback for the Yes team, the sixty-one-thousand-member Chambre de Commerce du Québec opted for neutrality. These decisions may have had something to do with the hostility faced by the Royal Bank in Quebec following its intervention on the Yes side. Many customers in Quebec closed their accounts in protest, *Non* stickers were plastered on many branches, and *Non* campaign leader Parizeau accused the bank of profiting by secretly speculating on the sharp decline in the Canadian dollar that the bank had helped to provoke.

But the most irreparable damage to the Yes campaign was the unravelling of support for the aboriginal self-government aspect of Charlottetown among some First Nations. The most positive feature of the Charlottetown Agreement for English Canadians and Québécois alike was the commitment to the inherent right to aboriginal self-government. Many in English Canada were inclined to support the deal just to affirm that right. From the outset, however, NWAC had strongly opposed the deal on the grounds that not only were aboriginal women excluded from the negotiating table, but also that the clause of the Agreement giving aboriginal culture and traditions primacy might prevail over gender equality rights.

NWAC was not the only organization in the aboriginal community to have doubts about the Agreement. By late September, the Council of Crees of Quebec and the Mohawks were proposing a boycott of the referendum, as were thirty First Nations in Alberta. Then the Manitoba chiefs began to express doubts. And there were rumours that the Union of B.C. Chiefs was moving toward support for a No. Elijah Harper also refused to endorse the deal. He indicated that if he had to vote, he would vote No, but it was better for aboriginals to boycott the referendum.

The chiefs' concerns were of fundamental importance. First, there was a fear that the Agreement might erode treaty rights as a result of constitutionalizing them. Second, there was a related concern that the devolution of power both to the provinces and to aboriginal governments might also weaken existing Crown treaty obligations and Ottawa's responsibility for them. Third, there was a growing apprehension that the "peace, order, and good government" concession to Quebec made the aboriginal self-government clause meaningless. Fourth, among treaty Indians there was some concern about the inclusion of the Inuit and the Métis in the aboriginal self-government clause. What impact would the inclusion of these groups have on the existing and future rights of status Indians? Where would the money for self-government come from? Finally, there was a feeling that too much power had been granted to Quebec and that the aboriginal people in Quebec needed stronger assurances. Among many chiefs, especially the Mohawks, there was also a principled rejection of the whole process on the grounds that they already enjoyed self-government on aboriginal lands, and always had. There was a final effort to secure the endorsement of the chiefs, but many remained unconvinced. Despite the fact that Ovide Mercredi and other aboriginal leaders continued to campaign for a Yes, the failure of the Assembly of First Nations to endorse Charlottetown was a mortal blow to the Yes campaign in English Canada.

There were a series of other events that nipped at the heels of the Yes campaign, undermining its credibility. There were the absentee premiers who failed to go on the campaign trail. Premier Wells of Newfoundland initially refused to campaign actively outside his own province and only agreed to do so later when he was satisfied that the legal text was acceptable. Premier Don Getty of Alberta had announced his retirement from politics right after the Agreement and did not take a particularly active part in the campaign, even in Alberta. Premier Gary Filmon of Manitoba failed to become active until late in the campaign. Premier Mike Harcourt of British Columbia spent so much of his time repairing the personal political damage he suffered as a result of the Agreement that he did not campaign outside the province. Premier Roy Romanow of Saskatchewan only made obligatory appearances and speeches. In the early phase of the campaign, the premiers' absenteeism had to do with overconfidence. Later, as the Yes campaign faltered, eagerness to campaign was tempered by the "Peterson factor" — memories of how the public had punished many of the incumbent politicians involved in Meech. Then there was the "Mulroney factor." If a large part of the reason that support was slipping for the Agreement had to do with Mulroney's un-popularity, the premiers doubted the wisdom of linking them-selves too clearly with the prime minister, who had largely seized for himself centre stage in the national Yes campaign.

Then there was the controversy over the legal text. While it was true that there would not be an enormous demand for a legal text among Canadians in general, those with a special interest re-quired one as soon as possible, if only to confirm that the legalese faithfully replicated the Agreement in letter and spirit. As Sep-tember came to an end and there was still no legal text, criticism mounted. Finally, at the end of September, Premier Wells of New-foundland, Deputy Premier Horsman of Alberta and Justice Min-ister McCrae of Manitoba clearly stated that a legal text was needed or their provinces would reconsider their support for the deal. The Agreement was only finally published in all daily news-papers on 3 October 1992, and Clark announced that the legal text would be available by mid-October. The text was not finalized until the Thanksgiving weekend, just two weeks before the vote.

By the time the legal text was generally available to the public there were only ten or eleven days left in the campaign. Yet the re-lease of the text did not lay the suspicions to rest — it was entitled "Draft Legal Text" and described only as "a best efforts text." Fur-thermore, there were some significant controversial changes to the original Agreement in the legal text. The democracy guaran-tees of the Charter were not to apply to aboriginal governments. Only the appointment of the governor of the Bank of Canada was definitely to be subject to Senate ratification, rather than the heads of all federal regulatory agencies and cultural institutions. Electri-cal power was added to natural resources as subject to Senate de-feat. The double-majority requirement in the Senate on matters of French language and culture was now defined in terms of a ma-jority of all senators and of all "French-speaking" senators rather than all "francophone" senators. Thus, the presumed veto of Que-bec's six senators was now dubious. Finally, the concession Wells wanted — that Senate laws defeated in the House of Commons would go to a joint sitting — was included. These were all serious last-minute changes and further undermined public confidence in the Agreement.

A further problem of credibility for the Yes campaign related to the very different versions of the meaning of the Agreement that were presented in Quebec and in English Canada. Every time Mulroney bragged loudly in Quebec about all the gains made for the province, the Yes campaign was hurt in English Canada. Yet when English-Canadian politicians told English Canadians that the deal gave Quebec very little, the Yes side was damaged in Quebec. When Premier Wells told a Calgary audience on 7 October 1992 that the Charlottetown Agreement was an improvement on Meech because it had put a "fence" around distinct society, giving it a more limited meaning than in Meech, the *Le Devoir* headline was *"Wells: le Québec s'est satisfait de moins que Meech,"* and another nail was hammered into the coffin of the Yes campaign in Quebec. The same was true when B.C. intergovernmental affairs minister Moe Sihota explained in Quesnel, B.C., on 6 October 1992 that Bourassa had "lost" and had run into a "brick wall" on "special status." The same was true on 14 October 1992 when Manitoba premier Filmon told a farm and business audience in Russell, Manitoba: "When Quebec said, 'We want all those other powers,' we said: …'No. This is as far as we'll go.'" Clearly, Wells, Sihota, and Filmon were trying to persuade English Canadians to support the deal on the grounds that Quebec had received comparatively little. Yet every such argument made in English Canada echoed back in Quebec and served to undermine the Yes side there. And such arguments did not finally help in English Canada because Mulroney continued to tell the Québécois about their thirty-one gains, the best deal for Quebec in 125 years. Thus, the Yes side faced a serious credibility gap in both Quebec and English Canada.

In an unforeseen irony, the Yes campaign's overwhelming superiority in media access turned into a liability. With its multimillion-dollar media budget, the Yes side, in ordinary politics, should have been a steamroller. With ample enough resources to insert one and two full-page spreads in all major dailies on at least two occasions, as well as to expose every Canadian television viewer to thirteen pro-Yes ads each week throughout October, the Yes side was confident. In addition, huge Yes billboards dotted Canada from coast to coast, Yes lawn signs sprang up and stood out sharply if only because of the near total absence of No signs everywhere but in Quebec, and pamphlets appeared in every single mailbox, all providing the Yes message with constant daily reinforcement. But the Yes propaganda campaign failed.

Many of the ads were misleading. Some ads claimed the new Senate was Triple-E. It was not, and only the ignorant or dishonest could claim otherwise. Others implied that the Social Charter clause provided clear protection to ordinary Canadians. It did not. Others boasted that the Agreement brought Canada an effective economic union. It did not. Many Canadians found the television commercials insulting. Yet the Yes campaign stubbornly persisted in playing these ads despite clear evidence they were counter-productive. An Angus Reid/Southam poll taken from 12 to 15 October found that 55 per cent of Canadians did not believe that a No would bring negative economic consequences, while 71 per cent did not believe a No would lead to Quebec's separation. The widely shared perception that Ottawa was misusing taxpayers' dollars to influence their votes in what was supposed to be a fair and democratic referendum process did not help the Yes side either.

The battle in Quebec was a separate, almost internal, event. Once again, the Québécois debated among themselves whether their vision of Quebec as one of two founding nations could be reconciled with English Canada's latest version of federalism. It was significant that Ottawa was conducting a separate referendum in the nine English-Canadian provinces under federal law, while Quebec was holding a separate vote under Quebec law. This difference was more than a matter of symbolism. The rules governing the referendum in Quebec were much fairer. While in English Canada the disparate, poorly organized No side seemed badly outmatched by the well-oiled Yes machine, in Quebec both sides were more evenly matched. As Mulroney declared, in Quebec he expected a "bare knuckled fight." On the Yes side was the Bourassa government and the Quebec Liberal Party, the preponderance of the business lobby and, at least initially, the formerly formidable federalist forces. On the No side were the sovereigntists, supported by between 30 and 40 per cent of the population and very well organized in the PQ and Bloc, a significant portion of the business lobby, and organized labour. As the campaign unfolded, the No side also picked up elements of the nationalist wing of the Liberal party and even a significant share of Trudeau federalists (including, according to one estimate, up to 20 per cent of Quebec's English-speaking minority). While the first post-Charlottetown polls gave the Yes side a large forty-one point lead in English Canada (61 to 20 per cent), in Quebec the Yes lead was a mere two points (44 to 42 per cent). At first, it was assumed that whichever side won in Quebec, it was going to be a close call, decided by a few percentage points. But then the Yes campaign in Quebec began to unravel.

The biggest problem was the Agreement itself. The Québécois had been prepared for some kind of serious resolution after Meech and were awaiting a referendum on renewed federalism or sovereignty. During the year prior to Charlottetown, more than five hundred thousand Québécois had signed a petition insisting that Bourassa hold such a referendum as promised. Thanks to the Allaire and Bélanger-Campeau reports, the Québécois had very definite ideas about what acceptable renewed federalism entailed, ideas that bordered on a popular consensus. When Bourassa agreed to go back to the table to negotiate the Charlottetown Agreement and then announced success, there was an initial misperception on the part of many Québécois. Obviously, they reasoned, Bourassa must have obtained something significant in the Agreement. Hence, the early September polls showed a two-point lead in public support in Quebec. But as soon as the Agreement was subjected to analysis, support began to collapse. The distinct society clause in the Charlottetown Agreement was weaker than the Meech Lake Accord. The Senate was still unacceptable. There was no new division of powers acceptable to Quebec. There was no clear veto, especially over the creation of new provinces.

As well, Bourassa's arguments for the deal were half-hearted and defensive. On one occasion he compared the deal to a lottery consolation prize: "*L'entente est comme un prix de consolation, acceptez-la et prenez des billets pour le prochain tirage.*" Or, he argued, it was better to accept the deal than to fight on: "*Ce n'est pas la perfection. Mais, c'est mieux que l'affrontement, les tensions et le recul.*" Or, as he once conceded in English, "It is not an absolutely extraordinary deal," though "there are substantial gains there for Quebec." Even the Yes slogan in Quebec suggested satisfactory resolution was put off for now: "*L'avenir commence par un Oui.*" Certainly, Bourassa participated in the scare tactics of Clark and Mulroney. Yet, his active defence of the deal itself was clearly tempered by the deal's self-evident flaws from the point of view of the Québécois.

The No campaign in Quebec was determined to make the deal itself the battleground and resisted all efforts to shift the terrain to other issues such as the contention that a No vote equalled a vote for sovereignty or that the political and economic consequences of a No would be disastrous. At one point, Parizeau said, "I won't discuss sovereignty. I'm discussing the constitutional proposal we have before us." The No slogan also zeroed in on the deal: "*A ce prix-là, c'est Non!*" The No side's approach was to lay the Charlottetown Agreement out like a corpse on a slab and to engage in a clinical dissection in full public view. Significantly, the first copies the Québécois received of a full text were distributed by the No campaign machine, with critical comments and remarks written on the margins throughout. From the outset, the No campaign saw its biggest asset as the deal and insisted on keeping the public's attention focused on the details.

Events at the Quebec Liberal convention on 29 August 1992 only confirmed the flaws in the Agreement. The resolution approved by the convention clearly damned the deal with faint praise: "That the Quebec Liberal Party recognizes that...the agreement...while beneath the party's program, represents a genuine progress that is concurrent with Quebec's traditional demands." The convention, which was open to all individual Liberals who happened to show up, was stacked with busloads of loyalists, including many non-francophone Québécois. It was widely acknowledged that there had been a last-minute brisk sale of memberships in the party. In protest, Mario Dumont, the leader of the Liberal youth wing, walked out of the convention and was followed by a few dozen youth delegates. Only later was it clear that he indeed represented the overwhelming majority sentiment among Quebec's young people. (A poll a few weeks later put No support at 66 per cent among the eighteen- to thirty-four-year age group). And when Jean Allaire, the author of the famous party report on the constitution, voted against the resolution and then later formally joined the No side, a large bloc of Quebec nationalist Liberals joined him. By the time Allaire had finished his quiet but lethally effective No campaign within the Liberal party, more than seventy local executive members had resigned. When Allaire earnestly said, "the offers...received amount to nothing less than a surrender by Quebec," people who would not give Parizeau or Bouchard the time of day listened.

The impact of close public scrutiny of the deal and the events at the Liberal convention were enough to turn the tide against it. By 6 September 1992, the No side in Quebec was leading the Yes by 39 to 34 per cent. A poll a week later found it was leading by 41 to 31 per cent. From late August to a week before the 26 October vote, twenty-six polls by a variety of polling firms were conducted in Quebec. Twenty of them gave the lead to the No starting from the first week of September to 19 October, when the No lead had increased to 58 per cent. In the early polls, there had been a large bloc of undecideds, but in the ensuing weeks, the undecideds began to break for the No as the Yes campaign in Quebec stumbled from one disaster to another.

One of the disasters was *l'affaire Wilhelmy*, which dominated the campaign in Quebec for a crucial period and lingered like a bad aftertaste until voting day. The controversy virtually killed any hope the Yes forces had of rallying its rapidly dwindling public support in a final push. At the centre was a tape of an electronically intercepted cellular telephone conversation between Diane Wilhelmy, Quebec's Deputy Minister of Intergovernmental Affairs, and André Tremblay, Bourassa's top constitutional advisor. Wilhelmy had been absent from the Charlottetown negotiations due to ill health, while Tremblay had attended.

Intercepted just days after the Agreement was concluded, the call caught Quebec's two top constitutional advisors commiserating with each other about the deal. They agreed it was a disaster for Quebec and that Bourassa had been an ineffective and weak negotiator, abandoning Quebec's traditional demands, collapsing under the relentless pressure from the English-Canadian delegations, and finally settling for far less than was defensible. In the course of the negotiations, Bourassa had ignored all the advice given him and agreed to a flawed package for no other reason than he was desperate to obtain a deal to present to the people of Quebec. The following excerpts capture the rawness of their exchange and their deep disappointment and shock at what had happened.

Tremblay: "[Bourassa] never wanted a referendum on sovereignty....We just caved in, that's all."

Wilhelmy: "It has taken me three days to accept the fact that we have settled for so little....We are walking on our knees..."

Tremblay: "It's a heavy burden to carry...with all these people against you. And the Ontarians...are the worse sons of bitches..."

Wilhelmy: "That is what we said last year, and it hasn't changed....It's a national disgrace....Mr. Bourassa should have taken a plane home right away. What a humiliation..."

Tremblay: "He had no choice. He wanted offers and he had to come home with offers."

These graphic images were serious affronts to Québécois national sensibilities: the premier on his knees to his domineering English-Canadian counterparts, compromising Quebec's historic demands, overly eager for any deal, and finally caving in to English-Canadian pressure.

The response of the Yes side ensured *l'affaire Wilhelmy* would remain uppermost in the public's mind. On 14 September, Wilhelmy obtained a court injunction preventing the printed dissemination of the transcript and the broadcast of the tape in Quebec. Portions of the transcript were, however, published in the 16 September *Globe and Mail* distributed outside Quebec. A few excerpts from the newspaper article, including quotations, were read into the record in the Quebec National Assembly. It became something of a farce, as English-Canadian editions of the *Globe and Mail* were passed hand to hand, while fax machines hummed throughout the province. Full-text transcripts were passed around in an almost clandestine fashion. Thereafter the public's right to know joined the content of the conversation itself in assisting the No side. When the court injunction was lifted on 30 September, allowing publication of the words used but forbidding the broadcast of the actual tape, there was another circus. Copies were printed and sold on street corners for five dollars and media outlets hired actors to perform the roles for broadcast. In addition to this pummelling, the responses of Bourassa's first ministerial colleagues didn't help. "Fraudulent and preposterous," intoned Mulroney, "Mr. Bourassa conducted himself with great skill and effectiveness." Virtually every premier leapt into the fray, giving glowing testimonials attesting to Bourassa's outstanding negotiating abilities. By protesting so much, the prime minister and the premiers only served to encourage scepticism, and many in Quebec found their comments patronizing and condescending. And in Quebec Tremblay was paraded at a press conference where he was forced to recant, though he retained some of his dignity by refusing to comment on certain key parts of the conversation.

Though the economic scare tactics of the prime minister at Sherbrooke were at least partly designed to divert attention from *l'affaire Wilhelmy* and to stop the slide in the polls for the Yes side, Trudeau's 1 October intervention was more effective than anyone expected. But in Quebec, where Trudeau's constitutional views were old news, the biggest impact of his speech was not his detailed analysis of the deal. The biggest impact was his attack on the economic scare tactics, and it struck a very responsive chord in Quebec that helped checkmate that issue. For a former prime minister of some stature, and one who himself had not hesitated to raise the economic issue when debating Quebec's sovereignty, to stand up in public and call the prime minister and the leading bankers of Canada liars was a strong antidote. The Yes team had anticipated Trudeau's constitutional criticisms, were prepared for them, and answered them quickly. But they did not expect that Trudeau would sandbag them with such a frank and frontal assault on the economic scare theme, a theme they had intended to make a central focus of their campaign.

The last hope of the Yes campaign became the 12 October ninety-minute live television debate between Bourassa and Parizeau. If Parizeau should stumble badly, or if Bourassa should shine brightly, there was still a chance. The debate was a big event in Quebec, the first debate between party leaders since 1962 when Liberal leader Jean Lesage badly mauled Union Nationale premier Daniel Johnson. More than 2.3 million viewers in Quebec watched the exchange and remained switched on for the post-debate analyses and commentaries. There were no surprises. No mortal blows were struck. Both men effectively exchanged point for point, with Parizeau putting Bourassa on the defensive in the early stages, and Bourassa rallying near the end. No new arguments were added, though Bourassa made a stronger-than-usual appeal to the doubting federalists who had been shaken loose from the Yes side by Trudeau and Allaire. The commentators and analysts were almost unanimous: neither man won; each held his own. But subsequent polls suggested the viewers had a different assessment. When asked to pick a winner, 46 per cent gave it to Bourassa, while only 15 per cent gave it to Parizeau. This was briefly reflected in a slight upward trend in the polls for the Yes side, accompanied by a slight decline for the No. But it was not enough. And any hope that this slight post-debate blip could lead to a rally was undercut a few days later in the pages of the 16 October edition of L'Actualité, Quebec's version of Maclean's.

L'Actualité obtained, from an unnamed source, a collection of Quebec government briefing documents for the Ottawa and Charlottetown meetings. These documents were highly confidential, normally secured in a locked safe. The documents filled in all the details and dramatically confirmed the earlier tantalizingly scant, but highly suggestive, telephone conversation between Wilhelmy and Tremblay. Bourassa had agreed to a deal that both surrendered Quebec's historical demands and succumbed to "domineering federalism." The deal repudiated Quebec as one of Canada's founding nations, shackled Quebec with the equality of provinces provision, and denied Quebec any form of special status. The deal contained far less than Meech, since the distinct society clause had been made trivial and virtually legally useless. The deal allowed even more intrusions by Ottawa into Quebec's affairs via the many administrative agreements to be negotiated under the Charlottetown Agreement. The documents revealed a certain envy that English Canada, with Bourassa's agreement, had allowed the aboriginal people to make great gains in achieving many of Quebec's basic constitutional objectives, including a clearly demarcated order of government with special status and a clear veto over constitutional changes affecting them. Since it was a province, therefore subject to the equality of provinces doctrine and with the diminished distinct society clause, Quebec was denied these gains. The documents advised that the Agreement would lead to "perpetual negotiations." Finally, it was confirmed that Bourassa's minimal demands for additional powers had been flatly rejected by the English-Canadian first ministers, reinforcing the statements made by Wells, Sihota, and Filmon.

The effect was devastating. Despite efforts by Bourassa to dismiss the documents as "anonymous allegations," and Mulroney to rant about "idiocies and absurdities regarding certain negotiations" while again defending Bourassa as "a remarkable Premier," the blow was fatal. Given the previous high levels of No support, defeat of the agreement in Quebec was already virtually assured. The publication of the documents in *L'Actualité* simply removed any hope of a comeback for the Yes side. Gallup carried out its last pre-vote poll from October 15 to 19. Not only did the poll suggest the Agreement was going down to heavy defeat in the West, but Yes and No were also tied in Ontario. Only Atlantic Canada remained firmly Yes. In Quebec, the No side was leading by an astonishing twenty-eight points — 58 to 30 per cent — with only 12 per cent undecided.

The last week of the campaign was one of bombastic desperation for the prime minister. In response to the published polls, Mulroney talked endlessly of internal polls that found great movement and a huge bloc of undecideds ready to stampede to the Yes side. He adopted a two-pronged contradictory strategy for the final drive to voting day. On the one hand, he appealed to Canadians to show tolerance and an acceptance of diversity by voting Yes. On the other hand, he continued a negative campaign of attacks, frequently very sneeringly personal, on the three major No figures: Manning for his intolerance and bigotry, Parizeau for his separatist agenda, and Trudeau for preventing Mulroney from "cleaning up his mess" left in 1982. He also continued to warn the Québécois, as he had from the outset: "You cannot have your cake and eat it, too. If you turn down the Charlottetown Agreement, the other English-speaking provinces are not going to the constitutional table to accommodate Quebec." In addition, he escalated his attack on the separatists: "*Le gang du Non* in Quebec...torpedoed Meech...are sabotaging Charlottetown and tomorrow will attack any agreement, no matter what, which does not ensure the division of Canada."

Bourassa, for his part, continued to pin his final hopes on the basic realism of both Québécois and English Canadians. He argued that, regardless of what the polls said, when people went out to cast their ballots they would "think twice" and in a "burst of lucidity" vote Yes. As voting day came closer, Bourassa made his strongest-ever pitch directly to federalists in Quebec, most importantly those in the Liberal Party influenced for opposite reasons by Trudeau and Allaire. Reminding the Québécois that a No vote would continue the impasse, pose a major setback for the federalist cause in Quebec, and represent a substantial moral victory for the separatists, he pleaded for support: "We can't say No all the time. We've said No many times. And now...this time we can say Yes. And I can only hope that the people will hear me."

The last week of the Yes campaign's national media strategy tried to salvage what could be salvaged. The Yes side persisted in focusing on the negative economic impact of a No vote, but did so in a more careful and restrained tone. As one strategist put it, "I don't think scare tactics are inappropriate if they are elegantly handled." The Yes side also embarked on a more aggressive strategy on the separatist threat. A third decision was to push a softer theme of national unity. Keeping Canada together was what the 26 October vote was most importantly about. Rather than a shotgun approach, the ads were focused to answer the major regional reasons for No support. Ontario and Atlantic Canada were hit mainly with the negative economic consequences and soft national-unity ads. Quebec and the West got top priority in exposure to the separatist bogey ads. Finally, a special ad was focused in the West, where the major reason for a No was a widespread belief that Quebec got too much in the deal, arguing that the concessions to Quebec were not only a reasonable compromise, but were more than adequately balanced by the West's gains.

In the final days, the Yes team toyed with focusing virtually the entire final propaganda campaign in Quebec on the separatist threat. Internal polls confirmed that the Québécois wanted a deal but rejected the Charlottetown Agreement. If the Québécois could be put in the position of believing that the choice was really between sovereignty and Charlottetown, and that Charlottetown was the best deal possible, there was a slim chance they would hold their noses and vote Yes. Clearly, fragments of this kind of thinking were present in the Yes propaganda during the final days, but no effort was made to polarize the whole situation by forcing such a choice. There was good reason for this hesitation. One poll found that if the Québécois were forced to choose clearly between Charlottetown and sovereignty, sovereignty was ahead by 43 to 36 per cent, with 21 per cent undecided. Another poll found that Charlottetown was ahead by 51 to 41 per cent, with 8 per cent undecided. With the numbers so close and contradictory, it was evident that to attempt to force a choice between sovereignty and Charlottetown might be a monumental tactical blunder. The Yes side, if the tactics failed, could have given Parizeau and the PQ what they had never dared to ask of the Québécois themselves — a No vote that would be interpreted as a Yes to sovereignty.

On 26 October 1992, 75 per cent of Canada's 18.5 million eligible voters rendered their final judgement on the Charlottetown Agreement, including 83 per cent of Quebec's 4.9 million voters. Turnout in English Canada ranged from a low of 54 per cent in Newfoundland to a high of 76 per cent in British Columbia. Nationally, it was a decisive No victory, 55 to 45 per cent, excluding spoiled ballots. In Quebec, the No victory, at 57 to 43 per cent, was substantial but failed to exceed the strongest No votes in English Canada. In British Columbia, No carried 68 per cent, in Manitoba 62 per cent, and in Alberta 60 per cent. The No side carried six provinces, including the four western provinces, Quebec, and, by a narrow margin, Nova Scotia (51 to 49 per cent). The Yes carried four provinces. The deal was given strong approval in Newfoundland (63 per cent), Prince Edward Island (74 per cent), and New Brunswick (62 per cent), and was passed by a narrow margin in Ontario — a mere twelve thousand votes of the 4.8 million cast. The North was split, with the Yukon voting No and the

Northwest Territories voting Yes. It was a decisive, irreversible defeat of the Agreement, forcing the Yes team to abandon the last hope of some premiers for salvaging parts of the deal under the 7/50 rule. If Yes had won in seven provinces, representing more than 50 per cent of the population, those elements of the agreement not requiring unanimity could be passed. The magnitude of the defeat firmly foreclosed such a controversial temptation.

Voters had been reminded one last time of the economic scare campaign in the lead story in the 26 October edition of the *Globe and Mail's Report on Business*: "Referendum stalls recovery by a least six months: Battle...has created monetary turmoil." Details of the terrible economic consequences suffered by Canada during the campaign were again presented. Canadians refused to listen and voted No. The next day interest rates fell by half a per cent, the dollar went up, and the Toronto stock exchange index improved. Two days after the No victory the real economic world passed an even clearer judgement, and it flatly contradicted the Yes message. The trend-setting Bank of Canada rate fell by another per cent, the dollar again went up, and the stock markets were even more buoyant. In fact, the Toronto Stock Exchange enjoyed one of its best three one-day gains in value of the year, while the one-day volume of shares traded had only been surpassed on five other days in the past. It appeared that Trudeau had been correct in his blunt assessment that the economic scare was a lie. On 29 October 1992, external affairs minister Barbara McDougall, who had participated in the scare campaign, held a private meeting with foreign diplomats in Ottawa. When asked by the media what she had said at the meeting, she replied, "I told them what had happened last Monday night was not a vote against Canada, but a vote against a specific set of complex constitutional reforms." Parizeau, Trudeau, and the entire No team had been saying exactly that during the previous two months.

Neither the short- nor long-term significance of the referendum was reassuring. At the simplest level, it was a clear rejection of a proposed constitutional amendment and a sharp repudiation of the incumbent politicians responsible for putting it together. But every Canadian knew it meant much more than that. And most Canadians knew what the referendum results did *not* mean. The vote was clearly *not* a rejection of the principle of aboriginal self-government. Gallup had reported that Canadians very strongly approved both the recognition of aboriginal people as a distinct society, and of the inherent right of aboriginals to self-government. Nor was the vote an indication of an acceptance of the *status quo*, as some of our bruised politicians suggested. On the contrary, a Decima poll taken on 26 October found that 54 per cent of the people of Quebec and 51 per cent of the people of English Canada wanted politicians to continue efforts at constitutional reform within a year. Canadians clearly wanted a resolution and expected their political leaders to try again and to do it right.

For a large group of Canadians — mainly in English Canada, but also a significant number in Quebec — the No vote was a vote *for* the Charter and the protections it provides individual Canadians. For another large group of Canadians the No vote was a vote *for* a strong central government, *for* national social programs with national standards, and *against* the devolution of too much power to the provinces. Together these two groups probably accounted for the biggest single bloc of No voters in English Canada — as many as 37 per cent of English Canadians voting No, according to the Decima poll done on voting day. The Charter and the strong central government and social programs arguments had been central to the failure of Meech. But the politicians refused to listen, and the same issues predictably proved central to the collapse of Charlottetown.

The greatest significance of the defeat of Charlottetown had very much to do with the possible resolution of the English-Canadian and Québécois conundrum. The No vote had, in fact, crystallized that conundrum even more clearly than the collapse of Meech. On 28 October 1992, Prime Minister Mulroney declared "no part of Canada voted against any other part of Canada." That, of course, was nonsense. In fact, a large bloc of English Canadians voted against the Québécois, particularly against the gains allegedly won for Quebec and the resulting impositions on English Canada. And for many Québécois, the No vote was seen as a national affirmation. As Parizeau asserted, "Quebec and the rest of Canada voted No for opposite reasons." Despite the self-serving exaggeration, Parizeau was partly correct.

The Charlottetown Agreement was presented to the Québécois as English Canada's final offer of renewed federalism. Bourassa, Mulroney, and Clark — and the English-Canadian premiers — made that repeatedly clear. If the Québécois rejected the deal, they were warned, there would be no repetition, no return to the table, the thirty-one gains for Quebec would be lost. It was a dangerous and risky game — final-offer politics always is — because there was no fallback position. When the Québécois answered with, as Parizeau described it, "the No that ends all Nos," it was for very clearly stated reasons. The final offer was not good enough. The Agreement was a poor deal because Quebec did not obtain the minimum the Québécois demanded in order to secure their nation. As Allaire put it on 26 October 1992, "We know what we want, so stop trying to sell us something else."

A disturbingly significant portion of the No vote in English Canada was clearly a vote against Quebec. According to Decima's voting day poll, 27 per cent of No voters in English Canada believed that Quebec got too much in the deal. Throughout the campaign this was clear, particularly in the West, and most especially in British Columbia and Alberta. An Alberta government poll taken during the last week of September found that 28 per cent of Albertans were against Quebec's guarantee of 25 per cent of House of Commons seats, and 14 per cent remained opposed to distinct society status for Quebec. A poll conducted by Angus Reid/Southam in mid-October found that 40 per cent of English Canadians believed Quebec got too much, registering strong opposition to "too much power" for Quebec, the 25 per cent seat guarantee, and distinct society status. Eighty-one per cent believed that if they voted Yes, Quebec would proceed to escalate its demands. Polling in British Columbia found the same attitudes, even more strongly expressed. Polls also found strong currents of western anger over the perception that the western premiers had betrayed their commitment to a truly Triple-E Senate by yielding to Quebec's sabotage. A national Gallup poll in September found that 72 per cent of English Canadians disapproved of the 25 per cent seat guarantee for Quebec, including 75 per cent on the Prairies and 80 per cent in British Columbia. Much of this, quite simply, was rooted in bigotry and ignorance. Mulroney's government house leader, Harvie Andre, after campaigning in the West, expressed surprise at how many he found who "hate French and French-Canadians," that he found "more bigotry and hatred than I thought existed." A significant portion of the No vote in English Canada, then, was opposed to any concessions to Quebec, regardless of the consequences. And now that stream of English-Canadian politics had a political vehicle in the Reform Party and had been legitimized as never before as a result of the referendum.

The day after the results were in, Parizeau claimed that the No vote in Quebec meant that the Québécois had returned, after a detour, to the "highway to sovereignty." He went on, "Canadian politicians tried to reconcile the irreconcilable, and it didn't work. And from both sides we told them it will never work." Bouchard said, perhaps more hopefully, "There were two roads for Quebeckers before the referendum — profoundly renewed federalism and sovereignty. These two options must now find a convergence." Granted, the Charlottetown Agreement failed, but is there no reconciliation to be found? Can there be a convergence? Can we reconcile the "individual rights" position held dear by Canadians such as Trudeau, Carstairs, and Coyne with the collective rights of the Québécois? Is there no way to satisfy the yearning in English Canada for a strong central government, a strong sense of Canadian nationhood, and secured and enhanced national social programs? Can Canada find no way to grant the Québécois the powers they believe they need to find a tranquil place in the federation? Can the very different regional concerns of the English-Canadian peripheries — the West and Atlantic Canada — not be reconciled with the special needs of Quebec?

The story of Canada has been to seek just such a reconciliation, just such a "convergence." Charlottetown was another failure to place in the archives alongside the Victoria Charter and the Meech Lake Accord. Hence, achieving reconciliation remained unfinished business that could not be allowed to remain unfinished. Events will force us to finish it, one way or another.

8

The Fallout from Charlottetown

The defeat of the Charlottetown Agreement ruined a variety of individual political careers and contributed to the collapse of both the Tories and New Democrats federally. The referendum battle catapulted the Reform Party in the West and the Bloc Québécois in Quebec into regional and thus national prominence, transforming Preston Manning overnight from a right-wing crank into a self-styled contender for prime minister and Lucien Bouchard from a relatively unknown cabinet minister into a central actor shaping the future of Canada. Ironically, a large role in shaping the destiny of Canada was thereby placed in the hands of two political leaders both hostile to what Canada had become, with contradictory views on the place of Quebec in Confederation. Preston Manning's "New Canada" had no place for a "special status" Quebec; Manning insisted that Quebec submit to the equality-of-provinces doctrine. Lucien Bouchard saw no future for Quebec in Canada in the absence of some kind of "sovereignty/new partnership" formula.

The first and most prominent casualty of Charlottetown was the prime minister. Though Brian Mulroney's support had collapsed long before the Charlottetown vote and his personal unpopularity helped ensure the Agreement's defeat, his fate, like that of Quebec premier Robert Bourassa, was inextricably linked to a resolution of the Quebec question. Mulroney's promise to bring Quebec back into the Canadian constitutional fold with "honour and enthusiasm" had set the stage for the *de facto* alliance with Québécois nationalists in his 1984 sweep. Furthermore, his efforts to salvage Meech won the continuing support of Québécois nationalists in 1988, an election he would have lost without Quebec. Although the Québécois nationalist pillar of Mulroney's unprecedented electoral alliance had begun to crumble, first with the defection of Bouchard and then very quickly with the failure of Meech, the success of Charlottetown remained his last desperate hope.

And it was certainly a desperate hope. Mulroney's determination to cling to office despite plummeting support became increasingly pathetic. He clearly waited to be driven out by negative public opinion. By the time Mulroney announced his resignation on 24 February 1993, his approval rating had remained at or below 21 per cent for three full years before it fell like a stone to 14 per cent after Charlottetown. No incumbent prime minister had been so reviled in Canadian history. By 1991, Tory support in Quebec had sunk to 16 per cent according to Gallup, while Bouchard's Bloc Québécois had reached 42 per cent. And while Mulroney's Quebec supporters were defecting and stampeding to the Bloc, his support among Tory westerners, the other pillar of his electoral alliance, also fell, though not as precipitously; much of it went to Preston Manning and the Reform Party. According to a national Gallup poll in 1992, Mulroney and the Tories held only 12 per cent support, while Reform enjoyed 15 per cent, largely concentrated in Alberta (39 per cent) and British Columbia (19 per cent).

Canadians turned against Brian Mulroney because of his policies and their effect on Canada. His loyal efforts to implement a corporate agenda were disastrous. His attacks on social spending placed Canada's social, education, and health infrastructures at serious risk and established in their stead a harsh, social Darwinist, two-tiered system of access: one for the rich and another for the poor. His programs of privatization and de-regulation crippled the national transportation system and put the public at risk in the air, while loosening the legislated bonds of social responsibility on corporate behaviour in a variety of areas, from drugs to the environment to advertising. Tax relief for the rich and the corporate sector, combined with his regressive taxation attack on ordinary Canadians dependent on wages and salaries, embittered middle Canada and set the stage for a mass, anti-government tax revolt carefully orchestrated by the business lobby. The free trade initiatives, which had only marginal public support, were economically catastrophic for the Canadian economy and Canadian wage earners, sending the country into a downward spiral of accelerating de-industrialization. In addition, Mulroney's clumsy constitutional initiatives deepened the chasm between English Canada and Quebec and led to the emergence of the Bloc Québécois. He deliberately weakened the federal power, encouraged the centrifugal assertion of provincial rights, and left Canada with a federal government incapable of governing, thus depriving the people of the instrumentality of a democratic state that could defend them from unrestrained corporate power in an unregulated global market. Victory in the Charlottetown referendum would not have saved Mulroney, but its defeat made his departure from politics before another federal election a foregone conclusion.

The late Robert Bourassa might have stayed on as Quebec premier after Charlottetown to seek vindication had he not been diagnosed with skin cancer in 1990. Bourassa's declining health led to his decision to leave politics, a decision he did not announce until 14 September 1993 in the midst of the federal election campaign. Yet the evidence is clear that even the old master, now federalist/now nationalist Bourassa, would have had to overcome enormous obstacles in order to win another term in the wake of Charlottetown. The image of the premier caving in to federal pressure, selling out Quebec's historic demands, and desperate for any deal in order to avoid a referendum on sovereignty left a bad after-taste in Quebec. The Quebec Liberals were trailing behind the Parti Québécois in the polls. The nationalist members of the Liberal Party had either left to fight the Charlottetown Agreement or had been ejected from any positions of influence. The two most influential disaffected nationalist Liberals, Jean Allaire and Mario Dumont, had declared their intention to launch a new political movement, which was formally registered with Quebec's Chief Electoral Officer on 19 January 1994 as l'Action démocratique du Québec. The Bourassa government had adopted Bill 86 legalizing bilingual commercial signs in June 1993, amid growing concerns about the security of the French language, which, when combined with the government's notorious failure to enforce existing language laws vigorously, made the government increasingly vulnerable to attacks by the Parti Québécois. Events since the Quebec Liberal convention to approve the Charlottetown Agreement on 29 August 1992 had placed the hard federalist wing firmly in charge of the party and the government. Consequently, in the next Quebec election the Liberal government would be forced to champion existing federal arrangements with no clear alternative. In such a context,

Bourassa's typical equivocation on the national question, his maybe-yes, maybe-no approach to Quebec and the constitution, was unlikely to succeed. Had Bourassa been healthy, it is hard to imagine a scenario in which he could have won another term.

Bourassa's resignation became an issue in the federal election. In a clear attack on the Bloc Québécois, Bourassa was uncharacteristically blunt about Quebec sovereignty: "Quebec independence is a geopolitical absurdity." Nevertheless, ever the vacillator, Bourassa declared his ongoing commitment to "a form of federation that could include a new political superstructure [in which] Quebec can achieve autonomy without dismantling the country." For their part, both Bloc leader Bouchard and PQ leader Parizeau insisted that Bourassa's career proved that Quebec cannot realize itself within Canada. Bouchard declared, "his failure is a living demonstration of the necessity to look elsewhere [for constitutional solutions]...the failure of Charlottetown slammed the door on all that." Parizeau was more blunt, stating that Bourassa's failures showed that federalism "is not reformable" and his resignation should "propel voters" to sovereignty.

The true extent of the deep malaise of the Quebec Liberal Party became clear after Bourassa's resignation. No one wanted the job of premier except Daniel Johnson, destined to repeat the fate of his brother, Pierre-Marc Johnson — a brief career as unelected premier followed by defeat at the polls. This reluctance was understandable. The Liberals continued to trail the PQ in the polls, especially among francophone Québécois voters. Two-thirds of voters were dissatisfied with the Bourassa government's performance. One-half the cabinet and many backbenchers declared an intention to leave politics. As a result of the failure of Charlottetown, the Quebec Liberal Party had no clearly defined election platform and no constitutional package to replace the defeated Agreement. The absence of the usually vigorous nationalist wing left the party stagnant and bereft of ideas. Even Johnson's over-eagerness for the post failed to flush out an alternative, despite the fact that he had run a poor third out of three when he last went for the leadership in 1983 and was widely seen as anti-labour, pro-big business, strongly in favour of *status quo* federalism, and harshly neo-conservative. In addition to these weaknesses, Johnson lacked basic political skills, suggesting that the party had already resigned itself to defeat in the next election and could not therefore find another candidate as an alternative. Consequently, there was no leadership contest and Daniel Johnson was quietly acclaimed as Quebec Liberal leader at a party executive meeting on 14 December 1993. On 11 January 1994, with only eight months remaining in his mandate, he was sworn in as premier of Quebec.

No one had anticipated the extent of the negative consequences of the referendum loss in the upcoming federal election, constitutionally required in the fall of 1993. The federal Liberals remained somewhat immune from these negative consequences, except in Quebec, largely because neither the Liberals nor their leader, Jean Chrétien, had played a central role in Charlottetown. In addition, many prominent Liberals, such as Pierre Trudeau and those who followed his lead, had attacked Charlottetown and urged a No vote. But the chief political architects of the Agreement, the Tories and the New Democrats, suffered terribly.

Granted, long before the Charlottetown referendum, the Tory ship of state was foundering, clearly a defeated government going through the motions, clinging to office to the end of its constitutional mandate, driven on by a desperate prime minister. The top Tories in the government knew this best of all — all the polls, both private internal polls and very public polls, carried the same message of a terrible, unavoidable defeat. The Charlottetown referendum transformed certain humiliation into virtual annihilation. The extent to which Tory insiders expected defeat was clear from the moment Mulroney announced his resignation. Not a single front-bencher wanted his job and even experienced ministers in the second row ran for cover. Mulroney himself, having already promoted Kim Campbell's candidacy, begged a number of prominent cabinet colleagues to run, without success. Having failed in the obvious choices, Mulroney then pleaded with Bernard Valcourt and Jean Charest. He failed to convince Valcourt, and it took two hours of charming wheedling at 24 Sussex Drive to persuade Charest; the clinching argument was Charest's future ambition. By the end of Mulroney's efforts, only two cabinet ministers and three back-benchers had agreed to stand. This was not the leadership race one would have expected in a party that believed that there was the slightest chance of victory.

The leading contender, defence minister Kim Campbell, was indecorous in her hunger for higher office and blithely unaware she was about to share the fate of her former colleague Rita Johnson (who was devoured at the polls in 1991 for Bill Vander Zalm's sins). Campbell's record inspired little confidence, although desperation among Tories and copy hunger among journalists gave her a brief boost. Campbell had been in public office since 1980, when she secured a seat on the Vancouver Public School Board as part of a right-wing slate. In 1983, she briefly served as board chair, just long enough to establish her reputation as a tough neo-conservative and prepare for her leap to better things. Unsuccessfully running for the Socreds that year, she entered the corridors of power by the back door, joining Socred premier Bill Bennett's staff. Campbell then tried to catapult herself into the elite of the provincial Socreds, running for leader in 1986 and winning fourteen votes. In the next election, she won a seat in the Legislature but Premier Vander Zalm, rankling from her unkind criticism of him, placed her firmly on the back benches where she languished only briefly.

Again using her back-bench seat as a springboard, Campbell secured the Tory nomination for Vancouver Centre and won a close victory in 1988. From there she caught the prime minister's favourable notice and glided easily to prominence — junior minister for Indian affairs, then justice minister, and finally defence minister — achieving overnight a seat in Mulroney's inner circle. Her record in the cabinet was not impressive. Her shifty position on negotiating Indian land claims — opposed in B.C., supported in Ottawa — undermined her credibility. As justice minister she executed a number of astonishing policy reversals. A self-declared pro-choicer, she tried to re-criminalize abortion. After the Montreal massacre of fourteen female university students in 1989, she became a passionate public advocate of gun control, while privately caving into the right-wing gun lobby by producing a law that was mostly public relations fluff. But perhaps the greatest disappointment was Campbell's record in defence, which alone should have barred the road to the prime ministership. After the loss of the Soviet menace and calls on all sides for a peace agenda involving deep reductions in military spending, Campbell became one of the new warhawks (carefully coached and tutored by senior military officers). At first she favoured spending billions on military helicopters; then, as a candidate facing public crankiness about such profligacy in hard times, she discovered reasons to re-think the helicopters, finally cutting seven at a saving of a billion dollars. In addition, her clumsy handling of the coverups in Somalia where Canadian soldiers were accused of homicide raised doubts about her fitness for high office.

Nipping at Campbell's heels, Jean Charest hoped to convince Canadians that his main claims to fame were youthful exuberance and fluent bilingualism. First elected in 1984 at the age of twenty-five, he was elevated to the safe post of Minister of Youth and Sport in 1986, giving him a lot of politically neutral public exposure. Charest's first misstep was telephoning a Quebec Superior Court judge. Unfortunately, the judge was about to render a decision in a case of a track-and-field coach who had been cashiered from Team Canada and was suing for reinstatement. The judge wisely refused to talk to the brash upstart and blew the whistle. Charest at first denied any wrongdoing. Only after a heart-to-heart with his mentor, Brian Mulroney, did he admit a serious violation of the cabinet's code of conduct. Cabinet ministers are not supposed to interfere in a judicial proceeding. In January 1990, Charest resigned in disgrace.

In April 1990, Mulroney gave Charest a chance at redemption, naming him to chair the special Commons committee to save the tattered Meech Lake Accord. The committee's hearings exploded in Charest's face in Saskatchewan when some members accused him of weeding out and harassing Meech opponents trying to appear before the committee in public session. When Charest presented his hurried report on 16 May 1990, Meech began its final unravelling. Charest proposed a series of additions to the Accord, which satisfied few in English Canada but deeply angered many Québécois due to a weakening of the distinct society clause. The day after the report was tabled, a Quebec Tory MP quit the caucus in disgust. The next day, Quebec premier Bourassa flatly rejected the proposals. On the fifth day, Lucien Bouchard, then still Mulroney's Quebec protégé and lieutenant, resigned from cabinet and, on the sixth day, from the Tory caucus. By the end of June 1990, eight Tory MPs had quit over Charest's compromise. The next month the Bloc Québécois was founded. Charest's role in these events had largely disappeared from public view, to his evident relief. He was, however, rewarded by Mulroney, who welcomed him back in the cabinet as minister of the environment. Nevertheless, it is clear that Charest shares in the dubious honour of having played a key role in provoking the chain of events that led to the emergence of the Bloc Québécois, the first Quebec separatist party successful in federal politics in Canadian history.

Given the records of the two top contenders for leadership of the Conservatives, it was clear why Chrétien kept smiling even as the interest in the Tory race created upward blips in the polls. The Liberal machine — in the House and on the hustings — would eat the lightweight Kim Campbell or Jean Charest for breakfast. Nevertheless, some Tories were hopeful that Campbell — a fresh face, a woman, a westerner, a relative outsider rather than a member of the elite old guard — could turn things around. The basis for this hope could be found in the polls. On 24 February 1993, a Gallup poll reported that 37 per cent of voters would support the Tories led by Campbell. This percentage was just two points behind the Liberals. An earlier poll had recorded a sharp drop in support for both the Reform Party and the Bloc. By April 1993, Tory support, though still seven points behind the Liberals, had reached the highest point in four years, with all other parties down significantly. Forty-four per cent of Canadians now believed Campbell would make the best prime minister, twice the percentage that supported Jean Chrétien.

It was these polls, as well as a series of internal polls and encounter group results, that persuaded delegates to select Campbell as leader at the June 1993 convention. Campbell, the early darling of the media and the prime minister himself, spent more than four million dollars to win the leadership (twice the amount spent by Charest). Even so, as a result of a poor performance in her speeches at the convention and growing doubts about her ability and depth among many, she was almost defeated by Charest, who won more than 47 per cent of the final delegate vote, having started his campaign with the support of only 5 per cent. At the point of victory, Campbell made the first of many gaffes — insulting Charest and his supporters — when she turned to him during her less-than-gracious victory speech saying, "Jean, I don't know whether I'm a rabbit or not, but you're one hell of a tortoise." This flippant remark and her failure to reach out to Charest and his supporters created a major public flap and raised doubts about whether Charest and his base would wholeheartedly work for her election. Only the personal intervention of Mulroney and an embarrassing public deal, in which Charest exchanged a declaration of support of Campbell for the positions of deputy prime minister and Quebec lieutenant, brought Charest on-side. This beginning was hardly an auspicious one for Campbell, who had, after all, promised to do politics differently, and it certainly did little to raise her stature in Quebec, where Charest had become a significant political force.

The Charest troubles and the lingering, unspoken doubts seemed to disappear from memory quickly after Campbell was sworn in as prime minister and began her summer tour. As she met responsive crowds and basked in extensive, positive media coverage during that summer honeymoon with Canadians, it almost seemed as if the albatross of the Mulroney years had been buried, as if Meech and Charlottetown had never happened, as if a new Camelot had dawned. By late August 1993, Campbell's approval rating among Canadians had soared to 51 per cent and Tory support levels had reached 36 per cent, just four points behind the Liberals. Campbell insisted, "I'm not going to be seduced by opinion polls...[but] I'll call an election as quickly as I can — pretty quickly," but it was clear to everyone that she and her advisers were just waiting for the best moment, particularly since her constitutional mandate was near its end. There were many sceptics, however, who were convinced that Campbell's support was ephemeral.

The federal NDP's fall from grace began with the Charlottetown Agreement. Despite ranging in the polls from 20 to 40 per cent from 1984 to 1992 and doing very well in 1988, the federal NDP effectively committed political suicide by supporting rather than opposing the Agreement. In June 1992, Gallup reported the federal NDP enjoyed the support of 21 per cent of voters. By October 1992, that figure had fallen to 18 per cent and by the next month to 14 per cent. By April 1993, the NDP appeared to have bottomed out at 13 per cent, still a respectable number and still well ahead of Reform. But the federal NDP also had to contend with the growing disappointment with the social and fiscal policies of the three NDP provincial governments, which, when combined with disillusionment over Charlottetown, was undermining the party alarmingly. All three NDP governments — Rae in Ontario in 1990, Harcourt in B.C., and Romanow in Saskatchewan, both in October 1991 — had been explicitly elected on platform promises to combat and reverse the neo-conservative agenda. All three failed to do so, instead joining the neo-conservative consensus and insisting that debt and deficit reduction and program cuts, rather than economic stimulation, tax reform, and an expansion of the social security net, were essential. As a result, all three provincial NDP governments lost significant support, especially the Rae government in Ontario where the NDP quickly fell to third place in the polls.

Federal NDP leader Audrey McLaughlin then compounded this loss by making another serious error. On 29 April 1993, McLaughlin fired Ontario NDP MP Steven Langdon as House finance critic when he publicly criticized the Rae government's Draconian attack on the deficit and debt by making massive cuts in spending on public sector programs and jobs. Langdon, acutely aware of the collapse of NDP support, realized some distance was needed between the federal party and the NDP premiers. His criticisms were not the uncontrolled outburst of a wounded ideologue. Rather, they constituted an astute effort to salvage the party's future in the looming federal election. As point man taking the flak, he provided McLaughlin a perfect opportunity to step in as federal leader to place a more diplomatic version of the same message at the centre of Canada's political debate. Langdon's public intervention, which understandably angered premiers Rae, Romanow, and Harcourt, provided McLaughlin with an opportunity to strut her prime-ministerial stuff. She could have swivelled her guns on the Mulroney/Campbell government, denouncing Ottawa for forcing the provinces to the wall by cuts in federal funding. She could have commiserated with the NDP premiers, the junior partners in a Tory-driven executive federalism, who did not have the fiscal and economic powers needed to do what social democrats would like to do and would do when federal power was won. She could have complained that, while she didn't much like what the NDP premiers were doing and she certainly wouldn't take any cues from them as prime minister, she understood why they might feel forced to do such distasteful things under fiscal pressure from Tory Ottawa. She did none of these things. Instead, McLaughlin blasted Langdon, sided firmly with the NDP premiers, and once again, just as during the Charlottetown debate, exposed herself as a captive of her party's provincial premiers. McLaughlin stumbled badly, forgetting that all Canadians — even Canadians who support social democracy — expect federal leaders aspiring to the highest office in the land to speak for all of Canada, not to be, or even to appear to be, captives of provincial politicians.

Justifying Langdon's firing on 29 April 1993, McLaughlin said, "I don't think there's anyone in Canada, in any province, in any territory, or indeed federally, who doesn't believe that we have to be conservative in the sense of addressing the budget and the deficit." Her observation gave aid and comfort to the NDP's business enemies. The NDP's major roadblock in its drive for electoral success had always been a public perception of the party as ineffective managers of the economy, a perception created and sustained by the business lobby and the media. By her firing of Langdon and her fateful words, McLaughlin inadvertently fed that perception. The business lobby and its loyal columnists delighted in suggesting the episode again revealed the NDP as woolly-headed and idealistic in opposition, while facing internal difficulty doing the right and necessary thing in power. Therefore, the media suggested the Langdon/Rae/McLaughlin episode revealed the reality and discipline of power, rather than emphasized the fundamental differences either in federal/provincial powers or between social democracy and neo-conservatism. Thus, the attention of the media and the public was effectively deflected from the federal NDP's strong economic policies, unveiled in February 1993, involving massive taxation reform, deep cuts in defence spending, and an ambitious job creation program in both public and private sectors through a national investment fund and public infrastructure renewal. Instead, the message to an already cynical and disillusioned public was and remained — there was no alternative, the business lobby was in command, even if the NDP wins power. Had Audrey McLaughlin and her federal caucus stood up to the three NDP premiers during Charlottetown and said No, had she moved behind Langdon both to put his comments in the context of federal/provincial differences in power and to distinguish herself from the fiscal neo-conservatism of the NDP premiers, the federal NDP's standing in the polls might have been very different in the spring, summer, and fall of 1993. But she did not, and as a result July and August 1993, a scant nine months after Charlottetown and three months after the firing of Langdon, the months of triumph for Kim Campbell, became months of panic for the New Democrats and Audrey McLaughlin. Support for the federal NDP collapsed to 8 per cent, threatening the party with its worst defeat since the Diefenbaker sweep of 1958.

On 8 September, when Prime Minister Campbell finally set the date for 25 October 1993, there began in effect two election campaigns, one in English Canada and one in Quebec. While English Canada debated the record of the Mulroney years and argued about who would be the best prime minister and which party would be the best for government, the people of Quebec argued about whether it was worth sending anyone but sovereigntists to Ottawa to represent their interests to prepare the ground for Quebec's final future exit from Canada. Initial theories that voters in Quebec were just "parking" their votes with the Bloc very quickly evaporated as support for that party not only held firm but increased as the campaign unfolded.

The day Campbell called the election, an Environics poll reported that the Tories and Liberals were virtually tied among decided voters at 34 to 33 per cent respectively, with 29 per cent undecided. That poll was the peak for the Tories; afterward it was all downhill. Campbell became a loose cannon whose verbal gaffes destroyed the Tory campaign from the outset. Despite the fact that 71 per cent of Canadians saw job creation as more important than the deficit, Campbell relentlessly made deficit reduction the major focus of her campaign, promising to reduce the deficit to zero in five years, a truly astonishing goal. Pressed for details on how this was to be done, especially on the costs of cuts in government spending, Campbell insisted she was "showing reality to the country." When pressed to respond to Canadian anxieties about unemployment and jobs, she bluntly declared that there were bleak prospects for any improvement in unemployment until the next century. As a result, she came across as arrogant, harsh, and uncaring.

As the campaign continued, Campbell was repeatedly questioned about the link between possible cuts to social programs and deficit reduction. In exasperation she blurted out the words that were to become fatal for her campaign: "You can't have a debate on such a key issue as the modernization of social programs in forty-seven days," referring to the election campaign's duration. When further pressed for details, she began to get visibly annoyed and accused the media of badgering her and failing to deliver her real campaign messages clearly and fairly. "I'll throw myself across the railway tracks to protect the system [of social programs]," she insisted.

The final blow to her campaign was the decision to use ads that attacked Chrétien personally, making fun of his appearance and speech and asking Canadians if they wanted such a man as their prime minister. Campbell denied knowledge of the ads before they were broadcast and pulled them off the air immediately, apologizing, but it was too late. Her "doing politics differently" claim became a public joke, and more and more references linked her to Mulroney and his style and record.

Allan Gregg, the Tory pollster, reported that in the week after the social policy blunder, their rolling polls recorded a twelve-point drop and that the day the attack ads were broadcast was followed by the Tories' worst night in the polls. By late September, the Tories were behind the Liberals by seven points (30 to 37), by mid-October by eighteen points (22 to 40), and by 21 October, four days before the election, by twenty-eight points (16 to 44). Early talk of a minority government had given away to talk of a Liberal majority and concerns about whether the Tories would hold the twelve seats necessary to retain party status in the House of Commons.

The Liberals were able to manipulate events to their advantage during the campaign. Having read the polls carefully, the party tailored its campaign to address Canadians' economic anxieties and anger about Mulroney's neo-conservative agenda and its consequences. The Liberals' Red Book carried messages of hope, of turning the corner, of reversing the neo-conservative agenda, of returning to a strong, caring, and interventionist central government. This persuasive package of promises was summed up in the Red Book as follows: "For far too many Canadians, after nine years of Conservative government, [the Canadian] dream has turned into a nightmare. Our economy is in disarray....Over a million Canadian children live in poverty. Many of our national institutions have been shaken. Our cultural and social fabric has been weakened....[H]ope for tomorrow has turned into fear of the future....For Canadians, the next election is about one simple question: what kind of country do we want for ourselves and our children?"

Everywhere Chrétien went he waved the Red Book, and repeated its promises, which had been carefully crafted to be vague and general. But the Liberals did not need to stick to their script, as Campbell's campaign gaffes gave them all the ammunition they needed. As Chrétien quipped when asked how late he had to stay up at night to prepare for the following day's campaign events, "I just go to bed and have a good night's sleep. Then I read the paper in the morning about Ms. Campbell and I have enough for the whole day." When pressed on the deficit, Chrétien attacked the Tory numbers and said he was also concerned about the deficit and would address it in a careful and responsible way, but creating jobs and turning the economy around were more important and would be the best thing for the deficit in the long run. In response to Campbell's social policy blunder, Chrétien exploited the opening to the hilt: "It's unbelievable that she doesn't want to discuss the serious issues of the nation during the election. Tell me when we would be able to discuss it? What is the hidden agenda?" When told about Campbell's remark about throwing herself on the tracks to save social programs, Chrétien retorted that such a promise was "very easy when you have closed down all the railways." On free trade, which a strong majority of Canadians still opposed, he promised re-negotiation and a refusal to sign the North American Free Trade Agreement (NAFTA) unless significant changes were made. He would get rid of the GST and bring in a fair tax system. In fact, just as Trudeau had in 1968 and 1974, Chrétien shrewdly wrote off the right — over which the Tories and Reformers were fighting — and went after the traditional Liberal centrist base, sidling left to woo the NDP's electoral base. For forty-seven days, Jean Chrétien sounded like a moderate and committed social democrat, slightly to the left of Bob Rae and Roy Romanow; with no hint that after the election he would become a passionate advocate of the neo-conservative business agenda.

The NDP was squeezed out in the election. The party's position on Charlottetown and the record of the three NDP premiers resulted in a sense of betrayal among supporters. The party couldn't get the troops out and money was hard to come by. It was squeezed by the Liberals, who had quickly occupied traditional NDP territory, stealing much of the rhetoric of the NDP's February 1993 economic program and presenting themselves as front-line fighters against the neo-conservative agenda. And it was squeezed by the Reform Party, which had replaced the NDP for many westerners as the region's defender and champion in national affairs. Even at the start of the campaign, the NDP had bottomed out at 8 per cent, falling further to 7 per cent in the last poll before the election. McLaughlin's campaign was like a funeral procession; few came to meetings, the media lost interest, the door-to-door canvass faltered, and the NDP had largely ceased to be a factor in the national election. One reporter complained that to be assigned to cover the NDP campaign was the equivalent of exile to Siberia, and another commented that covering the party was "like watching a dog die." In response to the crisis, the entire NDP campaign was devoted to holding enough of its traditional seats in order to cling to party status in the House. To do this McLaughlin embarked on a last-minute effort to beg for support in order to keep a Liberal majority government honest, focusing exclusively on saving medicare and fighting free trade. This was a potentially effective and wise course because, even though the NDP's national support had fallen to single digits, it was concentrated largely in urban working-class seats and rural areas dominated by small and medium-sized farmers, mainly in

B.C. and Saskatchewan, and could therefore translate into a significant if small number of seats.

The Reform Party had been on a roll since the Charlottetown referendum, and that roll continued throughout the election campaign. Starting the campaign in September with 13 per cent of decided voters, Reform finished four days before the election with 19 per cent, still largely concentrated in Alberta and B.C. Reform's campaign focused on keeping and increasing the western right-wing base that the party had already stolen from the Tories. Reform proposed Draconian measures to reduce the deficit to zero in three years and to enact punitive and conservative social policy reform. The party struggled to maintain its breakthrough as the champion of the West and of common sense, with its widespread use of shallow populist rhetoric and appeals to break with the "old line" parties, which now included the NDP. Reform, unfettered by running candidates in Quebec, also continued to appeal to the anti-Quebec stream in English-Canadian politics. It attacked bilingualism, condemned the separatists in Quebec, repeatedly and ominously raised Chrétien's Quebec roots, and warned that only a large group of Reform MPs could prevent the Bloc and the Liberals under Chrétien from negotiating a new pro-Quebec constitutional package or developing unfair programs to again pander to Quebec, Confederation's "spoiled child."

The 1993 federal election in Quebec seemed eerily unaffected by the campaign in English Canada. The basic issue was whether Quebec representatives in Ottawa should continue to participate seriously in governing the federation or should work diligently to accelerate separation. Ever since the separatist/sovereigntist option successfully emerged in 1966 as a serious democratic choice in Quebec, it had been clear that to be taken seriously politically and constitutionally, sovereigntists must win significant support in federal elections. The contradiction of electing sovereigntists in provincial elections and strong federalists in federal elections, which had characterized the Lévesque/Trudeau era, must be resolved. There had been many calls over the years for a revival of a nationalist/sovereigntist federal option in Quebec, inspired by the Bloc Populaire. Many adherents of the Rassemblement pour l'indépendence nationale (RIN) had repeatedly advocated contesting federal elections. After the formation of the PQ, such advocacy increased in intensity, ebbing and flowing with signals from Lévesque and the PQ leadership. One such stillborn effort was the Union Populaire, which gained only a handful of votes in the 1979 and 1980 elections. Immediately after the "Night of the Long Knives" in 1981, Lévesque and the PQ officially supported the formation of the Parti Nationaliste to challenge federal elections. Very soon thereafter, however, Lévesque reversed himself and embarked on *le beau risque* with Mulroney and the Tories. As a result, when Bouchard founded the Bloc Québécois in the wake of the Meech disaster, the political ground was well tilled, the theoretical principles had been repeatedly debated, and the tactical and strategic necessity of such an eventual move was widely accepted by sovereigntist intellectuals and activists. Furthermore, when the Bloc began to organize, it already had the PQ's political base and organizational infrastructure, making it possible, almost overnight, to move from a small group of MPs in the House of Commons to a mass party with mass support. Additionally, with support for sovereignty in Quebec soaring in the aftermath of Meech, the Quebec electorate was eager to embrace the sovereigntist option in federal elections. This was confirmed when the Bloc's Gilles Duceppe scored an overwhelming victory in the 13 August 1990 federal by-election in Laurier–Ste. Marie.

The reaction of many in English Canada to the founding of the Bloc, and to Duceppe's victory, was often outright hostile and angry. This only served to solidify Bloc support among the Québécois. There was a lot of nonsense about loyalty and disloyalty, particularly when Duceppe dismissed as a technicality the oath a newly elected MP must take in order to take his or her seat — "I do swear that I will be faithful and bear true allegiance to Her Majesty Queen Elizabeth the Second." Suddenly, the House of Commons and the ranks of newspaper columnists were full of instant constitutional experts insisting that it was not possible for a separatist to take a seat in the House of Commons because an honest separatist could not take such an oath. Reform party MP Deborah Grey led the charge, and many commentators picked it up. One Ottawa historian insisted, "One cannot profess to serve the state while trying to dismantle the state — it is a contradiction." Liberal MP John Nunziata had already set the tone by accusing Bouchard of being a "traitor" and many Reform MPs echoed the sentiment, some even suggesting Bloc MPs should be tried for treason.

Such facile and erroneous opinions only served to inflame the situation while purveying abysmal ignorance about the Canadian parliamentary system. The oath to the Queen, as head of state, implies neither an absolute personal loyalty to her or the Crown, nor an unqualified loyalty to the policies and arrangements of the existing state she symbolizes. Rather, the oath is a declaration that the elected person, on behalf of those he or she represents, will dutifully advise the Queen, and the state she represents, regarding policies to be pursued.[1]

When the election was called, Bloc support in Quebec stood at 45 per cent (Liberals, 24 per cent; Tories, 27 per cent). In the last poll four days before the election that support climbed to 50 per cent (Liberals, 31 per cent; Tories, 14 per cent). All parties except the Bloc avoided too much talk about constitutional renewal and the problems of national unity. They had surveyed the wreckage of Meech and Charlottetown, seen the polls suggesting the electorate wasn't interested in talk about constitutions, and were aware of the growing anger among a significant minority of English Canadians toward Quebec, an anger fanned repeatedly by the Reform Party. Nothing was on offer to Quebec — except administrative arrangements and vague promises of general decentralization. Having said loudly that Charlottetown was the final, "take it or leave it" offer, the three major parties had no room to manoeuvre. For its part, the Reform Party had always staked out the position that Quebec should take or leave the pre-Charlottetown *status quo*; Reform's "New Canada" involved dismantling many of the concessions made to Quebec and francophones since the Quiet Revolution. As a result, the Bloc had no competition on constitutional matters. The party's message was clear and simple, and the Québécois were receptive. The old domineering federalism hadn't worked for Quebec, and English Canada was not willing to offer any substantial concessions. Therefore, sovereignty and a new negotiated post-sovereignty partnership was the only road open. Bloc MPs would represent and defend Quebec's interests in the Canadian federation while undertaking to work toward a sovereign Quebec.

On other issues the Bloc took positions similar to the NDP and echoed many positions taken by Chrétien and the Liberals: reductions in defence spending; protection of social programs, especially medicare and unemployment insurance; and reforms to make the tax system more just, with a strong attack on loopholes and tax shelters. On economic matters, the Bloc endorsed free trade and advocated a more interventionist role for the government via public investment to create jobs, lower interest rates to stimulate the economy, and programs to enhance competitiveness. On the debt and deficit, the Bloc agreed on the necessity for reduction, but opposed severe measures that threatened social and health programs, arguing only a sovereign Quebec would have the tools to deal effectively with the debt and deficit. On the creation of a strong, globally competitive Quebec economy, the Bloc insisted that sovereignty would lead to a better economic future, freeing Quebec from the shackles of both a dying federalism and a series of disastrously ineffectual national economic strategies.

The alleged merits of sovereignty led to some sharp exchanges during the French-language leaders' debate. Campbell said to Bouchard, "You say you are a separatist. [It's] unacceptable that you should run as a candidate in a federal election." This left an opening for Bouchard that went down well in Quebec: "You're going to refuse to receive Bloc Québécois members in Parliament? Are you going to reject the democratic will expressed by Quebeckers?" In response to Bouchard's attacks on Chrétien's legitimacy as a Quebec leader given Chrétien's record of "betrayals," Chrétien, who was already very low in the polls in Quebec, rose to the bait: "I'm a proud francophone. I'm a proud Quebecker. I'm a proud Canadian. Does this indicate the level of intolerance that would exist in an independent Quebec?" The comment was well received in English Canada, especially among English Canadians and strong federalists in Quebec, but did little to help Chrétien among the plurality of Quebec voters. The attitudes Chrétien expressed were considered *passé* within Quebec sovereigntist and nationalist circles. Though the debates had little effect on the overall campaign, within Quebec public perceptions of Bouchard as the "best prime minister" doubled after the debate (14 to 28 per cent), increased only slightly for Chrétien (13 to 20 per cent), and collapsed for Campbell (44 to 19 per cent). By the end of the campaign it was clear that earlier federalist expectations that Bouchard and the Bloc did not have staying power were without foundation.

In March 1993, Gallup had reported that 52 per cent of Canadians wanted a majority government in Ottawa, but 54 per cent anticipated a minority government, most expecting a Liberal minority. Perhaps here we can find part of the reason for the unusual outcome of the 1993 election. Polling figures during the campaign, if projected based on past results, would indeed have produced a Liberal minority. There was clear evidence that the Reform Party would do well in the West. The party did even better than expected, as a result of the collapse of the NDP and the

Tories, and won 24 of 32 seats in B.C. with 36 per cent of the vote, 22 of 26 seats in Alberta with 52 per cent, and 4 of 14 seats in Saskatchewan with 27 per cent. Reform also picked up one seat in Manitoba and one in Ontario. Particularly gratifying for Reform was their popular vote in Ontario (20 per cent), which suggested they had come within a whisker of breaking out of their western ghetto. Nevertheless, with 51 of 52 seats, and 58 per cent of their total vote concentrated in the four western provinces, the Reform Party remained, in reality, a regional protest party. The Bloc also did better than expected in Quebec, winning 54 of 75 seats with just over 49 per cent of the vote, ironically winning the role of Her Majesty's Loyal Opposition in the House of Commons, perhaps the first time in history that a separatist party has won such a mandate in a federal parliament.

The collapse of the Tories and the NDP was worse than expected. The Tories were reduced to two seats — in New Brunswick and Quebec — and 16 per cent of the national popular vote, the worst defeat of a governing party in Commonwealth history. The NDP, though reduced to 7 per cent of the vote, was able to capture nine seats because its vote was effectively concentrated in the West — one seat in Manitoba; five seats in Saskatchewan; two in B.C.; and McLaughlin won her Yukon seat. The collapse of NDP support in B.C. was spectacular: there the party fell from 37 per cent and nineteen seats in 1988 to 16 per cent and two seats in 1993. The results in Ontario were crushing: the NDP fell from 20 per cent of the vote and ten seats in 1988 to 6 per cent and no seats in 1993. Significantly, the NDP candidate who did best in Ontario was Steve Langdon, fired by McLaughlin in April for criticizing the Rae government. He won 28 per cent of the vote in his Essex–Windsor seat, outstripping candidates in seats where the NDP vote was traditionally stronger.

The 1993 election is notable for two reasons other than the collapse of the Tories and New Democrats and the rise of Reform and the Bloc. First, the undemocratic nature of Canada's parliamentary system became grotesquely clear. Though winning 16 per cent of the vote, the Tories, with two seats, won less than 1 per cent of seats, rather than a representative share of fifty-one seats (based on assigning seats according to provincial shares of the popular vote). The Bloc, with 13.5 per cent of the vote, should have won thirty-seven seats in a fair and representative system rather than fifty-four. The NDP should have won twenty-eight seats rather than nine with its 7 per cent. Only Reform came close to a representative share of seats, winning 19 per cent of the vote, which should have delivered fifty-four seats rather than the actual fifty-two won by Reform. The clear beneficiaries of Canada's "first past the post" system were Chrétien and the Liberals with 41 per cent of the vote and 177 seats, giving them 60 per cent of the seats and a comfortable majority government (in a fair system the Liberals should have won 124 seats). According to the polls such distortions convinced 45 per cent of Canadians that Canada should move to a proportional system — indeed, Gallup found that of the 80 per cent of Canadians with an opinion on the question, 56 per cent wanted a proportional system. There was clearly something wrong with an electoral system in which it took an average of 31,000 votes to elect a Liberal MP and more than a million votes to elect a Tory MP, or where a similar level of support for the Bloc and Reform led to a triumphant electoral breakthrough, while the same support led to near annihilation of the Tories.

The 1993 election is also notable for being arguably the most effective case of spontaneous strategic voting by an electorate in Canadian history. Indeed, this strategic voting helps explain the regional electoral behaviour that contributed to the undemocratic distortions noted above. Prior to the election, Gallup had found that Canadians wanted a majority government, and a month after the election Gallup found that 64 per cent were happy with the result. An examination of the results suggests that many Canadian voters did what they could to give Chrétien and the Liberals a majority. They were aware and worried that the Bloc was winning in Quebec and that Reform was doing the same in the West, as well as attracting much of the right-wing, anti-Quebec Tory vote in English Canada generally. Voters in Ontario and Atlantic Canada, in particular, abandoned their traditional electoral loyalties in droves in order to ensure a Liberal victory. Only spontaneous, strategic voting on a mass level can explain the anomaly of the Liberals winning 98 of 99 seats in Ontario with 53 per cent of the vote, and 31 of 32 seats in Atlantic Canada with 57 per cent. Indeed, concerns about a hung parliament, with the Bloc and Reform tearing each other apart, contributed to a Liberal breakthrough in the West — 27 of 86 seats with more than 30 per cent of the vote, an unprecedented result in more than thirty years. Hence, a significant part of the collapse of both the NDP and the Tories, especially in Ontario and the West, can be explained by the migration of large numbers of their traditional supporters to the Liberal Party to ensure a majority government in response to the dual threat posed by the Bloc and Reform.

The Quebec results, however, were of most significance for the future of Canada. A sovereigntist party — with almost 50 per cent of the vote and 54 of 75 seats in Quebec — now represented the Québécois in the House of Commons. The Liberals won nineteen seats with 33 per cent, the Tories won one seat (Jean Charest) with 13.5 per cent. The Bloc won smashing victories in most seats in which francophones were a strong majority — frequently with majorities between 55 and 65 per cent. Fourteen of the nineteen Liberal seats were won on the Island of Montreal, resulting from overwhelming support for the Liberals among anglophones and allophones (people whose first language is neither English nor French), often with huge majorities (83 per cent in Mont Royal; 71 per cent in Notre Dame de Grâce; 61 per cent in St. Léonard; 65 per cent in Pierrefonds–Dollard, for example). In the five Liberal seats won off the Island of Montreal, two were in strong federalist territory (Gatineau–La Lièvre, Hull–Aylmer), one was the prime minister's seat, and the other two were tight races with the Bloc. And, of course, Jean Charest easily won his Sherbrooke seat. Bouchard had no doubt about the significance of the Bloc's victory when he said, "A new chapter has been opened. We are going to Ottawa to build something new, something that will prove beneficial to both nations." Other sovereigntists were more blunt. PQ leader Parizeau declared, "Two-thirds of Quebec MPs will now say in unison: 'We want our own country.'…In two years, Quebec will have its own country, Quebec will be sovereign, Quebec will be independent."

English Canadians were generally less than gracious in their response to the success of the Bloc, with 56 per cent believing the Bloc should be denied status as official Opposition in Ottawa (including more than 60 per cent in the West and almost 90 per cent of those who voted Reform). Ontario premier Bob Rae vowed to confront Bouchard: "Here's a guy who wants to break up the country….I think his policies should be confronted at every level. I think he's deluding himself if he thinks that the rest of the country is going to sort of sit back…and accept the breakup of the country. I don't intend to." Rae's comments signalled a series of hostile comments from the premiers of English Canada, most notably the NDP premiers. Such angry reactions, as well as continued sniping about the "treason" of Bouchard and the Bloc, could not, however, erase the ominous significance of the result.

Trudeau was well aware of that significance when he said, after voting in an advance poll before leaving for travels in the Far East, "If you weaken the government of Canada, which Bouchard intends [to do], you do no favour to Canadians; you do a favour to those who believe in separatism....Bouchard represents the disintegration of Canada. If that's what they want, they can vote for him." With the election of the Bloc, sovereigntists could now claim to have an overwhelming democratic and constitutional mandate to speak for the people of Quebec in the House of Commons. Success for the PQ in the coming provincial election and a majority vote in a future sovereignty referendum could set the stage for the democratic, peaceful, and orderly exit of Quebec from Canada. This was the most significant reality to emerge from the 1993 election — it gave Quebec sovereigntists the biggest positive push in the history of their struggle on the trajectory toward successful separation.

The next phase in the struggle was the Quebec provincial election. Although it was set for 12 September 1994, campaigning actually began on the heels of the federal election and particularly heated up when Johnson was sworn in as premier in January 1994. It was a provincial election but it was a national event of great significance, hence a number of premiers, business leaders, and federal politicians participated.

If the PQ won, Parizeau promised a speedy sovereignty referendum on a clear question. If the PQ lost there would be no referendum and sovereignty would be delayed until another provincial election, sapping the movement's momentum and leaving the Bloc to linger in Ottawa through another federal election. It was a tough fight, from the point of view of federalists. Bourassa and the Liberals, and then Johnson and the Liberals, were trailing the PQ in the polls. Bouchard and the Bloc had just won a smashing victory. Public support for sovereignty in Quebec was on the upswing. English Canada was cranky and appeared unwilling to offer a new constitutional deal to Quebec. Even if such a willingness could have been cultivated, there was a lack of political will among English-Canadian leaders to do so. Johnson and the Liberals would face the Quebec electorate with nothing but the *status quo* on offer.

In Ottawa, Bouchard and Chrétien competed for the hearts and minds of the Québécois, while Chrétien walked a trembling tightrope in English Canada between the contradictory demands and expectations of the general public and the neo-conservative business lobby. Chrétien initially made a few gestures based on his Red Book promises by cutting the controversial helicopter purchase, reversing the Tory-initiated privatization of Pearson International Airport, reducing defence spending, eliminating some unpopular tax advantages for the privileged and the corporate sector, and creating jobs through an infrastructure program. But finance minister Paul Martin was quickly converted to pursuing the neo-conservative agenda of attacking the deficit and debt through cuts in government spending. A few gestures were also made in this direction: reductions in unemployment insurance benefits, a clawback of income tax credits for seniors with incomes higher than $49,000, a public-sector wage freeze. Granted, this represented mere nibbling at the edges of the neo-conservative agenda and Martin promised the complaining business lobby that harsher deficit reduction measures were yet to come. Human resources minister Lloyd Axworthy was assigned the job of reviewing not only the entire unemployment insurance program but also all social programs, with a view to rationalization and cost savings. The signals were clear, as Martin kept reiterating, big cuts were coming and everyone knew they were put on hold due to the coming Quebec election.

The scene in Ottawa was dramatic and symbolic, especially for the Québécois. Here was a prime minister from Quebec, a committed federalist with approval ratings across English Canada that were so high they were unprecedented, but with much lower ratings in Quebec. There, across the floor in the House of Commons as leader of the official Opposition, was Bouchard, a committed sovereigntist, commanding support in Quebec and levels of public trust and adulation unknown since Lévesque. On constitutional issues, Bouchard and Chrétien agreed: neither wanted to talk very much about them, but for very different reasons. Chrétien, looking over his shoulder at the ugly mood in English Canada and the wreckage of Meech and Charlottetown, was trapped. To discuss the constitution in any way that appeared to re-open the negotiations or that appeared to offer Quebec concessions would be pounced on by the Reform Party and the largely francophobic English-Canadian media. Bouchard did not want to talk about the constitution because he believed that era was over. The only option to be discussed was sovereignty and a new partnership between two sovereign nations, perhaps modelled on the European Union. Bouchard did not, however, hesitate to extol sovereignty and attack Chrétien as the architect of Quebec's 1982 humiliation and as Trudeau's puppet. As the Liberals moved toward and then hesitated cutting and restructuring social programs, Bouchard attacked, declaring himself the defender of Canada's social safety net, saying, "It's a strange paradox that a sovereigntist party from Quebec will be the only party fighting to preserve the main value of Canada....The signals are quite clear. [The Chrétien government] will attack social programs." Bouchard also used his position as leader of the Opposition to raise his status as a statesman internally and externally, carrying the sovereignty message to Europe, the U.S., and western Canada. With the PQ well ahead of the Quebec Liberals in the polls, and with Bouchard carrying his "good news" messages about inevitable sovereignty across the country and around the world, Chrétien's strategy of non-interference in Quebec's election and his avoidance of the separatist issue seemed more and more risky, something Preston Manning never tired of pointing out.

During May and June 1994, in a move allegedly orchestrated by Chrétien and Ottawa, federal Indian affairs minister Ron Irwin and premiers Romanow of Saskatchewan and Harcourt of B.C. commenced a series of harsh attacks on the idea of Quebec sovereignty and on Parizeau and Bouchard personally. Given the brouhaha that developed over the subsequent days and weeks, it is difficult not to believe that Irwin, a minister in Chrétien's cabinet, and Romanow, a close confidant of Chrétien's, were acting as stalking horses (with the prime minister's approval) to test the effects of a hard line. On 16 May 1994, Harcourt expressed some harsh views on Quebec separatism, views very similar to those of Reform leader Manning: "If [the Québécois] decided to separate...we'd be the worst of enemies. The anger...felt by British Columbians...would be immense." He went on to suggest Quebec couldn't count on leaving with its present borders intact. "It's you're in or you're out...it's much, much clearer." He accused Bouchard and Parizeau, dubbing him "the Pied Piper," of misleading the Québécois by suggesting that Quebec's separation would be amicable. "Oh, it would be terrible consequences for everybody....[Bouchard and Parizeau] think it's going to be logical and civilized. Forget it, it won't be. There will be great bitterness and a nasty split. And they'll suffer, not just economically but they'll suffer every which way, the people of Quebec."

The following day in an address at a two-day meeting on self-government between Quebec aboriginal leaders and federal and provincial officials in Quebec City, Irwin promised that Quebec's aboriginal people could choose to remain part of Canada in the event of separation. He also insisted that Quebec was not a nation and had no legal claim to sovereignty. This was followed on 18 and 19 May by a series of personal attacks on Bouchard and Parizeau. During a meeting of the four western premiers in Gimli, Manitoba, Romanow accused Bouchard and Parizeau of being the "master illusionists of Quebec politics...advancing a con job...about separation. They say it's inevitable — that's a con job. That it's going to be easy — that's a con job. That there's going to be some economic association thereafter — that's a con job." Romanow explained that he was provoked into commenting by "the spectacle of Her Majesty's Loyal Opposition travelling to Washington and Paris and other parts of the country preaching the virtues and inevitability of Quebec separation." Harcourt and Romanow were unable to persuade their two Tory colleagues — Gary Filmon of Manitoba and Ralph Klein of Alberta — to put together a joint public response to the separatist threat. By that time, Preston Manning had joined in the war of words: "An example of a nonsensical statement is Mr. Bouchard saying the boundaries of Quebec are inviolate but the boundaries of Canada are not. Either they're both inviolate or they're both subject to negotiation." Despite such a strange bedfellow, Romanow and Harcourt refused to back off from their comments; indeed, Romanow escalated the confrontation in late May by insisting that a Yes vote on sovereignty in a Quebec referendum was not sufficient grounds for separation and that the constitution contained no mechanism for separation. And a few days later, Romanow attacked Bouchard again, saying his actions were "malicious," "contributing to economic uncertainty," and his role was "fundamentally flawed and...illogical." Even Prime Minister Chrétien, who had insisted on staying out of Quebec's debate on separatism because it was a "hypothetical" question, was drawn briefly into the fray, when he said, "The best protection...for Quebec's territory is to stay within Canada." Later he also reiterated that he had no intention of discussing separatism prior to a referendum should the PQ win the coming election, but nevertheless took the opportunity to suggest that the sovereigntists would mislead the people of Quebec: "If [the PQ] win the election and hold a referendum I hope they will not try to hide their real option. They have to say that it's separation that they want. They call themselves sovereigntists and it's not even a French word. It's not in the dictionary."

The reaction in Quebec to these comments — especially those on territory — was as predictable as it was instantaneous and u-nanimous. Parizeau restated his 1991 position that Quebec's borders "are what they are....There's no way the federal government will say...we are going to carve out pieces of you. Nobody does that in a country where the rule of law applies." Accusing the federal government and the premiers of using aboriginal people as pawns in a cynical anti-separatist campaign, he said, "As the sovereignty of Quebec becomes more probable, they are angry....I've got to say periodically, 'Pipe down...a great deal of your ill will, of your hollering, has absolutely no legal or constitutional basis. And, therefore, as ministers or premiers, keep your shirt on.'" Bouchard was also blunt, declaring that any attempt to re-draw a sovereign Quebec's borders would unite all francophones: "If there is one thing sacred in Quebec, as in any other country, it is territory....Even Robert Bourassa would get angry." Finally, given the reaction in the province, Quebec premier Johnson made a solemn declaration in the National Assembly: "We will defend Quebec's territory no matter what happens."

In the midst of this war of words, Johnson asked politicians outside the province to keep their noses out of Quebec politics. "We're not in a mode where we're into scare tactics or scenarios now. We want to keep the temperature down." Only Preston Manning ignored this advice, despite a specific request from Liberal strategists who told him his meddling would only help Parizeau. This advice was understandable: every outburst from outside had been met head-on by sovereigntist leaders whose stature among the Québécois was thereby elevated as defenders of Quebec. Federalists in Quebec and experienced analysts of Quebec politics warned that such attacks, threats, and warnings by English Canadians from outside Quebec only inflamed passions and made the sovereigntists' job easier. A successful attack on sovereignty must come from within Quebec from federalists and non-separatist Québécois nationalists. The prime minister also intervened, suggesting that everyone, especially his own ministers, should stop responding to hypothetical questions about the future of Quebec and get on with the real, pressing work they had to do. That the premiers took this to heart became clear in the remaining months prior to the election as the rhetoric was toned down, if for no other reason than it clearly didn't help Johnson and only boosted the popularity of Bouchard and Parizeau among the Québécois. The premiers became so disciplined that at their annual premiers' conference, held in Toronto at the height of the Quebec election late in August, they even refrained from blasting Ottawa for fear of helping elect Parizeau and went out of their way to praise Johnson. Only New Brunswick premier Frank McKenna broke ranks and put his foot in his mouth, saying, "If we end up with a separatist government in Quebec, there's no interest in solutions. What they want is to establish a separate country and throw all of us into a vortex of debt and despair."

This war of words, provoked by English-Canadian politicians and responded to with such enthusiasm and alacrity by Bouchard and Parizeau, raised a number of important issues and intensified the polarization between English Canada and Quebec. Romanow's and Harcourt's comments, in particular, gave credence to the dreary stream of dangerous nonsense that had emanated from English-Canadian extremists ever since the collapse of Meech. Groups such as the right-wing Alliance for the Preservation of English in Canada and many in the Reform Party, to which the Alliance was closely linked, talked loosely of the use of military action to support the establishment of non-francophone ethnic enclaves in west Montreal and the north, to force a territorial corridor through a sovereign Quebec to link Ontario and Atlantic Canada, and even to suppress the move to sovereignty as treason. Comments such as those of Romanow and Harcourt tended to add considerable weight and credibility to such extreme and dangerous talk. Raising the territorial question in that context — of talk of anger and enemies — was extremely provocative. It was also dishonest. Regardless of the history of Quebec's boundaries, particularly the lands transferred to Quebec by federal statute in 1898 and 1920 — the northern territories beyond the Height of Land, taking the province's borders to Hudson and Ungava bays and the Hudson Strait — the Canadian constitution stipulates that a province's borders cannot be changed without the province's consent. Hence, Quebec's boundaries must remain intact until the moment of sovereignty, at which point territory and boundaries become a matter among many others for negotiation. The PQ's 1994 sovereignty program, while making the case for Quebec's territorial integrity after sovereignty, proposed that "the framework for questions of [Quebec's] territorial integrity will be international law," thus presumably making a commitment to submit such issues to arbitration by the UN's International Court of Justice in the case of an impasse. Threats to Quebec's territory were thus not only premature but also bellicose posturing of the most dangerous kind, given the role territory has played in provoking strife in world history.

The manipulation of the aboriginal issue was also questionable. Granted, most aboriginal nations in Quebec, with the exception of the Huron, understandably have grave concerns about their future rights and entitlements in a sovereign Quebec and have consistently opposed Quebec sovereignty. Despite reassurances by Bouchard and Parizeau, despite the relatively good record (compared to English Canada) Quebec had had prior to Oka, and despite the 1975 James Bay Agreement, aboriginal leaders want the matter resolved and do not want to separate. Sovereigntists would be compelled to deal with aboriginal rights and to do so under close international scrutiny. Yet for English Canada to use the aboriginal issue as a trump against Quebec sovereignty smacked of hypocrisy, given its own record of treatment of aboriginal people, and it was clearly seen as such both by the aboriginal communities and by the Québécois.

Taken together, and putting the best possible light on them, these episodes in the campaign were serious errors in judgement. Putting the worst possible light on the situation, it was a deliberate effort to test the effectiveness of scare tactics in persuading the Québécois to step back from the precipice of sovereignty. If scaremongering was the intent, the episode provided an opportunity to assess the political effects and consequences of English Canada's use of threats on a sovereign Quebec's territory. The evidence was clear. Such an approach was counter-productive, and served only to exacerbate the fear and anger of those opposed to separation, to stiffen the resolve of those committed to separation, and to compel those in Quebec who struggle diligently to reconcile federalism and Québécois nationalism to walk a tightrope from which they inevitably fall.

Although the economic costs of separation continued to be raised throughout this war of words, Quebec sovereigntist leaders, perhaps having learned from two decades of confronting economic fear campaigns, met the negative claims head-on, just as they had during the Charlottetown referendum campaign. The soil for a successful economic fear campaign was certainly not as rich as it had been in the past. The free trade agreements had their expected effects, as Quebec trade shifted more and more southward and as economic links to Canada become less and less important. A study conducted for the Caisse de dépôt found that

Quebec exports to the U.S. between 1988 and 1992 had surged in all economic sectors, and this growth had been significantly greater than that experienced by Canada as a whole. Another study found that between 1981 and 1995 Quebec's exports to the rest of Canada grew by 67 per cent, while international exports grew by 208 per cent. This changing economic reality was accompanied by a shift in public opinion. In January 1994, Gallup found that although 53 per cent of Québécois believed the Canadian economy would be worse off without Quebec, opinion regarding the province was almost equally divided, with 35 per cent of Québécois believing their economy would be better off and 37 per cent believing it would be worse off. Meanwhile, 74 per cent of Canadians outside the province believed the Quebec economy would be worse off, another example of the two solitudes. The depth of this economic disagreement was confirmed when a poll found that 60 per cent of non-francophones blame Montreal's high unemployment levels on the sovereignty debate, while only 28 per cent of Québécois share that view.

Further evidence that federalism and bilingualism may not have delivered economic justice to francophones was reported by the *Globe and Mail* using hitherto unpublished data from Statistics Canada that showed that between 1977 and 1991 the income gap between individual francophones and anglophones in Canada had more than doubled, while among francophone and anglophone families the gap had grown by 50 per cent. In Quebec, francophone incomes had reached the level of anglophone incomes in 1992. Indeed, in the case of men, francophone incomes had edged ahead of those of anglophones — but a large part of the explanation lay in the decline of anglophone incomes, on the average, between 1977 and 1992 as a result of the flight of head offices and higher income anglophones from the province in the wake of the 1976 PQ victory and the new, tough language laws. In fact, the anglophone share of Quebec's population fell from 13 per cent in 1971 to 9 per cent in 1991; in absolute numbers, from 789,000 to 626,000. It was not surprising, therefore, when Gallup reported once again, just as it had in three previous polls since Meech, that 54 per cent of Canadians believed that the federal bilingualism policy package had failed, including 61 per cent of Québécois and 58 per cent of all francophones in Canada.

Unlike Lévesque and earlier sovereigntist leaders, Parizeau and Bouchard were not at all defensive about the economic issue. On the contrary, both leaders aggressively insisted that both Canada and Quebec would benefit economically in the long run from Quebec separation. Parizeau, a distinguished economist, a top-level career civil servant and academic, and a member of the economic elite himself, was particularly confident in his knowledge and experience and dealt easily with complex economic issues, preferring to attack federalism as a drag on Quebec's economy rather than apologizing for sovereignty or agreeing there might be large costs involved. Indeed, Parizeau consistently blamed federalism and the constitutional deadlock for Quebec's stagnant economy and high unemployment and poverty figures. Parizeau also insisted on keeping the politics of sovereignty separate from business issues, continually reassuring the business community that economic life in Quebec, especially secure and profitable investment, would not be jeopardized by sovereignty. Whenever prominent business leaders or financial institutions warned about the heavy costs of sovereignty, such as one Toronto bond house that forecast a sixty-seven-cent dollar, a 10 per cent prime rate, and a loss of twenty thousand jobs if the PQ won and held a referendum, Parizeau and Bouchard were both quick to rap their knuckles for "fear-mongering." As Parizeau said in June 1994 in response to a negative comment by Canada's banking regulator, superintendent of financial institutions Michael Mackenzie: "Why don't you handle the money and we will handle politics? Whenever they start playing the political game, someone must step on their toes and say, 'Watch Out.'" In response to a claim by the Bank of Montreal's chief economist that a PQ win on the proposed sovereignty program would "create a great deal of fear" in financial markets, Parizeau counter-attacked vigorously: "Some of [the bankers] have tried to frighten Quebeckers. I will always be on the side of Quebeckers. I will always defend them." When the Royal Bank joined the doomsayers, Parizeau accused Canadian banks of using Québécois money to finance a fear campaign against the PQ and of using Québécois savings to finance a Liberal victory indirectly: "Some Canadian financial institutions are trying to play politics with our own money. Fair enough, but we don't have to believe them....It will pass in a few weeks like it has passed for thirty years." Parizeau and PQ candidate Daniel Paillé implied that banks, brokerage houses, and other financial institutions that persisted in such economic fear tactics in the runup to the Quebec election would pay a price after a PQ victory by a loss of business. The result was fewer negative interventions from the business community.

The 1994 election was unprecedented because it presented the Québécois with a stark and clear choice: *status quo* federalism or sovereignty. Johnson was the first Quebec premier since the Quiet Revolution to wrap himself in the Canadian flag as an unambiguous champion of Canada and federalism. And Parizeau was the first sovereigntist leader to be unapologetic and determined in his absolute devotion to separatism "first, last, and always," even unafraid of embracing the term "separatist," offering nothing but a quick referendum on sovereignty and, of course, better government than the Liberal "clowns" provided. Throughout the campaign, the PQ maintained its lead in the polls, just as they had since Charlottetown, beginning in the third week of July with 51 per cent and ending a week before the vote with 49 per cent, while the Liberals fell from 44 per cent to 38 per cent. Parizeau also consistently outscored Johnson on issues relating to leadership competence. This was the obvious reason Johnson agreed to the 29 August televised debate with Parizeau, the first since 1962 when Johnson's father, Union Nationale premier Daniel Johnson Sr., lost to Liberal leader Jean Lesage. History repeated itself when according to the post-debate polls Parizeau easily won.

Johnson and the Liberals decided to make independence the central issue of the election. A vote for the PQ was a vote "to initiate the process toward sovereignty and independence....We will be at a turning point....There would be eight, ten, twelve, or even fifteen months of uncertainty and constitutional turmoil...a fate worse than recession." Johnson also hammered away at the economic problems posed by the PQ's obsessive pursuit of sovereignty, noting that the choice was between "the strengthening on the one hand and the rupture and division on the other of the Canadian economic and political union," warning that "the economic recovery is really here...in spite of a certain fragility." In response, Parizeau and the PQ embraced the sovereignty issue and turned it back on the Liberals, reminding voters that the election was not really about sovereignty because that would be decided in a referendum in less than a year; nevertheless sovereignty was Quebec's "destiny," was achievable, and would turn the economy around. At every opportunity, Parizeau flaunted his commitment to sovereignty, puzzling Liberal strategists, because they expected to put the PQ on the defensive by making independence the central issue. From time to time expressing exasperation at the media's insistence on pursuing the sovereignty issue relentlessly, Parizeau nonetheless never once deviated from his confident, pro-sovereignty message, despite always reminding voters that the final decision was theirs to make in a separate referendum. In the last half of the campaign, Bouchard intervened to help the PQ by warning the Québécois that the election of Johnson and the Liberals would lead to the submission of Quebec to Ottawa. "Elect Johnson and that's handing the destiny of Quebec to Jean Chrétien," said Bouchard, making it clear that the battle was not just between the PQ and the provincial Liberals but between Quebec and English Canada. Polls continued to show that the Liberal effort to make the election a vote on separation failed and continued to fail throughout the campaign — the Quebec electorate wanted to toss the Liberals out and their first purpose in voting was to get change and good government.

Late in the campaign, facing certain defeat, Johnson broke his own taboo by raising constitutional matters. He criticized Bourassa's strategy for seeking constitutional change, which had ended in Meech and Charlottetown, and distanced himself from Trudeau's vision, saying he would push for greater autonomy for Quebec as well as accelerated decentralization. "All my political career is based on a defence of Quebec's interests," he said, though his basic "constitutional policy is to provide job opportunities for Quebeckers." In late August, he stated that Quebec's position with him as premier would remain to "exercise our own jurisdiction with more and more autonomy, that the federal government gets out of the way…and that we make sure [the federal system] is as efficient for the taxpayer as possible."

Then, in early September, still facing defeat, Johnson appeared to convert to Québécois nationalism when he reversed his earlier Canada-first defence of federalism. Speaking to the Quebec City Chamber of Commerce, Johnson said that he could conceive of being a Québécois without being a Canadian, but not of being a Canadian without being a Québécois. He went on to describe himself as a Québécois above all, dismissing his earlier comment about being a Canadian first as an "unfortunate use of words." Delighted, Parizeau described Johnson's late conversion as "revolting," attacking him on two fronts: first, for being opportunistic enough to adopt "any position…to be popular at any time," and second, for continuing the confused and indecisive ambiguity for which Quebec federalists had become famous.

Virtually ignored by the media in English Canada, the disgruntled nationalists who had abandoned Bourassa over Charlottetown had founded the ADQ. Led by the prominent Jean Allaire and the former Young Liberal leader Mario Dumont, the ADQ ran eighty candidates in the election. Allaire and Dumont, who at twenty-four became the youngest leader of a credible registered political party in Quebec history, were uncomfortable with Parizeau's hard line on sovereignty, preferring Lévesque's earlier, softer "sovereignty-association" approach. As Dumont put it, "I think we can be sovereigntist without being separatist. I'm certainly a sovereigntist in the sense that I want Quebec to have its powers. But I'm not a separatist because I believe in a new partnership with the rest of Canada." Not unlike Bouchard, he pointed to the supranational parliament of the European Union as a model. Rather than seeing a successful referendum on sovereignty as a final decision, Dumont believed that it would provide Quebec the political clout to persuade Canada to negotiate a new partnership. If Canada refused to negotiate, however, he believed Quebec would separate because, as he said in a clear reference to Bourassa's humiliation in the closed sessions on Charlottetown, "I won't walk on my knees for that." The ADQ was seen as a minor spoiler, but its support grew from 3 per cent at the beginning of the campaign to 9 per cent a week before the election.

On 12 September 1994, Parizeau and the PQ won 77 of 125 seats with 44.8 per cent of the vote, while the Liberals, gaining significantly in the last days of the campaign, took forty-seven seats with 44.4 per cent. The big surprise of the election was the election of Dumont in his seat and the ADQ's 6.5 per cent of the popular vote. Though only 0.4 per cent separated the PQ and the Liberals, the wins for the PQ were spread primarily among the francophone population, whereas the Liberals' vote tended to be largely concentrated in anglophone and allophone seats where Liberal candidates won by large majorities but the overall vote did not translate into a fair share of seats. The results suggested that Johnson's tactics of trying to turn the election into a vote on independence, to worry voters about the PQ's sovereignty process upon victory, and to raise the economic uncertainty issue had closed the gap with the PQ. But most of the votes that had been scared off the PQ had gone to Dumont and the ADQ, not to the Liberals. At the outset of the campaign, PQ popular support rested at 51 per cent. Thus the party lost approximately 6 per cent by election day. The Liberals, on the other hand, began with 44 per cent and ended with that level of support. The ADQ began with 3 per cent and ended with 6.5 per cent. Meanwhile other parties, such as the anglophone Equality Party and a gaggle of others, rose from 2 per cent at the outset to approximately 4.5 per cent at the end.

Many in English Canada refused to recognize the significance of the results, responding to the outcome with equal measures of ill grace and wilful blindness. Indeed, many English-Canadian politicians and commentators embarked on a systematic and creative re-interpretation of the outcome. The result was not a vote for sovereignty, they maintained, just one for change and good government. Of course, Parizeau and the PQ had never claimed the provincial vote was on sovereignty, even though Johnson had done so repeatedly. Furthermore, English Canada by and large continued to ignore the very real fact that Parizeau presented his priority commitment to sovereignty frequently, firmly, and with candour. Hence, he clearly had a mandate to establish the agenda and to set the process in motion, with the clear democratic blessing of the Quebec electorate, which had granted him all the power of the Quebec state to do so. The election result was a moral defeat for the PQ, some commentators crowed, because the popular vote was so close. Whether we like it or not, the objective in a parliamentary democracy is to win seats, and here the PQ's victory was decisive. Furthermore, English-Canadian commentators tended systematically to overlook the 6.5 per cent of the vote won by the ADQ and deliberately to ignore the fact that Dumont ran on a sovereignty-association platform. Hence, the pro-sovereignty vote had been over 51 per cent of the electorate, nearly the percentage the PQ had at the beginning of the campaign. Hence pro-sovereignty support in the election was hardly at a level to inspire confidence in the outcome of the looming referendum. Yet that is what many in English Canada began to express — an ungrounded confidence that, given the closeness of the vote, the approaching sovereignty referendum was doomed to defeat. English Canada's capacity for self-serving delusional thinking on the Quebec question again seemed remarkably immune from repeated doses of reality. As incredible as it seems in retrospect, many in English Canada breathed a sigh of relief after the PQ's victory, yet another reflection of an abysmal ignorance of Quebec politics.

Granted, some of this misdirected optimism in English Canada might have had to do with poll results in Quebec on separation. Those in favour ranged from a high in May 1994 of 44 per cent to a low of 32 per cent just before the election. Yet as soon as the PQ won, the polls began to shift, up to 34 per cent in favour in October 1994 and then to 38 per cent in December 1994. Perhaps more significant, given the context, was that those clearly opposed fell from 61 per cent in August to 43 per cent in December, pointing to a sharp rise in those undecided (9 per cent in August; 19 per cent in December). Furthermore, this was Gallup's hard separatist question (which had only 11 per cent support in 1968). On a more ambiguous question using the word *sovereignty* rather than *separation*, with a new partnership being offered post-independence, the chances of victory for the Yes side in an early referendum had in fact never been better.

Notes

1. The Magna Carta of 1215 first affirmed that loyalty to the Crown was not unqualified and that the Crown, or the state, was required to abide by the law. The Bill of Rights of 1689, after a bloody civil war, established the supremacy of Parliament over the Crown, or the state, leading finally to our form of fully responsible and democratic government. The Queen is head of state and appoints her representative, the Governor General. The cabinet comprises the Governor General's closest advisers and, though technically appointed by him or her, must be nominated by the prime minister and have the confidence of the House of Commons. The House of Commons as a body advises the head of state through the cabinet and prime minister. Elected members are obliged to proffer their best advice according to their conscience to ensure good government. The practical reality, by constitutional custom, is that the prime minister is the *de facto* head of state. The prime minister selects the Governor General, the cabinet, and senators. But the prime minister must answer to the House of Commons and, at least every five years, to the people. To say that the MP's oath is an expression of loyalty to the state is in fact to say that the oath is an expression of loyalty to the current prime minister. In a democracy, this is patently untenable, since the prime minister holds office at the pleasure of the House of Commons and, ultimately, the people. Again, we are back to 1689 when, in the aftermath of a civil war and the execution of a king by Parliament, the British Crown itself clearly existed (and exists) at the pleasure of Parliament — Parliament was and is, within the constitution and the common law, supreme. Therefore, when a person is elected a member of Parliament or a provincial legislator, and takes the prescribed oath, he or she merely affirms that he or she will support the constitution and the laws. But in that constitution and in those laws, as well as in the theory and practice of democracy itself, are the necessary mechanisms for change — whether it be a minor amend-

ment to a law, a revolutionary change in constitutional arrangements, or the very dismantling of the state itself. The limits on an MP's actions are the same as on the rest of us — they must be lawful actions. Futhermore, an MP can be removed from his or her seat only by the House of Commons itself, as occurred with Louis Riel, or by the voters in a general election. The problem with a complex federal democracy such as Canada is that loyalty is inevitably divisible. Each of us, in one way or another, divides our loyalties according to gender, family, class, ideology, ethnicity, region, and nation. The secret of Canada's success has always been rooted in a commitment to recognize, to accept, and to reconcile our divided loyalties. Words such as "disloyalty" and "treason" and calls for an indivisible loyalty to the state destroy that process of reconciliation. People who use such words are neither friends of democracy nor of Canada.

9

The 1995 Sovereignty Referendum

Immediately following the election in Quebec, the major players began to position themselves for the coming referendum. Initially, there was an effort by English Canada's premiers and federal politicians to warn Parizeau that, given his narrow win, he did not have a mandate to pursue his sovereignty agenda. The usual economic debate emerged, focused on the heavy costs to Quebec of separation, the terrible effects of economic uncertainty on the entire economy, and the benefits of federalism for Quebec. One study suggested the minimum annual cost to Quebec of sovereignty would be $3.4 billion, but these costs would begin to decline after the first three years. The PQ government released confidential economic studies done by the Johnson and Bourassa governments, alleging the federal system cost Quebec three billion dollars a year. Federalists countered with statistics that proved Quebec benefited from federalism to the tune of six billion dollars a year. Pro-federalist business leaders indicated that though they had been relatively silent during the election, they would campaign very actively in any future referendum. Chrétien tried to bait the PQ into an early date for the referendum but the PQ declined. At first, the party held to Parizeau's ten-month timetable, but later modified it to twelve to fifteen months, after an intervention by Bouchard. Parizeau rejected Dumont's suggestion that a referendum be put off until Quebec's economic house was in order. Johnson, the Opposition leader and official leader of the No campaign, called for modifications to the federal system, noting that a vote against sovereignty was not a vote for the *status quo*. He insisted that Ottawa would eventually renew federalism and "adjust the constitutional framework."

Undeterred, Parizeau and the PQ adhered to their promised timetable. In early December 1994, the premier tabled a draft bill on sovereignty in the National Assembly that opened with section 1 declaring that "Quebec is a sovereign country." In brief and clear terms, the bill laid out the PQ's plan for achieving sovereignty. It also provided assurances: it authorized the government to seek an economic association with Canada, guaranteed the rights and freedoms of anglophone and aboriginal citizens (including a self-government guarantee for aboriginal nations), and proposed an orderly transition plan. After lengthy debate and public consultations, the bill would eventually be amended and approved by the National Assembly, but would not come into force until "one year after its approval in a referendum." This referendum, to be successful, would require a majority of votes cast in favour of the following question: "Are you in favour of the Act passed by the National Assembly declaring the sovereignty of Quebec?" This was clearly a very different question from the one asked in 1980, which was long, convoluted, and confused, and asked only for a mandate to negotiate sovereignty-association. If successful, the referendum would have the effect of triggering sovereignty within one year. In a sense it was a unilateral declaration of independence by referendum.

Not unexpectedly, the bill was roundly condemned by federalists across Canada and by aboriginal leaders in Quebec. It was described as "not democratic," "a scam," "flawed," and "dishonest" by the prime minister; "a unilateral denial of all aboriginal and Cree rights" by Matthew Coon Come, leader of the northern Cree; and "a fraud" by deputy prime minister Sheila Copps. "Parizeau has broken his word," intoned Romanow; "trickery," ventured McKenna; "illegitimate" and "propaganda," declared No leader Johnson. Parizeau's response was blunt, "Quebec is on the fast track to sovereignty and there is nothing the rest of Canada can do to stop it....You're a Canadian or you're not....This thing has to be settled." The issue for Quebec sovereigntists was clear: "The more time goes by, the more the Canadian majority is determined to act as though there is but one nation in Canada, as though all provinces are equal. This is the Canada of tomorrow. Do we want to be part of it? Absolutely not."

The Quebec referendum campaign had four phases. The first phase was the early stage of preparations and positioning for the referendum, during which Parizeau was the key leader and Bouchard was absent from the scene due to his near-fatal bout with "flesh-eating disease" (necrotizing fasciitis) that kept him sidelined until late February 1995. The second phase was the period of confusion and disagreement in the ranks of the sovereigntists, which was not resolved until April 1995. The third phase was the period with Parizeau leading the Yes campaign, including its formal launch, until Bouchard took over the *de facto* leadership of the campaign on 9 October 1995. Finally, the fourth phase was the period with Bouchard at the helm, during which support for the Yes side began to grow and panic set in among the No forces.

During the first phase, Parizeau and the PQ government put the process in motion. Fifteen regional commissions were established to hold public hearings throughout Quebec in order to get feedback and proposals for modifications to the sovereignty agenda. At first, Johnson refused to participate and suggested that federalists boycott the commissions since they were just a propaganda exercise. Very quickly, however, he changed his mind when it became clear that people were taking the consultation process very seriously and intended to participate (more than fifty-three thousand would take part by the end). Parizeau and the PQ focused their strategy on winning over the "soft nationalists," the middle 20 per cent. In the months leading up to the actual campaign, the media were full of claims and counter-claims: debates among legal experts about constitutional matters; warnings of the dire consequences of separation by some economic experts, by others reassurances that the economic impacts would be insignificant; proposals that a Yes vote be denied recognition; debates about whether 50 per cent-plus-one vote is enough to break up a country; arguments over sharing the debt and dividing up federal assets. As one would expect, for every claim or threat made by federalists, there was a counter-claim and a response by sovereigntists in this tit-for-tat battle for the hearts and minds of the soft nationalists. By late February 1995, when Bouchard returned from his convalescence, Yes support was stuck at 45 per cent, with 55 per cent for the No. Though this was an improvement on Lévesque's 1980 showing, polls clearly indicated that the No was coasting to an easy win.

The problem was Parizeau's hard line and his insistence on a clear, tough question. Determined not to give English Canada the means to interfere directly in the Quebec debate (as Lévesque had done with his mandate to negotiate and his hyphen in sovereignty-association), Parizeau was making it very difficult for the soft nationalists to move his way. These were the sovereigntists who feared a rupture that might be messy and difficult, who still wanted links with Canada, who wanted any breakup to be amicable. Sovereigntist arguments that these links would be inevitable after a Yes vote and that most English Canadians wanted some association with a sovereign Quebec did not provide this group with enough reassurance, particularly in the face of repeated threats and warnings from English Canada. Parizeau appeared willing to fight on, hoping that by the end of the day the sheer weight and passion of the arguments for sovereignty, combined with the pro-sovereignty momentum since Meech, would be enough to succeed. Nevertheless, continuing resistance from aboriginals in Quebec, dire economic predictions, harsh comments from English Canadians, the prospect of endless turmoil and uncertainty were all taking their toll, keeping the soft vote from embracing Parizeau's sovereignty project in the numbers he needed.

On 19 February, in the first interview after his surgery, Bouchard suggested that the referendum question be modified in order to find a question a majority of Québécois could embrace with some comfort. During March and April, Bouchard amplified his remarks by suggesting the question be changed to include some reference to political and economic association. He made it clear that he was not happy with the proposed tough question, and he had grave concerns that the referendum would be lost. Dumont agreed and insisted, as he always had, that some form of political and economic association be clearly tied to sovereignty. There was even some talk that the referendum be delayed until a more auspicious time. Ever hopeful, English-Canadian media analysts and politicians did not hide their delight at this rupture in sovereigntist ranks, painting it as a power struggle between the PQ and the Bloc (a rather silly idea, given that the two parties had virtually the same membership). In reality, the disagreement was about tactics and strategy, a disagreement as old as the sovereignty movement itself. Parizeau took the harder line, as he had since he broke with Lévesque and led the undoing of Pierre-Marc Johnson. He continued to insist that Quebec opt clearly and unambiguously for sovereignty. If a sovereign Quebec then opted for an association, Parizeau would not be opposed; indeed, he would favour such an arrangement. But after 1980, he refused to make Quebec sovereignty contingent in any way on English Canada's willingness to agree to an association. Bouchard, for his part, did not want to hold a referendum unless victory was reasonably certain, and he was willing to toy with the concept of linking association in some way to sovereignty. Bouchard believed that a referendum victory on a softer version of sovereignty was preferable to a defeat on a hard question.

Both men had strong cases that were doubtless argued out thoroughly in private. Parizeau could point to four polls taken since the election that gave the Yes 45 per cent and the No 55 per cent. Hence support for the Yes side had stabilized at 45 per cent, not an insignificant level of support with which to go into a referendum campaign. Furthermore, polls had shown that party preference had shifted significantly against federalist forces: the PQ had remained stable at 45 per cent; the Liberals had dropped eight points to 35 per cent; Dumont's ADQ had jumped to more than 17 per cent. These figures suggested that the momentum for sovereignty was in fact building and gave Parizeau a reasonable argument that a clear question could win in the fall.

Bouchard could point to the same numbers, arguing that victory on a soft question was assured, given that more than 60 per cent of Quebec voters preferred one of the two sovereigntist parties. Defeat on a hard question could set the movement back a decade, while victory on a soft question would be better for the momentum of the movement, even if the result would be more ambiguous. What gave Bouchard the argument was that without Dumont, defeat was certain. Dumont must be brought clearly on side with the Yes team if there was to be any hope of victory. The clinching argument was the results from the fifteen commissions: they indicated that tying sovereignty to some form of association or new partnership was essential for victory. Faced with such pressure, Parizeau relented and agreed to link sovereignty to some form of association in the question, but refused absolutely to delay the referendum beyond 1995, which was something Bouchard and Dumont were prepared to consider. Polls in late April helped buttress Parizeau's decision. One poll showed that if sovereignty were linked to association with Canada, Yes support would rise to 53 per cent and No would fall to 47 per cent, whereas a question just on sovereignty would lose 44 per cent Yes to 56 per cent No. Suggestive of things yet to come was another poll that found that with Bouchard leading the Yes team, support increased to 46 per cent for Yes to 42 per cent for No, regardless of the question; with Parizeau at the helm, the Yes enjoyed only 36 per cent compared to 52 per cent for the No.

The new agreement among the three sovereigntist leaders was laid out in formal terms and signed with great fanfare on 12 June 1995. The new question, which was later tabled in the National Assembly, was much fuzzier than Parizeau's original one: "Do you agree that Quebec should become sovereign, after having made a formal offer to Canada for a new Economic and Political Partnership, within the scope of the Bill respecting the future of Quebec and the agreement signed on 12 June 1995?" In practical terms, the question made little real difference, since in the event that Canada refused to negotiate such a deal Quebec would become sovereign on 30 October 1996. It was still a unilateral declaration of independence by referendum. Furthermore, the English-Canadian premiers and the prime minister had repeatedly stated that there would be no such offer from Canada. Nevertheless, the question contained the required reference to sovereignty in the context of a commitment to forge new links, or associations, with Canada. And, as had been clear in 1980, no matter what question was posed, the No side would campaign as if a Yes vote meant an automatic, dangerous, immediate, and messy separation. Politically speaking, the debate remained a clear debate on sovereignty.

The campaign was officially launched on 11 September with voting day set for 30 October. During this period, the debate became much more bitter. Though most federalists were confident, especially after a late June poll put the Yes for sovereignty with association at 48 per cent and the No at 52 per cent, some warned of overconfidence given the shift in the pro-sovereignty balance of forces since 1980. Claude Ryan, the leader of the No side in 1980, warned that the referendum would be difficult to win without a commitment to return the veto to Quebec. Former prime minister Joe Clark warned that the polls were so close that the Yes might win and he feared that the federalists were fumbling the ball. With the addition of association to the question, the gloves came off as federalists warned that a Yes meant separation and there would be no association. Saskatchewan premier Romanow asserted Quebec would be "a foreign country with no special treatment"; at a meeting in St. John's, the premiers said a sovereign Quebec could not expect to continue with existing trade links with the rest of Canada; Johnson, the leader of the No side in Quebec, declared a clear Yes or No on sovereignty was required, because "separation means borders"; Manitoba premier Filmon flatly stated there would be no negotiations on association; finance minister Martin said there would be "no economic partnership…no favours….Quebec would be just another country"; Prime Minister Chrétien repeatedly stated the only issue up for discussion was "the separation of Quebec"; Alberta premier Klein joined the chorus, as did premier Mike Harris of Ontario, saying there would be no ties with Quebec if the Yes side won. This response was part of the federal strategy to counter the sovereigntists' agreement to include a reference to association in the question; the intent was to make it unmistakably clear to the people of Quebec that there would be no discussion of association after a Yes victory and that a Yes vote meant separation, complete and unqualified. "A one-way ticket to separation" was the way the prime minister put it.

This campaign of political refusal was supplemented by the usual economic fear campaign, especially after the kickoff of the official campaign. The Chamber of Commerce warned that a Yes victory would put 470,000 jobs at risk. The federal finance minister warned that Yes would jack up interest rates and cause the dollar to collapse. Johnson claimed that a Yes win would lead to average tax increases of three thousand dollars a year and a sixteen-billion-dollar deficit. Later he claimed a Yes would lead to an immediate loss of 92,000 jobs, with more to go. As federal concerns rose, the claims became more fantastic. By 17 October, Martin warned that a Yes victory would put one million jobs at risk. Again, the sovereigntists' response was to release contrary figures and studies to bolster their claims that there would be no dire economic consequences and that Quebec would benefit economically from sovereignty. The sovereigntists also accused big business and the federalists of trying to destroy Quebec's sovereigntist and social democratic experiment and warned that the federal government would begin cutting the social safety net right after a No victory. On the practical side, the Quebec government bought up hundreds of millions of Canadian dollars in the midst of the campaign to prevent a sharp fall in the dollar, which they expected to be engineered by federalist forces in an effort to frighten the Québécois.

The business lobby did not participate as directly in this campaign as it had in the past. Indeed, much of the Charlottetown economic fear campaign had been carried out by members of the business elite, and it had failed. Furthermore, some, such as the Royal Bank, had paid a price in lost business in Quebec as a result of a boycott because of the economic fear document released by the bank during Charlottetown. Many business leaders, therefore, stayed silent. In the previous year's election, Parizeau had warned financial institutions of losing business if they interfered. This warning carried over into the referendum, such as when the Standard Life Assurance's Claude Garcia called on the Québécois to "crush" the separatists in the referendum in order to put the sovereignty issue permanently to rest. After that intervention, the PQ government opened up bids for the $11.5 million insurance contract formerly held exclusively by Standard Life and stripped Garcia of his duties as chairman of the board of the University of Quebec at Montreal. Furthermore, the business lobby was deeply divided, as indicated by the very prominent business leaders now in the ranks of the PQ government, such as Jean Campeau, former head of the Caisse de dépôt, Daniel Paillé, a top executive with Québecor Inc., and Richard Le Hir, former leader of the Quebec Manufacturers' Association. (Le Hir, sidelined by Parizeau due to a patronage scandal, renounced his sovereigntist past in September 1996 and began seeking a federal Liberal nomination.) In addition, the public was suspicious of negative economic preaching by business leaders as a result of Charlottetown; companies were concerned about losing business if they offended an aggressive government quite prepared to use its power against its political adversaries; and there was a desire not to give Bouchard and Parizeau any highly visible big business targets for emotional attacks. The overall result was that the business lobby stayed largely out of the public fray and worked behind the scenes by contributing financial and personnel resources to the No campaign.

By early October, it was clear the campaign was not going well for the Yes side. ADQ leader Dumont complained publicly of the "loser mentality" rampant among the Yes forces. This was confirmed in the polls: on 30 September, Yes 46.8 per cent, No 53.2 per cent; on 6 October, Yes 47 per cent, No 53 per cent. Though an improvement over the stalemate prior to linking sovereignty to association, it was still not enough to win. On 9 October, Parizeau named Bouchard to be "chief negotiator" for Quebec sovereignty after a Yes victory and Bouchard assumed the effective helm of the Yes campaign, becoming its main figure. By 12 October, Bouchard had re-defined the meaning of a Yes vote to include a strong mandate for him to negotiate with Canada. This mandate became one focus of the Yes campaign from then on: if the Québécois gave Bouchard a strong hand to negotiate, the new economic realities would force Canada to the table. Another focus remained independence and sovereignty, including a continuing hard line from Parizeau. Thus, during the last phase of the referendum campaign, the Yes side gave the Québécois mixed messages from which to choose. There was Bouchard at the helm playing soft cop, and Parizeau, still the official leader of the Yes team, playing hard cop. The effectiveness — partly due to the softened message, partly due to the trust and affection enjoyed by Bouchard, partly due to the ineptitude of the No team — had a dramatic impact as Yes fortunes began slowly to turn around: on 14 October, Yes 49.2 per cent, No 50.8 per cent; on 20 October, Yes 50.2 per cent, No 49.8 per cent; on 28 October, Yes 50 per cent, No 50 per cent. The referendum had been transformed from a certain defeat for the Yes to a dead heat.

English Canada, after a deluge of propaganda that the No would win easily, was ill prepared for the sudden prospect of a Yes victory. Indeed, leaders of the No forces, especially those in Ottawa and most particularly the prime minister himself, reacted with poorly concealed panic. As Canada tottered on the edge of the abyss, federalist arrogance was now coupled with near begging, as English Canada tried to pull the Québécois back from what was repeatedly described as a final and irreversible decision to separate. Although the dual No campaign of political refusal — absolutely no association after a Yes — and economic fear had an effect in Quebec (for example, polls revealed that approximately 66 per cent of voters in Quebec would easily say Yes to sovereignty if Ottawa and the nine English-Canadian provinces promised association), it seemed to have more effect in English Canada. Indeed, English Canada had convinced itself with its own propaganda that a Yes vote would be an economic catastrophe and reacted shrilly when a Yes victory became a real possibility.

After the 20 October poll put the Yes ahead at 50.2 per cent to 49.8 per cent, the No message became decidedly mixed: there were promises of love and big changes if Quebec voted to stay; threats of the dire consequences of a Yes vote. Finance minister Martin promised a No would bring significant changes to the federal system to address Quebec's concerns. After some open begging by No leader Johnson, the prime minister first rejected and then three days later declared his support for recognition of distinct society for Quebec and for a qualified constitutional veto for Quebec. This was followed by a nationwide television appeal by a visibly shaken prime minister pleading with Quebec to stay in

Canada. On 27 October, a large unity rally — estimated at any-
where from 30,000 to 150,000 people, depending on the source —
in Montreal's Canada Place was engineered by the No campaign
using subsidized bus and airline tickets to bring in Canadians
from all over English Canada. Participants in the rally emotionally declared love for Quebec and urged the people to vote No
and stay in Canada. At the same time, the prime minister warned
Quebec of the ugly mood in the rest of the country in the event of
a Yes vote and of the possible loss to the Québécois of their pensions, currency (putting their savings at risk), and passports. Furthermore, he again suggested that a narrow victory for the Yes
would not be enough to break up the country. In the midst of this
crisis atmosphere, a mood deliberately orchestrated by the No
campaign, the results of referendums held by the Cree and the
Innu on sovereignty were announced — a massive vote for a No.
Meanwhile, hundreds lined up at the Montreal passport office to
get their passports before the vote. In response to this growing
federalist panic and a climate of crisis, Bouchard and Parizeau
held firm, appealing finally to the national pride and confidence
of the Québécois. As Bouchard put it in one of his last speeches of
the campaign, "Seize it and vote Yes…say Yes to ourselves. Say
Yes to the people of Quebec."

On 30 October, the Quebec electorate narrowly voted against
sovereignty as 94 per cent of the eligible voters trooped to the
polls. The final tally was 50.6 per cent for No against 49.4 per cent
for Yes. Only fifty-three thousand votes separated the Yes and the
No. Opinion remains divided on what finally saved federalism in Quebec: some point to the unity rally (later found by
Quebec's Chief Electoral Officer to be a flagrant violation of
Quebec's referendum law on spending limits); others to Daniel
Johnson's eleventh-hour plea for a commitment to grant Quebec
distinct status and a veto, first refused and then embraced by the
prime minister; others to simple fear of the unknown and the unpredictable in the midst of a contrived crisis atmosphere. Efforts
have also been made to re-interpret the Yes vote in ways other
than a vote for sovereignty: it was a vote for change, a vote to give
Bouchard a strong hand in negotiations with Ottawa and the rest
of Canada, a vote for sovereignty-association, a vote against
English-Canadian bullying and intransigence, a vote to affirm
Québécois nationalism in the face of English-Canadian attempts
to deny the existence of the Québécois nation. All of these, of
course, contain some truth: the Québécois wanted change, chose

to assert their pride, wanted association with Canada, resented bullying and threats. But all this rationalization does not erase the enormous democratic political significance of the vote. The fact remains that 60 per cent of Quebec's francophones voted for sovereignty in a political context that had demonstrably hardened and clarified the choice. Had the percentage of Yes voters been slightly higher, given the PQ government in Quebec City and the Bloc's prominence in the House of Commons, Quebec would have been on an irreversible trajectory to separation, especially if English Canada had continued its refusal to negotiate association.

In his address to the Yes rally on the night of 30 October, Premier Parizeau expressed his sadness and frustration at the result with some ill-chosen and inflammatory remarks: "It's true we have been defeated, but basically by what? By money and the ethnic vote. All it means is that next time round, instead of us [francophone Québécois] being 60 or 61 per cent in favour, we'll be 63 or 64 per cent." Almost as soon as the words escaped from his mouth, Parizeau was subjected to a barrage of criticism from all sides. Montreal's ethnic leaders accused him of racism, while many sovereigntists described his words as unfortunate and unacceptable. The remarks, however, were consistent both with Parizeau's previous bluntness and with certain political and sociological truths. The PQ's efforts at a breakthrough in winning support among the so-called "ethnic," or allophone, communities had failed consistently to climb much beyond 10 per cent. The PQ had only slightly better success among the anglophone minority.

That the anglophone and allophone votes go *en bloc* to federalists during elections and to the No during referendums remains an axiom of Quebec politics. This should not be surprising. Indeed, a massive vote by anglophones and allophones for sovereignty would have settled the question for sovereignty back in 1980. Given these groups' anti-sovereignty sentiments, the question had always been whether the sovereigntists could ever hope to achieve the nearly 65 per cent required among francophone Québécois to win a referendum. After the 1980 referendum, there was much learned opinion that sovereignty was demographically doomed because it could never hope to break the federalist bloc of anglophones and allophones, and because older francophone Québécois would remain forever cautious and unwilling finally to take the risk of sovereignty. Since the francophone share of Quebec's population was slowly declining and aging due to the low birth rate, and the "ethnic" population was slowly rising due to immigration, over the long run sovereignty would never win the required 50 per cent-plus-one. Lévesque and some of his advisers had largely bought this analysis, doubtless a factor in his temporary abandonment of sovereignty after the 1980 loss.

But Parizeau and others did not agree and doggedly insisted that sovereignty could be won, a stance to which the PQ had returned when Parizeau became leader. After an analysis of the results of Charlottetown referendum, Parizeau had announced to a PQ national council meeting in January 1993 that sovereignty could be achieved without the support of allophones and anglophones. The implication was clear: the sovereigntists should give priority to developing support among francophones and worry less about pursuing an unattainable breakthrough among non-francophones. These comments caused as much of a storm in 1993 as his remarks did on 30 October 1995. The next big eruption over the issue had occurred in January 1995 when Pierre Bourgault, advisor to Parizeau after the PQ's 1994 victory, warned that a volatile and dangerous situation would be created if a rejection of sovereignty resulted largely from non-francophone bloc voting. (Bourgault was the founder and leader of the Rassemblement pour l'indépendence nationale, which first presented the democratic separatist option to voters in 1966.) The furore that resulted from Bourgault's remarks led him to resign in order, as he said, to prevent further embarrassment for Parizeau and the PQ government.

Efforts by English-Canadian political leaders and commentators to use the "ethnic" issue to smear Quebec sovereigntists reflect another dimension of the hypocrisy and double standard so common in English-Canadian reactions to Québécois nationalism. Recent federalist strategy in Quebec has been built on the cornerstones of "ethnic politics" and bloc voting, as have historical English-Canadian efforts to erase or contain the "French fact" from the Conquest onward. In recent Canadian history it was the Liberal Party — commencing most notably with Clifford Sifton's immigration policies in the West — that used "ethnic" or "recent immigrant" politics to help secure its domination of federal politics from 1896 onward. The use of ethnic politics was also evident in federalist actions in the 1995 referendum, although it was not mentioned in the English Canadian media, leaving most Canadians in ignorance. (The exception was an op-ed piece in the *Globe and Mail* by Montreal writer Robin Philpot, published on 20 November 1995, twenty-one days after the vote.) For the first time in history, in the runup to the referendum vote during the autumn of 1995, Ottawa cut red tape to facilitate the rapid creation of 15,000 new voting citizens in Quebec prior to 30 October. Ottawa's immigration and citizenship department distributed information to new citizens explaining voter registration procedures, and official newsletters to recent citizens instructed them that they had a duty to fight for a strong and united Canada. In the spring of 1995, a former MP and Liberal Party organizer in Quebec publicly requested the re-establishment of deportation laws targeted at refugees and immigrants who supported sovereignty, taking aim directly at Bloc MP Osvaldo Nunez, who had escaped from Pinochet's Chile. In the days preceding the referendum, leaders of various ethnic communities in Quebec correctly bragged that 90 per cent of their communities would vote No. Furthermore, Prime Minister Chrétien's warnings about the loss of passports, pensions, and currency, finance minister Martin's hyperbole about the loss of one million jobs, and repeated warnings from English-Canadian politicians and the media about chaos and instability were clearly aimed at the ethnic and recent immigrant vote, who feel more vulnerable and insecure during tempestuous political times. While Canadians of long standing in Quebec and the rest of Canada could laugh at such outrageous claims, immigrants and refugees in Quebec, many of whom had fled countries and regions characterized by serious economic and political instability, would understandably be deeply affected, perhaps even frightened.

The dangers of the manipulation of ethnic politics in Quebec were obvious. The federalist strategy of using the ethnic vote as a reliable pawn opened the door to scapegoating by Québécois nationalists. Sovereigntist failures to break the allophone and anglophone bloc vote led to an exclusive focus on developing the francophone bloc vote, a dangerous "us against them" scenario, as suggested by Parizeau's comments after Charlottetown and as stated explicitly in his 30 October speech. Parizeau's remarks encouraged such scapegoating and smeared the ethnic communities as the saboteurs of Québécois aspirations. This position was dangerous and irresponsible. Obviously, in his speech Parizeau could have mentioned the many other reasons for the referendum's defeat: the 40 per cent of francophones who voted No; the 85 to 90 per cent of anglophones who voted No; the Cree and Innu who voted No. An analysis of how the resistance of these social elements to sovereignty could be overcome, how future reassurances and guarantees would have to be more effectively developed, and so on, would have transformed his speech from an inflammatory and irresponsible bombshell into a thoughtful political analysis. Instead, it gave aid and comfort to the racist and xenophobic extremists among Québécois nationalists, provided federalists with brickbats to hurl at sovereignty and Québécois nationalism, and discredited the sovereignty movement at a crucial moment when the world's attention was focused on it.

On 31 October 1995, Premier Parizeau resigned, expressing regret for his "harsh comments" and repeating his disappointment at the failure of the sovereigntists to win more ethnic voters to their cause. He insisted that "the words were too strong but the reality doesn't change." While it was evident that the storm over his comments had accelerated the timetable, Parizeau insisted he had always intended to resign quickly if the Yes side failed and had in fact announced earlier that even if Yes won he would only stay on long enough to see the sovereignty negotiation process through to a conclusion, insisting that at age sixty-five he shouldn't outstay his welcome. As expected, Bouchard was crowned as uncontested PQ leader and sworn in as Premier of Quebec in January 1996. Once described by Lévesque as a "Napoleonic strategist," Parizeau had served sovereignty well, bringing the PQ back from post-Lévesque oblivion, reasserting the PQ's central commitment to sovereignty, masterminding the 1992 Charlottetown campaign, playing a key role in the Bloc's 1993 victory, securing the PQ's re-election in 1994 on a hard sovereignty position, and bringing the movement to the threshold of victory in the 1995 referendum. His intellectual distance and arrogance, his undisguised wealth and privileged background were forgiven due to his political commitment and principled adherence to sovereignty, allowing him to win the respect of the Québécois but never their affection. According to some Quebec commentators, his successor, Lucien Bouchard, comes close to combining the best elements of the political persona of Lévesque and Parizeau. Like Lévesque, Bouchard enjoys the affection of the Québécois, rivals Lévesque's charisma and inspiration in public oratory, and, like Parizeau, is reputed to be a shrewd tactician and strategist. Bouchard's accession as premier, barring an unprecedented catastrophe for the sovereigntists, assures the PQ's re-election, making another sovereignty referendum inevitable after the next Quebec election, due in 1998 or 1999.

Many on both sides of the sovereignty debate inside and outside Quebec greeted the result of the referendum with relief and naive expectations that the narrow victory for Canada would lead to dialogue, change, and renewal. After all, this was what the federalists had promised in the panic stage of the referendum campaign and what Bouchard's repeated emphasis on the concept of a new partnership seemed to call for. A significant portion of sovereigntists expressed relief that the result had not been reversed, giving the Yes a narrow victory, particularly as revelations emerged about the many No votes that had been designated as "spoiled" by overzealous pro-Yes officials at polls in some of the strong pro-federalist ridings. Many federalists were disturbed by the failure of Chrétien to read the situation correctly, pointing to his unfounded overconfidence until the last ten days of the campaign; they expressed doubt that the "take Canada or leave it, no concessions, no negotiations" approach had been the wisest course.

The hope that the referendum would lead to rational dialogue and reasonable negotiations proved to be wishful thinking. Though the public mood in English Canada had softened a bit on Québécois aspirations, it was not enough to push English Canada's political leaders to make concessions and open up negotiations in good faith with the sovereigntists. For example, a November 1995 Gallup poll reported that 44 per cent of Canadians would agree to grant Quebec distinct society recognition in the constitution, but 46 per cent would not. The close national figures, however, concealed the polarization between Quebec and English Canada. All regions of English Canada strongly opposed distinct society, from a low of 51 per cent in B.C. to a high of 63 per cent in the Prairie provinces, while 70 per cent of Québécois supported the concession. Figures on support for a veto for Quebec were worse — a low of 68 per cent opposed in Ontario to a high of 78 per cent in the Prairie provinces. Meanwhile, in Quebec, an omnibus poll carried out by Gallup in the same month found that 79 per cent of Québécois wanted significant changes in Quebec's place in Canada, including 38 per cent who expressed a preference for sovereignty and 41 per cent who preferred to stay in Canada if significant changes were made. At the same time, 56 per cent expressed no confidence in Chrétien's ability or willingness to negotiate "real change." Dramatic confirmation of this inability came in December 1995 when the Chrétien government "delivered" on the prime minister's referendum promises of distinct society and a constitutional veto for Quebec: a resolution in the House of Commons that recognized Quebec as a distinct society and Bill C-110, which guaranteed the federal government would not initiate amendments to the constitution without the approval of Canada's five regions, were passed. These gestures, which were largely symbolic and legally and constitutionally meaningless, were viewed by Québécois nationalists as either a joke or an insult, and probably both. With Bill C-110 passed, Chrétien declared his commitments to the people of Quebec made during the referendum to have been fully discharged and proceeded to get even tougher with the sovereigntists. In this exercise in duplicity and aggressive posturing the prime minister was not alone. Indeed, if anything he was loyally carrying out the wishes of English Canada, which had, after all, elected him in 1993 and, according to the polls, would re-elect him again as long as he remained a faithful servant of the interests of English Canada *vis à vis* Quebec and Québécois nationalism.

Just days after the referendum, the "provincial rights" premiers began to circle the barely resuscitated federal corpse. At an early November 1995 meeting in Yorkton, Saskatchewan, the four western premiers proved they had learned nothing from the crisis. Determined once again to exploit the urgent need to provide constitutional accommodation to Quebec, as provincial rights premiers have done during all previous crises, the western premiers proposed to eliminate an effective central government in Ottawa as the price for accommodating Quebec. Once again, as in the past, to save the Canadian federation, they proposed to destroy it. In a suggestion that contained equal measures of effrontery and bad faith, given the negative catharsis Canadians had just experienced, the western premiers proposed to convene a first ministers' meeting without the prime minister. There, Canada's federal powers would be dispersed, while the powers of the provinces would increase accordingly. Echoing the process that brought Charlottetown, the western premiers, hungry for power, appeared prepared to sandbag the discredited federal government while presenting themselves as the "saviours" of the federation.

Not to be outdone, Manning and the Reform Party began to provoke the Québécois nationalists and sovereigntists in an effort to sustain the anti-Quebec anger in English Canada that had served them so well in 1993. In December 1995, the party released a document, *Twenty Realities of Secession*, that laid out harsh terms for Quebec's departure. The most provocative included re-drawing the borders to accommodate "local self-determination" through partition if desired by anglophone, allophone, and abo-riginal minorities; a denial of dual citizenship; a corridor through Quebec to Atlantic Canada; and the preparation of emergency measures and plans in the case of violence. At a press conference in Vancouver to release the document, in response to reporters' questions Manning declined to rule out the use of force if Quebec tried to secede unconstitutionally after a Yes victory. The Reform leader insisted that by the year 2000 Quebec would have to finally decide to stay or go and that Reform and the West were "promot-ing a vigorous defence of federalism" but were determined to "drive it to resolution....Either the country is going to go into the twenty-first century as a bigger, greater single nation, or...as two lesser nations." Then, in late December, Manning proposed meas-ures to impeach and remove Chrétien as prime minister should a Yes win, on the grounds that a prime minister from Quebec could not be trusted to negotiate for Canada. In the new year, Reform presented a resolution in the House of Commons calling for an in-vestigation into a fax sent by Bloc MP Jean-Marc Jacob prior to the 30 October referendum to all Quebec military bases to invite Québécois soldiers to switch their allegiance to their "new coun-try" in the event of a Yes victory. Reform insisted that this action was "seditious and offensive" and constituted "contempt of Par-liament." (Clearly the action was provocative and almost adoles-cent in its adventurism, but it could hardly constitute sedition, defined in the criminal law as the use of force to overthrow the government — unless, as new Bloc leader Michel Gauthier put it, sedition now included efforts to overthrow a government by fax and press release.) References to Quebec sovereigntists as traitors and to their actions as treasonous continued to be commonplace in Reform rhetoric about Quebec. During six federal by-elections held on 26 March 1996, the Reform Party based its campaign on the slogan "Boot the Bloc," unsuccessfully appealing to voters to help remove the Bloc as official Opposition by supporting Reform candidates. Such provocations, of course, served only to increase support for sovereignty in Quebec. As Tory leader Jean Charest put it: "Manning is planning Canada's funeral...vying for the po-sition of Canada's number-one undertaker." Actually, Manning's likely motives were clarified by Tom Flanagan, Reform's former chief advisor and strategist fired by Manning. In his book, *Wait-ing for the Wave*, Flanagan pointed out that one of the likeliest scenarios for Manning's ascension to the prime ministership involved exploiting the crisis provoked by Quebec's separation.

The Chrétien government, having superficially fulfilled the promises it made to win the referendum and stinging from Reform's criticisms that the government was weak and vacillating, proceeded to get tough. In 1996, Ottawa began a two-track approach to fighting Quebec sovereignty, which was widely touted as Plan A and Plan B. Plan A, the carrot, involved carrying the good news about federalism to the Québécois via a new $43-million propaganda effort (with $23 million earmarked for free Canadian flags). The passage of the distinct society resolution and the veto bill, as well as the administrative devolution of power for employment training programs, were also part of this soft and positive approach to win hearts and minds. Furthermore, Chrétien used the March 1996 by-elections, three of which were in Quebec, to bring into his cabinet "two wise men" from Quebec, Stéphane Dion and Pierre Pettigrew. It was their job to spearhead the fight against sovereignty in Quebec and enhance the weight of Quebec francophones in Chrétien's cabinet. Dion and Pettigrew had been selected only after efforts to get more prominent and respected non-sovereigntist Québécois nationalists to run had failed. Neither new minister had a significant political following in francophone Quebec. Commentators in Quebec predicted this effort would be as unsuccessful as the 1994 decision to bring "one wise woman" from Quebec, Lucienne Robillard, into the cabinet to fight the referendum. She had been unsuccessful (again lacking significant credentials among francophone Québécois) and had got into hot water with other federalists for her public declaration that Ottawa would honour and respect a Yes majority in the referendum. (Clearly, Chrétien's attitude remained situated in the 1960s when the simple gesture of giving francophone Québécois cabinet seats in Ottawa was a significant act and an effective mollification of Québécois resentments.) Such were the changes outlined in Plan A: a propaganda campaign; a House resolution on distinct society; a bill on a veto; some minor administrative devolution; and the appointment of two new, strongly anti-nationalist Québécois cabinet ministers with little political credibility among francophone Québécois. Nothing else was on offer to Quebec.

Plan B, the stick, was chock-full of a series of aggressive measures designed to bully Quebec. All the measures involved threats to use superior federal powers variously to interfere in the referendum process, to deny Quebec the right to act upon the result if there were a sovereigntist victory, and to tamper with Quebec's borders in the event of separation, including the partition of Quebec in support of minority claims by anglophones, allophones, and aboriginals. The most provocative for Québécois sovereigntists were Ottawa's threats to Quebec's post-sovereignty territorial integrity. The federal government supported the concept of partitioning parts of Montreal and claimed that aboriginal lands were legally excluded from any move to a sovereign Quebec. The government also asserted that any future referendum on sovereignty and any move to sovereignty if a referendum were successful were unlawful and unconstitutional and therefore legally foreclosed.

In addition to strong words and threats, Ottawa's August 1996 appointment of Senator Jean-Louis Roux as Quebec's lieutenant-governor indicated further preparation for a possible use of maximum federal powers to thwart any drive to sovereignty. In this case, it was the power of reservation (a refusal to sign laws passed by a provincial legislature) vested by the constitution in the office of the lieutenant-governor, and last used against the Alberta Social Credit regime in the 1930s. Premier Bouchard and his cabinet were not consulted by the prime minister on the appointment, as is the convention. Roux is known as a strong federalist and fervent anti-nationalist who said in 1995 "nationalism is a movement that diminishes the spirit and can lead to intolerance" and who threatened to leave Quebec if the Yes side won in 1995. Roux resigned in November 1996 in the wake of revelations that he participated in a 1942 anti-conscription demonstration with pro-Nazi, anti-Semitic elements. Chrétien insisted Ottawa would appoint a replacement without consulting Quebec, rejecting Premier Bouchard's call to allow the National Assembly to appoint the lieutenant-governor, a position he described as a "colonial relic."

Ottawa helped undermine the legality of Quebec's drive to sovereignty and asserted federal powers by joining Jean-Guy Bertrand's legal challenge of the constitutionality of Quebec's plans. Bertrand, a former PQ cabinet minister who was now a zealous born-again federalist, unsuccessfully attempted to obtain an injunction against the 30 October referendum. In that case, the judge had ruled that any attempt to secede was indeed unconstitutional, but refused to stop the referendum on the grounds that democratic principles insist that the Quebec people had a right to be consulted in a referendum by the Quebec government. Not satisfied, after the referendum Bertrand launched another suit to ask the courts to stop future referendums on sovereignty, to declare that Quebec's right of self-determination stops short of any right to secede from Canada, and to rule that unilateral secession would be unconstitutional. Up until the moment when Ottawa decided to intervene formally, the case was a curious sidebar in Quebec politics, a sort of family feud between an ex-sovereigntist and his former colleagues. With Ottawa's intervention, the stakes were raised since a victory for Ottawa and Bertrand would provide the legal pretext for Ottawa to intervene with a heavy hand in the next referendum. Premier Bouchard initially reacted by threatening to call a quick election and referendum in response to Ottawa's legal challenge, but then wisely backed off, thus avoiding a confused tangle of what would have become a legal and political crisis in the context of aroused passions. The decisions of both the Quebec government and Ottawa to formally withdraw from the continuing Bertrand case further defused the immediate situation. However, Ottawa's decision to refer the whole issue to the Supreme Court for a final determination of the legal and constitutional issues raised by Quebec's drive for sovereignty only postpones the confrontation until the Supreme Court makes the inevitable ruling against the sovereignty project.

Ottawa's legal challenge is a political provocation pure and simple, an explicit and gratuitous threat both to the Quebec government and to those in Quebec contemplating voting for sovereignty. Challenges to the legality and constitutionality of a successful referendum leading to sovereignty and warnings about partitioning and/or constricting Quebec's territory imply a willingness to back up such threats with force. Falling back on the rule of law regardless of democratic outcomes also implies a willingness to use force to back up the imposition of the law against the democratic will of the people. Similarly, to declare support for the right of minorities to partition Quebec after a Yes vote, as both Chrétien and Dion have done, implies a willingness to use force to impose the will of the minorities against the will of the majority in Quebec. To turn Montreal into a Jerusalem and Quebec as a whole into another Ireland would require a willingness to resort to violence and would cultivate the political soil for civil war. This raises the question of whether Ottawa has a Plan Z sitting in a safe in the Privy Council Office, a plan for sending military forces into a separating Quebec, as well as the political and administrative measures necessary for such an event to occur: the suspension of the Quebec government and National Assembly, the arrest and imprisonment of Bloc MPs and PQ MNAs, the disarming of military and police units of questionable federalist sympathies, the necessary plans and personnel to take over the political administration of Quebec. All of these things could be lawfully done in terms of the maximum powers granted to Ottawa by the constitution, provided the support of the House of Commons could be sustained.

All this seems bizarre and far-fetched, particularly given the Chrétien government's assurances that Quebec would never be kept in Canada against the will of the people. Nevertheless, Ottawa's current rhetoric and actions lead logically to a final resort to legal force. Furthermore, the constitutional challenge to Quebec's drive to sovereignty is redundant. It is clear that any court will inevitably find that secession, especially unilateral secession, is unconstitutional. Indeed, to say it is unconstitutional only states the obvious. Moreover, Canada has already qualified and hedged any constitutional initiative to outlaw a sovereignty referendum or to refuse to honour the result. Having allowed three referendums under Quebec's referendum law — in 1980, 1992, and 1995 — any effort to disallow that law retroactively would be difficult if not impossible to justify legally, politically, and morally. The active participation of many premiers and three prime ministers in previous referendums implies not only a respect for the process, but also a willingness to honour the outcome. In the Charlottetown referendum, all players — premier, prime minister, legislatures, House of Commons — accepted the expression of the will of the people as final without any qualification. And, back in 1970 when the federal government imposed the *War Measures Act*, it sent a clear message to the Quebec sovereignty movement that undemocratic and illegal methods, such as force and terror, would not be tolerated in a campaign for sovereignty. As a result, Quebec nationalists put all their energy into the democratic drive for independence, the results of which — victories in provincial elections for the PQ, two referendums, and the election of Bloc MPs — were respected and recognized. To challenge that thirty-year history of democratic struggle as unlawful and unconstitutional now is an act of bad faith and will prove impossible to impose and sustain either in Canada or abroad.

When constitutions cannot or will not accommodate the aspirations of a people — in this case a democratic decision by the

Québécois nation to secede — the obvious response is a unilateral declaration of independence followed by orderly negotiations in the context of international law and democratic principles. Since what Ottawa seeks is legally redundant, self-evident, and serves no legal purpose, and since Ottawa has already promised not to force the people of Quebec to stay in Canada against their will, the only conceivable motive for Ottawa's current position and actions is intimidation. It hopes to bully and threaten the Québécois to submit and to refrain from continuing down the dangerous and unacceptable democratic road to separation.

The escalation of Ottawa's rhetoric has given aid and comfort to anti-Québécois extremists inside and outside Quebec, encouraging the growing acceptability of public expressions of hatred and hostility against sovereigntists. As a result, views and attitudes that used to be limited to the cranks of the Reform Party, or a few of the English-Canadian extremists in Quebec, have become commonplace in our public discourse. In the 22 July 1996 issue of *Maclean's*, Diane Francis felt free to write with exaggerated hyperbole and irresponsible disregard for facts or balance about the "seditious behaviour by separatists regarding our military" and "separatist attempts to get military personnel to defect." She called for a witch-hunt against pro-sovereigntists in the military and for the expulsion of Bloc defence critic Jean-Marc Jacob from the House of Commons. To take another example, *Saturday Night's* editors felt free to use the following headline in the July/August 1996 edition: "The writing's on the wall: Things are not getting better in Quebec. They're getting worse, and fast. Chaos, terrorism and violence are now a safe bet." The partitionist movement in Quebec is growing and becoming more aggressive and outrageous in its rhetoric. It has aggravated the issue of commercial signage in an effort to polarize Montreal and build support for partition, all with the public endorsement of the prime minister. Liberal MP Anna Terrana can say to a Vancouver *Sun* journalist: "What is happening now is what happened before the war in Germany....First [the Nazis] founded the party, then they got hold of the institutions, including the unions. They got themselves a charismatic leader. And now, they're going through ethnic cleansing....The PQ has the same strategy of trying to get rid of those who are not *pur laine.*" Challenged the next day by journalists, she repeated her outrageous comments. Only after a *tête à tête* with the prime minister did she issue a heavily qualified retraction: "I may be definitely wrong, but there is a similarity."

Deeper down in the foul muck of hate politics lurks the Anglophone Assault Group, which has issued death threats against Bouchard and his two sons and has declared its intention to use violence to win Montreal's secession from a sovereign Quebec.

The danger is that English Canadians outside Quebec will begin to see the province through the extremists' eyes and begin to believe that the situation is volatile, unstable, and moving toward violence. As extremist views gain routine expression in the mainstream media and among moderate and responsible politicians, all with the apparent blessing of the Chrétien government, it will be easy to persuade English Canadians outside Quebec to give unquestioning support to harsh methods and to believe every exaggerated and nonsensical claim made by anti-sovereigntist extremists. At the worst, once again, the soil is tilled for legal violence and civil war; at best, the chasm between the two solitudes widens and reasoned dialogue becomes futile.

Reactions in Quebec to Ottawa's hard line have been drearily predictable: in January 1996 support for a Yes in a sovereignty referendum stood at 52.4 per cent; by July 1996 it had increased to 53 per cent. As of 1996, 75 per cent of Québécois expect a sovereign Quebec in the future, 60 per cent in the next ten years, and more than 47 per cent in the next five years. PQ support has risen to 50.5 per cent, Quebec Liberal support has fallen to 29.7 per cent, and ADQ support has gone up to 9.4 per cent, giving pro-sovereignty parties 59.9 per cent in total. Bloc support has largely stayed in the forties despite Bouchard's departure as leader, while the federal Liberals hover around the 30 per cent mark. As premier, Bouchard had promised to focus his government's efforts on jobs and the economy and on deficit reduction; he held out olive branches to Quebec's minorities and suggested the sovereignty issue be debated with reason. To facilitate this, the Bouchard government has begun to prepare a more elaborate draft of its 1995 partnership proposal, now described as "a new Canadian union" based on a two-nation partnership. It hopes to provide more details and reassurances in order to win some hearts and minds in English Canada. It is clear that, as Ottawa fulminates and hardens, the Bouchard government intends to carry its proposal, when drafted, directly to the English-Canadian premiers and voters, thus bypassing Ottawa. The PQ perhaps hopes that by proposing a radical decentralization of federal powers, involving the premiers directly in the discussions from the outset, and advocating an autonomous provincial presence in the structures of the new partnership, they will win the "provincial rights" premiers over in a grotesque and desperate alliance against Ottawa.

Meanwhile Quebec politicians have felt compelled to respond to Ottawa's provocations. Responding to Chrétien's threat to use disallowance powers, Bouchard said: "He must be desperate to say such an enormity. I can't understand why a man who knows politics and is supposedly a democrat would resort to the grandmother of the *War Measures Act* to stop Quebec." Bouchard sharply attacked Ron Irwin, the Indian affairs minister, when he speculated about aboriginal land not being included in a sovereign Quebec and the possibilities of post-sovereignty violence against aboriginals by an independent Quebec; he called Irwin "an imbecile, an idiot, a perfect idiot." Quebec's inter-governmental minister Jacques Brassard had more to say: "It's one of two things. Either Mr. Irwin is an irresponsible arsonist who dangerously sets fires everywhere, or he is an ignoramus, prophesying nonsense." Responding to Ottawa's musings about setting the required vote for a Yes victory at 55 to 66 per cent and about partition and changing borders, Bouchard declaimed, "If the federal government and federalists continue to attack the territorial integrity of Quebec, they will provoke...an extraordinary unity and solidarity that will trigger support for sovereignty above the levels they will have set in order to stop it." Bouchard also expressed surprise at the "audacity" of Chrétien's "encroachments on democracy" in supporting partition. In response to these and the other threats, Bouchard appealed to Ottawa to cease provoking "a dangerous debate" and to desist from its "intimidation, provocations and scare-mongering tactics"; he warned that such an approach could only "backfire" and lead to a growth in support for sovereignty and Quebec's accelerated departure from Canada. In the midst of this brouhaha, ADQ leader Dumont appealed to the rest of Canada, saying he had an "open mind" about proposals for reforming Canadian federalism, but that any change must be "deep, serious and rapid," that "symbolic" measures weren't enough, and that the situation was "much more urgent" than Canada realized. Yet the young man who, just a few months earlier, had naively hoped that the close referendum result would lead to a willingness to change, now sadly expressed the view that there appeared to be "no real hope" that Ottawa and English Canada were prepared to meet even the minimum expectations of Quebec.

Federalists in Quebec found themselves mercilessly squeezed by Ottawa's tough line. Liberal leader Johnson, under attack by Ottawa federalists for his alleged inadequacies as the No leader, in turn attacked Ottawa for its failure to promise constitutional change on distinct society and a veto until defeat became nearly certain. Furthermore, Johnson attempted to distance himself from Ottawa's position, declaring his support for the right of Quebec to self-determination and telling Chrétien to stop discussing the illegality of separation and unilateral declarations of independence. "Trying to stop Quebec from separating after a Yes vote would be like ordering a man who has jumped off a bridge to fall back up," Johnson observed. In response to Chrétien's determination to sustain a polarized debate on sovereignty, Johnson expressed frustration and anger: "Let's be practical here. There isn't a referendum in the offing, there's not even an election in the offing....So why is the prime minister today worrying about what's to happen in the future instead of working on the mandate for change that the referendum has given him?" Why was Chrétien encouraging a "destructive debate" about partition? The best way to avoid another referendum, Johnson reminded Chrétien, was to meet Quebec's constitutional minimum of distinct society and a veto. Insisting that despite the distinct society resolution and the veto bill passed in the House of Commons, Johnson noted "we are still far from there." In response to attacks from federalists in Ottawa, such as André Ouellet, and only lukewarm support from Chrétien, Johnson declared that he wouldn't be "a valet, an echo, a loudspeaker" for Ottawa's views and that his "preoccupation [was] the interests of Quebeckers." As a counterpoint to Johnson's remarks, Gerald Tremblay, a leading soft nationalist in the Quebec Liberals and a man who could have succeeded Bourassa had he wanted the job, announced he was quitting politics due to his "disgust" with Ottawa's refusal to offer constitutional change to Quebec. Even the dying Robert Bourassa was pulled into the debate, insisting that native lands would clearly fall under the jurisdiction of an independent Quebec, since control of the lands had been settled in the James Bay Agreement, to which Ottawa was a signatory in 1975. Furthermore, Bourassa spoke out against partitionist rhetoric and Chrétien's support for the idea, insisting that "partition is nonsense legally and administratively." It appeared that Ottawa's tough stance was singularly unsuccessful, at least in Quebec, where it provoked a polarization that favoured sovereigntists. Indeed, Ottawa's political base in Quebec, according to the polls, seemed to be shrinking rapidly, as francophone Québécois were pushed to support both sovereignty and sovereigntist parties in response to Ottawa's hectoring and bullying.

By the fall of 1996, the Chrétien government's strategy was clear. It involved a monumental gamble, a "roll of the dice" for much higher stakes than Mulroney's gamble over the Meech agreement. It involved a gamble with the survival of the Canadian federation itself. The strategy was Plan B all the way, one very much in the legacy of Trudeau's approach to Québécois nationalism and separatism — no negotiations, no concessions, expressions of contempt for Québécois nationalism and sovereigntists, continued threats of the assertion of superior federal powers to forestall separation. The main difference was that, unlike Trudeau, Chrétien had very little support among francophone Québécois.

The strategy had three elements. The first was destabilization. By forcing the Bouchard government to continue to deal with crises provoked by threats from Ottawa and internal challenges from partitionists and English-language-rights groups, the strategy deflected the PQ from providing orderly, good government and from getting on with, and receiving credit for, the practical agenda of dealing with the economy and the deficit. The maintenance of a crisis atmosphere destabilized the economy by reenforcing business jitters, by discouraging new investment, and by encouraging established firms to leave Quebec, put off expansion plans, or expand capacity elsewhere. Furthermore, such provocations went down well on Main Street in English Canada, undermined the Reform Party, and solidified English-Canadian support for the Chrétien government. The second element was polarization. Polarizing the situation in Quebec maintained a crisis atmosphere and hampered the Bouchard government's efforts to return to normalcy, to succeed with initiatives to reassure Quebec's minorities and to calm business fears. This polarization, particularly with Ottawa's approval and sanction, gave further encouragement to the anti-sovereignty movement, including extremist elements, to keep up the pressure on the Bouchard government. Furthermore, maintaining a crisis atmosphere or the appearance of a crisis atmosphere in Quebec kept English Canadians on side, forcing them to choose between a strong, majority Liberal government or chaos. The third element in the strategy — and perhaps most risky for the Chrétien government — was writing off Quebec for the purposes of the next federal election and focusing most of its political energy on appeals to English Canada.

In late October, the Chrétien government added another dimension to Plan B through a judicious combination of high profile business patronage underlining the tangible rewards of supporting federalism, with a continuing emphasis on the negative economic consequences of the political uncertainty resulting from a determined pursuit of sovereignty. Ottawa granted an $87-million interest-free loan to Bombardier Inc., headed by Laurent Beaudoin, an aggressive partisan of the federalist cause in Quebec who had publicly defied the sovereigntists repeatedly. The message was clear: those business leaders who publicly fought sovereignty could expect federal largesse, those federalist business leaders who had remained largely silent during the referendum should re-examine their position, and those business leaders who embraced sovereignty could expect nothing from Ottawa. Coming on the eve of premier Bouchard's tri-partite economic summit with business and labour leaders to seek co-operation in developing an economic plan for Quebec, Ottawa's message was not lost, and those business leaders willing to exchange economic co-operation with Bouchard for an abandonment of sovereignty were emboldened to increase the pressure. Meanwhile PQ and labour activists were increasingly angry at Bouchard's apparent willingness to embrace an approach to deficit and debt reduction involving large cuts in social, health, and education programs. These combined pressures created a political crisis within the sovereignty movement, as the spending and tax cuts and the downplaying of sovereignty demanded by the more aggressive among the business lobby as the price for help in tackling Quebec's debt, high unemployment, and a stagnant economy provoked sharp resistance from former premier Parizeau and the more militant sovereigntists and social democrats in the PQ. Ottawa's fondest hope was that this process would both deeply divide the sovereignty movement and begin to destroy Bouchard's charisma, undermining his personal popularity. Such outcomes would make Bouchard's almost certain re-election in 1998 or 1999 something less than a popular coronation and Bouchard himself might begin to reconsider plans for another referendum in 2000 or 2001.

The Chrétien government's strategy sought to re-shape the political landscape in the next federal election by taking a hard line against the Bouchard government and the sovereignty movement. The objectives were clear: to maintain enough support in English Canada to ensure another majority Liberal government; to undercut the Reform Party and reduce it to a western, red-neck rump by stealing its anti-Quebec and fiscal conservative rhetoric; to keep the anglophone and allophone minorities in Montreal on side while trying to win frightened francophones in an effort to reduce the Bloc's share of Quebec's seventy-five seats by polarizing the situation in Quebec and using threats and a fear campaign; to increase the economic pressure on Quebec and encourage the Quebec business elite to rejoin the very public campaign of economic blackmail and reprisal. If the strategy succeeds in 1997 or 1998, the Chrétien government will be in a better position to defeat the Bouchard government and thus prevent another referendum. A search in political history for parallels to this risky strategy immediately brings to mind Lincoln's political strategy leading up to the American Civil War and, more recently, Boris Yeltsin's pre-invasion approach to Chechnya.

If the strategy fails — if English Canadians decide to withdraw their strategic support for a Liberal majority, if the Bloc retains a clear majority of Quebec seats or, worse for Chrétien, increases its share and remains the Opposition, if Reform, though in decline, retains a large bloc of western seats — the crisis of the federation will be deeper, the chasm between Quebec and English Canada wider, and the good-faith opportunity provided by the result of the October 1995 referendum will have been squandered, like all opportunities before it. Furthermore, if the Bouchard government is returned in Quebec in 1998 or 1999 with a strong majority of seats and sovereigntist parties win a share of the popular vote that approaches 60 per cent, then the outcome of a sovereignty referendum in 2000 or 2001 could be a Yes victory in the appalling context of an aroused, angry, and fearful population in English Canada and a besieged English-Canadian minority in Quebec where extremists have been thrust into the leadership.

At that point, Canada will be on the threshold of civil war and the dynamic, so cynically and irresponsibly set in motion by the Chrétien government after the 1995 referendum, will be irreversible, or very nearly so.

10

Separation or Special Status?

From the beginning of the Quiet Revolution, the Québécois have appealed to English Canadians to understand their national grievances and to provide the minimum accommodation necessary to allow Quebec to find a secure place in Confederation. And it was clear to all but the most wilfully blind in English Canada that Quebec would eventually separate unless large structural concessions were made to the new progressive Québécois nationalism. The demands of the Québécois were simple — a recognition of the right to national self-determination and a willingness to negotiate a new, mutually acceptable set of relationships between the two nations.

Rather than rising to the challenge, English Canada papered together a federal system based on historical misperceptions, a rejection of the reality of Canada's two nations, and a trivialization of Quebec's fears as merely questions of language. Furthermore, English Canada commenced first to construct and then to embrace a series of political and constitutional myths. These myths concealed the reality of Quebec as the political and constitutional home of the Québécois nation, while providing a false but reassuring sense of Canadianism.

English Canadians must free themselves of these myths, presented as inviolate axioms, that make a settlement impossible. One of these is the assertion that the Québécois are only one small piece in the Canadian mosaic, no more or less distinct than other groups in other provinces. This belief is untenable. We cannot make a constitutional choice about whether or not Quebec is a distinct society, as if this were simply a matter of opinion. Quebec is a distinct society and always has been. What we are debating is whether our constitution will explicitly recognize that reality in a meaningful way. And it must be said from the outset that constitutions that refuse to recognize reality are recipes for continuing political strife. Trudeau's eloquent sophistry convinced us that if we refused to recognize Quebec's distinctiveness constitutionally, it would somehow not exist; that if we denied the existence of the Québécois nation, it would somehow not exist. This is the talk of lawyers who believe that legal texts make things so. In fact, sensible legal texts are those that help us deal rationally with reality, rather than irrationally deny it. Throughout the entire Trudeau era, the reality of Quebec was denied. The constitutional recognition of Quebec as a distinct society is a minimum demand of the Québécois. In Quebec, it is seen as merely a recognition and affirmation of a historical and sociological fact.

The second myth we need to abandon is multiculturalism. Before we can reach a successful resolution of our differences, English Canadians must stop embracing multiculturalism as an alternative to the reality of Canada's three nations — English Canadian, Québécois, and aboriginal. Section 27 of the *Constitution Act* of 1982 says, "This Charter shall be interpreted in a manner consistent with the preservation and enhancement of the multicultural heritage of Canadians." This is an important principle with which no one should quarrel — the rich, cultural, and ethnic diversity of Canada should be maintained, encouraged, and protected. But we must recall how the doctrine of official multiculturalism emerged, was used to bludgeon the Québécois (and later, the aboriginals), and found final reflection in the constitution that Quebec rejected.

In October 1971, Trudeau promulgated the doctrine of official multiculturalism in a clear effort to avoid a central recognition of non-aboriginal Canada's binational, bicultural, and bilingual reality. The doctrine stems from *The Cultural Contribution of the Other Ethnic Groups*, volume IV of the Report of the Royal Commission on Bilingualism and Biculturalism. This formal official statement by the prime minister in the House of Commons retroactively rewrote the mandate of the B and B Commission, flatly rejecting the thrust of the commission, which recommended not multiculturalism as a state policy but integration of the diverse ethnocultural groups into one or the other of the two main founding nations. The multiculturalism doctrine, in contrast, proposes that *the* key feature of Canada is its composition of a variety of diverse ethnocultural groups, among which Canada's francophones are but one among many. While ethnocultural diversity is a key feature of Canada, it is a malicious fiction to insist it is the key feature of Canada, when almost seven out of ten Canadians have British or French roots, and when all Canadians have integrated with either the English- or French-language groups.

The most convenient aspect of multiculturalism, which was used quite cynically by Trudeau, is that while it masks the reality of anglophone domination, it diminishes the significance of the French fact in Canada. The doctrine has proven a potent weapon against Quebec. English Canadians, and the many ethnic minorities that justifiably feel excluded, grasp the concept to offset demands both from francophone minorities across English Canada and from the Québécois nation.

The doctrine is not in accord with historical and contemporary fact, and its promulgation has only served to increase tensions. Canada is composed of two nations. The Québécois nation enjoys the province of Quebec as a political and constitutional home. The English-Canadian nation enjoys a considerably stronger political and constitutional home: nine provinces and two territories. It dominates in the House of Commons, the Senate, and all other federal institutions, and it has a well-protected and privileged minority status in Quebec. More recently, Canadians have also conceded we must add a third founding nation to Canada's constitutional design: the aboriginal nations. Because Canada's aboriginal people do not have a clearly defined and established constitutional and territorial home, because small populations are scattered across the country, and because the aboriginal peoples themselves are composed of diverse nations and language groups, Canadians, including aboriginals, have yet to agree on how to deal with the First Nations principle fully, other than by recognizing aboriginal rights, conceding the inherent right of self-government, and making a vague promise of fairness in land-claim settlements. Canada's two-nation reality, however, is recognized in the *Official Languages Act* and in the language rights enumerated in the constitution. It was also recognized at the founding of Canada in the *British North America Act*. To live and work comfortably in Quebec, one must speak French. To live and work comfortably in the rest of Canada, one must speak English.

Finally, before English Canada can resolve its differences with Quebec, it will have to give up the myth of the equality of provinces. Confederation was not premised on the doctrine of the constitutional equality of the provinces as a federal principle. Indeed, such a principle was explicitly rejected in favour of enumerating a limited list of provincial powers, while granting the federal government a list of specific powers, a series of key dominant powers, and all "residual" powers. All provinces were constitutionally equal in the exercise of the powers assigned to them within their borders, but that notion of equality did not extend to an equal say in the federation or to an equal share of power in the central government. On the contrary, the basic doctrine underlying the federal power was a slightly modified version of "representation by population." That is, each province would enjoy and exercise a share of power in the central government commensurate with the size of its population. This principle was modified to the extent that when readjustments were made in representation in the House of Commons after each census, the number of MPs for any province was not to be allowed to fall below the number of senators designated for that province. This provides the safeguard that, despite the principle of "representation by population," each province will continue to enjoy reasonable levels of representation in the House of Commons.

Not all provinces were equal at the time of their entrance into Confederation. Each of the four original provinces — Ontario, Quebec, New Brunswick, Nova Scotia — entered Confederation under somewhat different arrangements in 1867, including a very special and "distinct" status for Quebec, and different deals were struck as each additional colony opted to join. The three Prairie provinces were in an entirely different constitutional category. Ottawa acquired the region as a colonial possession, and the Prairie provinces were simply the constitutional creations of the central government. Upon their creation, Ottawa denied them control of their lands and natural resources, a clear provincial power enumerated in the *BNA Act*, yet successfully withheld by Ottawa until 1930 "for the purposes of the Dominion." Nothing makes clearer the historical supremacy of Ottawa than this power to create provinces by federal statute and, furthermore, to create a different constitutional class of province, that is, those whose attainment of full constitutional provincial status could be delayed at the pleasure of Ottawa.

A further confirmation of federal supremacy lies in the fact that Ottawa retains key powers that can be exercised in the national interest and at the peril of provincial powers. These include the power to disallow or reserve any provincial statute, all residual powers, the general power "to make laws for the peace, order, and good government of Canada," and the power to declare that any local work in a province is "to be for the general advantage of Canada or for the advantage of two or more of the provinces." The federal powers of disallowance and reservation have not been exercised since the heady days of Social Credit under Alberta's William Aberhart in the 1930s. But these powers have not atrophied from a lack of use. Indeed, they are designed not to be used. Their mere existence imposes a certain self-discipline on the provinces, particularly in the face of an assertive federal government. The federal declaratory power has been used more frequently to establish central authority over things such as railways, the grain trade, telecommunications, and nuclear energy. Any federal system that abandons such powers will slowly bleed to death as a result of a self-inflicted wound.

The recent emergence of the doctrine of the constitutional equality of the provinces was another device in the arsenal developed by Trudeau to deal with Quebec. By insisting that all provinces were constitutionally equal, Trudeau was able to insist that Quebec was a province just like the others. Therefore, Quebec's demands should simply be put on a list along with the demands of all other provinces. In this way, Trudeau was able to sidestep Quebec's demand for a bilateral negotiating process between Ottawa, which represents English Canada, and the Quebec government, which represents the Québécois nation. But it was a doctrine that Trudeau invoked with deft opportunism. To Quebec he would say he couldn't give it what it wanted when the other provinces refused. Yet he was equally able to plead with Canadians to elect a strong central government "to speak for Canada." On one day he would use Ottawa's power unilaterally to patriate and amend the constitution. Yet on another, when Lévesque appealed to him after the 1981 débâcle to return Quebec's veto, for example, he could insist that though he personally favoured such a concession to Quebec, the other provinces would have to agree and until that agreement was obtained, his hands were tied. In the post-1995 sovereignty referendum period, Chrétien has proved to be a good student of Trudeau's, invoking promises of constitutional change for Quebec in order to defeat the Yes, yet pleading powerlessness in the face of the other provinces right after the vote.

Ironically, Trudeau's opportunistic use of the doctrine gave it a degree of respectability, turning it into a Canadian constitutional convention and achieving a degree of realization in the amending formula adopted in 1982 (which states that changes in the constitution require the consent of Ottawa and seven of ten provinces representing more than 50 per cent of the population). Mulroney and those premiers who espoused provincial rights were able to use the doctrine in nearly successful efforts to transform Confederation into a loose amalgamation of powerful provinces presided over by an increasingly impotent central government. Furthermore, the doctrine allows these premiers to insist that Quebec obtain nothing not granted to all the other provinces. This doctrine makes our current Quebec/English-Canada impasse insoluble. To give all provinces exactly what Quebec needs to advance and protect its uniqueness will destroy the federation. Yet not to give Quebec at least some of what it needs also risks the breakup of Canada.

This brings us to the final logical expression of the doctrine of the equality of the provinces — the Triple-E Senate, composed of equal numbers of senators from each province, democratically elected, and with some real and significant powers to exercise. The Triple-E Senate was first proposed by Manning and the Reform Party and imperfectly expressed in the defeated Charlottetown Agreement. As we have seen, Quebec will never agree to such a proposal, nor will most English Canadians, who would prefer abolition. In arguing the Triple-E case, some have suggested that one of the original intentions of the Canadian Senate was to provide, in an imperfect way, a place to deal with regional grievances in the federation. Nothing could be further from the truth. The Fathers of Confederation explicitly rejected the model provided by the American Senate. They wanted neither a powerful nor a regional body. Although the *BNA Act* distributes an equal number of senators to each of the four regions — Ontario, Quebec, the Maritimes, and the West — the Senate was never conceived as a house of the regions. Rather, it was seen quite explicitly, as John A. Macdonald stated, as "the representative of property" and the place for second thoughts regarding the actions of the Commons. The Senate has no real, effective power, other than that of delay and inconvenience, and the Commons can always finally prevail in any clash. In practice, the Senate became and remains simply a secure place at the public trough for former party bagmen and hacks, public figures past their partisan usefulness, and assorted cronies of prime ministers past and present. As such, it has long outlived its usefulness and deserves to

| | Total Seats | Conservative | | | Liberal | | |
		Vote %	1988 Result (seats)	PR (seats)	Vote %	1988 Result (seats)	PR (seats)
			1988 Federal Election: Estimates of Seats under				
Que.	75	53	63	41	30	12	23
Ont.	99	38	46	40	39	43	38
Man.	14	37	7	5	37	5	5
Sask.	14	36	4	5	18	0	3
Alta.	26	52	25	14	14	0	4
B.C.	32	35	12	11	20	1	6
N.B.	10	40	5	4	45	5	5
N.S.	11	41	5	5	47	6	5
P.E.I.	4	42	0	1	50	4	3
Nfld.	7	42	2	3	45	5	3
Yuk.	1	35	0	0	11	0	0
N.W.T.	2	26	0	0	41	2	2
	295	43%	169	129	32%	83	97

be abolished, a point on which there appears to be a near consensus in post-Charlottetown Canada.

The remedy is available, if Canadians seriously want to address the problem of regional representation and deepening Canadian democracy by coming closer to realizing the principle of representation by population without offending Quebec or most English Canadians. First, abolish the Senate and establish a constitutional minimum number of seats in the House of Commons below which a province or a territory cannot fall should its population decline (say, for example, two seats for each territory, two seats for Prince Edward Island, eight seats for the western and other Atlantic provinces at five hundred thousand or below, with representation by population operating for anything above that number). Second, amend the constitution to require that the Commons seats granted to each province be assigned on a proportional basis to each political party according to levels of popular support. This would ensure that each province, or at least each region, would send MPs from all major political parties to Ottawa and force each party caucus to grapple with and reconcile regional and national interests at the same time. It would also ensure that splinter parties and regional protest parties, though small, would obtain a platform in the Commons sooner rather than later. Furthermore, in the event that a regional protest party

Popular Vote, Seats Won, and Proportional Representation (PR)					
NDP			Reform		
Vote %	1988 Result (seats)	PR (seats)	Vote %	1988 Result (seats)	PR (seats)
14	0	11	-	-	-
20	10	21	-	-	-
21	2	3	3	0	1
44	10	6	1	0	0
17	1	4	15	0	4
37	19	13	5	0	2
9	0	1	-	-	-
11	0	1	-	-	-
7	0	0	-	-	-
12	0	1	-	-	-
51	1	1	-	-	-
28	0	0	-	-	-
20%	43	62	2%	0	7

becomes strong, proportional representation would ensure a fair representation of all points of view among the voting population and avoid a sweep of seats based on a plurality of votes in a "first past the post" system. The results of the 1988 and 1993 elections, roughly calculated according to this system of proportional representation, would have been quite different under such a system, as the tables on these pages show.

The House of Commons would also be quite different if these had been the 1988 and 1993 results. Our recent political history would probably have been less divisive and crisis ridden, and the principles of fair and democratic representation would have been more perfectly realized. There would be the clash of debate along class, regional, national, and party lines. Each party would have to deal with regional issues — language for Quebec, energy resource policy for the West, the fisheries in B.C. and Atlantic Canada — in the context of the party's ideological line. On occasion, cross-party regional alliances could occur. The chance of the kind of regional polarization that allowed Trudeau to write off the West and the pre-Mulroney Tories or the Chrétien Liberals to write off Quebec would be greatly lessened; indeed, it would be highly unlikely.

A House of Commons based on proportional representation would be difficult to effect in Canada. The major parties would re-

		Conservative			Liberal		
				1993 Federal Election: Estimates of Seats under			
	Total Seats	Vote %	1993 Result (seats)	PR (seats)	Vote %	1993 Result (seats)	PR (seats)
Que.	75	14	1	11	33	19	25
Ont.	99	18	0	18	53	98	54
Man.	14	12	0	2	45	12	7
Sask.	14	11	0	2	32	5	4
Alta.	26	15	0	4	25	4	7
B.C.	32	14	0	5	28	6	5
N.B.	10	28	1	3	56	9	6
N.S.	11	24	0	3	52	11	6
P.E.I.	4	32	0	1	60	4	3
Nfld.	7	27	0	2	67	7	5
Yuk.	1	18	0	0	23	0	0
N.W.T.	2	16	0	0	65	2	2
	295	16%	2	51	41%	177	124

*There was one independent elected in Quebec.

sist it, and critics allege it would be a disaster. There would rarely be a majority government, the "Italian disease" would afflict us. Prime ministers would constantly jockey for majorities, governments would fall, and we would have annual elections. Canada would become ungovernable. One easy remedy would be to have fixed election dates: elections would occur on the second Monday of June every fourth year, for example. In between, the parties would have to work harder at putting together ministries with the confidence of the House, which, after all, is the basic principle of parliamentary democracy and responsible government. Furthermore, Canada's experience with minority governments — Diefenbaker from 1957 to 1958, Pearson from 1963 to 1968, Trudeau from 1972 to 1974 — has not been bad. Some argue such governments are the most sensitive and productive. They must work harder at governing and refrain from arrogant assertions of undiluted power. Indeed, one could argue that the governments of Mulroney in 1988 and Chrétien in 1993 may prove to have been the worst in our history. Both governments won strong parliamentary majorities with minority popular support and proceeded to brutally impose controversial, divisive, and damaging

Popular Vote, Seats Won, and Proportional Representation (PR)								
NDP			Reform			Bloc		
Vote %	1993 Result (seats)	PR (seats)	Vote %	1993 Result (seats)	PR (seats)	Vote%	1993 Result (seats)	PR (seats)
2	0	1	0	0	0	49	54	37
6	0	6	20	1	21	0	0	0
17	1	2	22	1	3	0	0	0
27	5	4	27	4	4	0	0	0
4	0	1	52	22	14	0	0	0
16	2	12	36	24	10	0	0	0
5	0	0	9	0	1	0	0	0
7	0	1	13	0	1	0	0	0
5	0	0	1	0	0	0	0	0
4	0	0	1	0	0	0	0	0
43	1	1	13	0	0	0	0	0
8	0	0	8	0	0	0	0	0
7%	9	28	19%	52	54	14%	54	37

policies contrary to the popular will and contrary to much of what was promised before election.

We should contemplate the answers to a series of questions about our recent political history had the results of 1988 and 1993 been expressed in a proportional system. Would the free trade agreements have been put in place and retained in their present form? Would Meech have occurred? Would the GST have passed? Would our tax system, which favours corporations and the wealthy, have remained unreformed? Would our social, educational, and health programs have been cut as severely and would responsibility for these programs have been downloaded to the provinces? Would we have been subjected to the divisive Charlottetown referendum? Would Brian Mulroney have remained prime minister after the 1988 election, particularly given his betrayals of the electorate on the "sacred trust" of social programs and his 1984 opposition to free trade? Would Chrétien have remained prime minister after his flagrant reversal on his Red Book promises? Would the undiluted corporate, neo-conservative agenda of successive governments remain in place, despite explicit and repeated rejections of that agenda by the electorate in provincial and federal elections?

Would Chrétien be able to continue his bullying and scare tactics against Quebec?

English Canadians want and need a strong central government, one able and willing to share power in good faith with the regions and the provinces on issues of vital provincial and regional concern. But after a failure of good-faith efforts to reach a national strategy with regional support, English Canadians want a central government with the power to do what is best for Canada as a whole. Unlike Quebec, where a clear majority of residents feel a primary allegiance to their province as a result of Québécois nationalism, in the English-Canadian regions residents feel a primary allegiance to Canada as a whole. The nine English-Canadian provinces need and want a strong federal government to maintain a sense of Canadian nationhood through a series of national strategies, particularly to offset regional disparities as well as resist the American pull, a pull that has increased dramatically in this era of free trade and "harmonization." They want and need a prime minister and a House of Commons at the centre that can not only speak for Canada but can also act decisively on its behalf. Canadians in English Canada want a government at the centre that can maintain existing national programs, such as medicare and post-secondary education, and develop new ones in areas such as day care and culture. They want an effective national government able to act on the popular will in the face of globalizing forces of the coming corporate millennium, not one incapable of governing, fearful of asserting itself against the forces of economic dictatorship, characterized by so many checks and balances that popular desires cannot be realized in national policy.

Canadians in English Canada can never achieve such a strong, central government until the Quebec question is resolved satisfactorily. Québécois fears continue to block the realization of a more potent national government. Intrusions of federal power, such as federally funded programs in areas of provincial jurisdiction, have always been viewed as threatening by the Québécois. English Canada desperately needs a more aggressive national strategy on culture, something the Québécois resist. English Canada cries out for a well-developed, co-ordinated program in secondary and post-secondary education, training, and job strategies; again there is profound resistance in Quebec. English Canada urgently needs a new national economic policy: the regional pillars of the old policy are collapsing — forestry in B.C., agriculture in the West, industry in Ontario, the Atlantic fishery

— as global corporate power seeks to impose its anti-social market logic on us. Yet Quebec, recalling a century of exploitation as a source of cheap labour and cheap resources, as well as its exploitation as a captive market, would undoubtedly resist such an initiative if it was merely one of ten provinces at a table chaired by Ottawa. Intrusions of the federal spending power in various areas of Québécois life have always provoked resistance, whereas, despite resistance from their provincial premiers, English Canadians realize that such assertions of federal power have been essential in bringing us medicare, fairer access to university education, public pensions, unemployment insurance, and programs to fight regional disparity. It is as a result of this federal power that all Canadians are assured a reasonable minimum standard of living and access to universal, publicly funded programs with national standards. Thus, something that may be sorely needed and wanted in English Canada is blocked or only done by half-measures because of Québécois resistance. Typically, English-Canadian premiers in favour of provincial rights, eager to expand provincial power at the expense of federal power, opportunistically ally themselves with Quebec in order either to bring Ottawa to a standstill or to extract additional revenues and administrative powers. As a result, the national government has become increasingly ineffectual and more and more the object of scorn among Canadians. It is, therefore, in the interest of all Canadians in English Canada who yearn for an effective and responsive national government to join together in a final resolution of the Quebec question, if only as a necessary first step toward allowing us to address our national question with the same devotion and focus with which the Québécois address theirs.

English Canadians have two choices, now starkly clarified. Either we grant Quebec special constitutional status within Confederation or we reconcile ourselves to Quebec's ultimate separation. Perhaps it is too late. Certainly, Parizeau believed so, though Bouchard and Dumont appear willing to contemplate a new arrangement that does not include the first, rupturing act of separation. But we have squandered so many opportunities; we may squander this last one. Had English Canada responded to the B and B Commission, the Quiet Revolution, the October Crisis, the election of the PQ, the results of the 1980 sovereignty referendum, the post-Meech crisis, and the defeat of Charlottetown in both Quebec and English Canada, we might not have reached this point. But we did not respond, and now we are forced to confront a situation in which the Bloc has triumphed federally, the PQ has triumphed provincially, and the Quebec electorate has come within a handful of votes of saying Yes to sovereignty. And so we stand on the edge of a precipice we have been marching toward for thirty years.

What sort of special status will satisfy Quebec? In the first place, most Québécois who support separation or sovereignty-association are, like Lévesque, Dumont, and perhaps Bouchard, reluctant separatists who yearn for even a minimal settlement with dignity. Bourassa clearly believed that his government's five conditions derived from Meech were the minimum. These were: 1) recognition of Quebec as distinct society in the constitution; 2) more power over immigration; 3) limits on the use of the federal spending power; 4) a veto; and 5) a say in the appointment of Quebec's three judges on the Supreme Court. Obviously, clear and unfettered constitutional authority over language, education, culture, and immigration are bottom lines for Quebec. Furthermore, a special mechanism to deal with intrusions of the federal spending power into Quebec (the ability to opt out with financial compensation) would need to be developed. In addition, a Quebec veto over constitutional changes that have a significant impact on Quebec would need to be granted. The point is that the precise form of the special status would be negotiated. It might include some form of special status or asymmetrical federalism, or a confederal system, both of which would see the withdrawal of Quebec MPs from the House of Commons during consideration of those matters that have been devolved to the Quebec National Assembly. But the reality is clear: either we negotiate special status while Quebec is still part of Confederation, or we will negotiate with an independent Quebec the terms of the association we will inevitably want.

Certainly, the Charlottetown Agreement went some distance toward Quebec's minimum, but it proved finally insufficient. The recognition of Quebec as a distinct society was so heavily hedged and qualified that the Québécois decided it was not enough. The special status granted Quebec, such as it was, was not the sort Québécois nationalists had in mind, though it was enough to offend Trudeau. They never asked for a perpetual guarantee of 25 per cent of the seats in the House of Commons. They never asked for a reformed Senate and a double majority on language and culture. Special status for Quebec was never seen as more power at the centre, power to threaten or frustrate the aspirations of English Canadians; rather, it was seen as uniquely granting the province of Quebec the special powers necessary to sustain the Québécois nation. Not only were the Charlottetown provisions insufficient for Quebec, but they also provoked profound concern in English Canada. That concern was certainly a mixed ideological bag that included anti-Québécois sentiment at its rawest; fears of losing too many powers by Ottawa; a desire for a strong, central government to articulate a vision of the country acceptable in English Canada; a yearning for new national social programs in areas such as day care and maintenance of existing national social programs; concerns that the rights of women, especially aboriginal women, would be given short shrift under the deal; and so on.

The failure of Charlottetown and the narrow victory for the No in the 1995 sovereignty referendum can set the stage for another effort on the part of English Canada to resolve the Quebec crisis before the country breaks apart. And this time English Canadians must not confuse the Quebec issue with all the other constitutional issues crying out for resolution, as if there could be one organic settlement of all matters like the one attempted in the Charlottetown Agreement. Let us proceed one careful step at a time: the Quebec crisis, the aboriginal question, the vision of English Canada in the context of the grievances of the English-Canadian peripheries or of Atlantic Canada and the West, the Social Charter, expansion of gender-equity measures, and so on. This way our constitutional reconstruction can be deliberate, careful, and solid, rather than haphazard jerry-building in a crisis atmosphere. Above all, constitutional reconstruction should not again be allowed to be made part of the personal, urgent re-election agendas of incumbent politicians, as was the case in Meech and Charlottetown. One approach worth considering is that of the constituent assembly, elected popularly and assigned the task of formulating constitutional solutions for presentation first to the people in a referendum and then to the House of Commons and the provincial legislatures for ratification. Given the urgency of the situation, the first task assigned such an assembly might be to formulate recommendations for reconciling the national question in the Canadian constitution, including special status for the Québécois nation and the aboriginal nations.

Critics have contended that special status for Quebec, no matter how limited initially, will turn out to be a half-way house to separation. This argument has considerable merit. Given any form of special status, the argument goes, Québécois nationalism will simply use these unique powers as levers to win more and more. In the end, only full sovereignty will be enough, followed by bi-national negotiations on association. The argument has become more compelling as Quebec's demands have escalated in response to English Canada's repeated rebuffs, so compelling that it has taken on the character of a self-fulfilling prophecy. Perhaps we in English Canada have refused Quebec once too often; perhaps we have denied the Québécois nation too repeatedly and with too much hostility and contempt. Perhaps the trajectory of the Québécois cannot now be deflected from ultimate sovereignty. If that is true, we in English Canada, or our descendants, will be forced to deal with it. But to use it once again as an argument for yet another refusal is to ensure that English Canada fulfils its own worst prophecy about Quebec.

Despite the 1995 sovereignty referendum results, relations between English Canada and Quebec have not yet reached the point that puts the Québécois on an irresistible and irreversible path to sovereignty. It is not too late, but it is nearly so and will be certainly so if the Chrétien government and the English-Canadian provinces persist with their hard stance. Together, Québécois and English Canadians have forged one of the best places on the planet in which to live. If we can continue our unique experiment in seeking unity through diversity, if we can retain the two great cultures together in one federal or confederal structure, Canada could yet become a model for all the world. But if we fail, it will not be a disaster. Life will go on, our economies will continue to function in much the same way, and Quebec and Canada will then compete for the United Nations title of the most desirable place in the world to live. We will muddle through, seeking some practical working arrangement. But the Canada we could have become, had we achieved an effective reconciliation between the two nations in a single federal or confederal state, will be lost, perhaps forever. After all, it is always easier to take things apart than it is to put them back together. Events of the last few years in the former Soviet empire should constantly remind us of this fundamental truth.

The Québécois nation has the political will to seek a reconciliation. It always has had. Indeed, the last thirty-five years have been characterized by increasingly urgent appeals from the Québécois for just such a reconciliation. But it cannot be on English Canada's terms as it always was in the past. The reconciliation sought by the Québécois insists that we in English Canada accept the fundamental legitimacy and correctness of their historical grievances. It also insists that English Canada abandon its notorious habit of declaring sympathy for the Québécois while imposing measures smugly judged by English Canada to be sufficient remedies. Just as English Canada reluctantly accepted the Québécois nation's right to self-determination only after the election of the PQ, English Canada must now yield the powers that nation needs to protect, strengthen, and enhance itself. To do otherwise, to try to turn back the clock and again deny the Québécois nation's existence, to threaten and bully it with the use of legal technicalities and superior federal power, will provoke a fast-track either to separation or to extreme civil disorder.

As we have seen, English Canada and Quebec have two quite different versions of the same history. Understandably, this makes dialogue difficult. English Canadians, searching for positive, upbeat themes and justifications, prefer versions of history that ignore or diminish the oppression of the Québécois. Undeniably negative events — military conquest and suppression; the use of exile, prison and the noose; insults and degradations — are overlooked or attributed either to the actions of defective individuals who happened to hold power or to the temper of the times. As victor, English Canada wrote the official history, selected the national symbols, and controlled the myths, rituals, and rites of official national self-celebration.

The Québécois, for their part, carefully husbanded their own history, holding it close to their hearts. Even when it was absent from official versions or reflected badly, it became deeply embedded in their collective consciousness. It was passed down from generation to generation in the private circle of family, neighbourhood, and parish. The myths and symbols of that history became the litmus test for local political leaders. Efforts by English Canada to distort or sanitize the history of oppression had an opposite effect. The Québécois resented what they saw as an arrogant attempt to rob them of their heritage and clung to the truths they had learned at their parents' knees with even greater determination. English Canadians saw this tendency as evidence of backwardness and romanticism, an imprisonment by tradition, heaping insult on the original injury.

This circle can only be broken only with the greatest effort and only when English Canada admits the injustices done to Quebec. For English Canada to admit publicly that the Québécois have been oppressed will involve the acceptance of critical public scrutiny and the humbling admission that all along much of what they said was true. It will also involve a fundamental change in self-perception. There will be shame and guilt and, inevitably, a need to make amends, an effort to pay historical debts.

Do English Canadians have the political will to go through this process? A crucial step toward achieving that political will is for us to admit there are debts yet to be paid to the Québécois. Persuading English Canadians of this fact has been the purpose of this book. Do we acknowledge a debt to the descendants of those we conquered, re-conquered, and oppressed? Do we owe anything to the descendants of those we exploited as cheap labour? Can we be called to account again for the years of English privilege in Quebec? Have we settled accounts with Quebec regarding the *War Measures Act,* or the dirty tricks of our secret police against the PQ, or the mole we placed in the Lévesque cabinet, or the premiers' gang-up of 1981–82? Have we erased the impact of the insults and affronts when Meech fell? Did we really test our limits in the Charlottetown Agreement? Are we prepared to use domineering federal powers and the threat of force in an effort to checkmate a democratic decision by the Québécois to separate? Can we in English Canada truly say that our collective conscience as a nation is now clear and that we have made a full historical accounting to the Québécois nation?

The Québécois nation does not believe we have yet paid our debts. Nor do many of us. We can pay them now, or we can pay them later. But pay them we must.

BIBLIOGRAPHIC NOTE

When I first proposed the idea for this book to the publisher, I had in mind an essay that would make the basic "debts to pay" and "denial of nation" arguments, while providing a re-interpretation of the well-known events of Quebec's history. As I began to write, I found myself forced both to revisit a variety of old sources to refresh my memory and to visit some new ones to update myself on more recent events. I have included a list of those sources most heavily relied upon. However, the book is still first and foremost an essay.

Additionally, I made a great deal of use of my own newspaper clipping files from the *Globe and Mail*, the Regina *Leader Post*, *Maclean's*, and selected editions of *Le Devoir*, particularly for the periods of the October Crisis of 1970 and the rise and fall of the Meech Lake Accord and the Charlottetown Agreement. I also made frequent use of *The Gallup Report*, to which I have subscribed for many years. I followed the constitutional debates between the demise of Meech and the Charlottetown effort in *The Network*, the newsletter of the Network on the Constitution, published out of the University of Ottawa and edited by Donald G. Lenihan. And I followed the extent and impacts of federal budget cuts through the *CCPA Monitor*, published by the Ottawa-based Canadian Centre for Policy Alternatives. The material on the Charlottetown Agreement and the 1992 and 1995 referendums is based on coverage provided in the *Globe and Mail*, Regina *Leader Post*, *Maclean's*, the Montreal *Gazette* and *Le Devoir*, as well as on the CBC-TV and CTV national networks.

My discussion of the October Crisis might provoke some controversy. The facts on which I base the characterization of the events of October 1970 are all now on the public record. For the sceptical among you, I refer you to the books on the crisis by Haggart and Golden, Pelletier, Rotstein, Smith, and Vallières. Some excellent investigative work, including interviews with paroled FLQers, was published in the *Globe and Mail* on the tenth and fifteenth anniversaries of the crisis (October 1980 and October 1985). I found John Twigg's unpublished paper to be very useful, and I kept a very detailed clipping file during the crisis. One cannot overlook the information contained in the report of the McDonald Commission on the RCMP Security Service and the press clippings about the Quebec Keable Commission.

For basic statistics, which I tried to use sparingly, I appealed often to Urquhart and Buckley's *Historical Statistics of Canada*, Langlois's *Recent Social Trends in Quebec, 1960–1990*, to census reports, and reports by various electoral officers. Additionally, I found myself forced to re-visit some of the major government reports regarding Quebec, most importantly the reports of the Royal Commission on Bilingualism and Biculturalism, the Task Force on Canadian Unity, and Quebec's Gendron Commission.

Selected Bibliography

Armstrong, E. *The Crisis of Quebec, 1914–1918*. Toronto: McClelland and Stewart, 1974 (1937).

Arnaud, N., and Dofny, J. *Nationalism and the National Question*. Montreal: Black Rose, 1977.

Arnopoulos, S.M., and Clift, D. *The English Fact in Quebec*. Montreal: McGill-Queen's University Press, 1980.

Behiels, M.D. (ed.). *The Meech Lake Primer*. Ottawa: University of Ottawa Press, 1990.

——. *Prelude to Quebec's Quiet Revolution: Liberalism versus Neo-nationalism, 1945–1980*. Montreal/Kingston: McGill-Queen's University Press, 1985.

Bercuson, D.J., and Cooper, B. *Deconfederation: Canada without Quebec*. Toronto: Key Porter, 1991.

Berger, C. (ed.). *Conscription 1917*. Toronto: University of Toronto Press, n.d.

Bergeron, L. *The History of Quebec: A Patriote's Handbook*. Toronto: NC, 1971.

Bernard, A. *What Does Quebec Want?* Toronto: Lorimer, 1978.

Bernard, J.P. (ed.). *Les Rébellions de 1837–1838: Les Patriotes du Bas-Canada dans la mémoire collective et chez les historiens*. Montreal: Boréal, 1983.

Black, C. *Duplessis*. Toronto: McClelland and Stewart, 1976.

Bliss, J.M. (ed.). *Canadian History in Documents, 1763–1966*. Toronto: Ryerson, 1966.

Boris, S.T. *The Language of the Skies: The Bilingual Air Traffic Control Conflict in Canada*. Montreal: McGill-Queen's University Press, 1983.

Bouchard, L. *A visage découvert*. Montreal: Boréal, 1992.

————— (dir.) *Un nouveau parti pour l'étape décisive*. Montreal: Fidès, 1993.

Brebner, J.B. *Canada: A Modern History*. Ann Arbor: University of Michigan Press, 1960.

Brown, R.C., and Cook, R. *Canada, 1896–1921: A Nation Transformed*. Toronto: McClelland and Stewart, 1974.

Browne, G.P. (ed.). *Documents on the Confederation of British North America*. Toronto: McClelland and Stewart, 1969.

Brunet, M. *La Présence Anglaise et Les Canadiens*. Montreal: Beauchemin, 1964.

Buchanan, A. *Secession: The Morality of Political Divorce from Fort Sumter to Lithuania and Quebec*. Boulder: Westview Press, 1991.

Burroughs, P. *The Colonial Reformers and Canada, 1830–1849*. Toronto: McClelland and Stewart, 1969.

Burt, A.L.R. *The Old Province of Quebec*. Toronto: McClelland and Stewart, 1968.

Campbell, K. *Time and Chance: The Political Memoirs of Canada's First Woman Prime Minister*. Toronto: Doubleday, 1996.

Canada. First Ministers' Meeting. *Consensus Report on the Constitution*. Ottawa, 1992. (Charlottetown Agreement.)

—————. Royal Commission on Bilingualism and Biculturalism. *Preliminary Report*, 1965; *The Official Languages*, Vol. I, 1967; *Education*, Vol. II, 1968; *The Work World*, Vol. III, 1969; *The Cultural Contribution of the Other Ethnic Groups*, Vol. IV, 1970. Ottawa: various years.

—————. The Task Force on Canadian Unity. *A Future Together*. Ottawa, 1979.

Carens, J.H. (ed.) *Is Quebec Nationalism Just?* Montreal/Kingston: McGill-Queen's University Press, 1995.

Chaput, M. *Pourquoi je suis séparatiste*. Montreal: Editions du Jour, 1961.

Chodos, R., and Hamovitch, E. *Quebec and the American Dream*. Toronto: Between the Lines, 1991.

Cleroux, R. "L'affaire Morin." *Canadian Forum*, June 1992.

Clouthier, E., Guay, J.H., and Latouche, D. *Le virage: l'évolution de l'opinion publique au Québec depuis 1960, ou comment le Québec est devenu souverainiste*. Montreal: Editions Québec/Amérique, 1992.

Constitutional Forum Constitutionnel. "Perspectives on the PQ Plan for Sovereignty, 'Quebec in a New World,'" Special issue. Edmonton: Centre for Constitutional Studies, University of Alberta, Fall 1994.

Conway, J.F. *The West: The History of a Region in Confederation.* Toronto: Lorimer, 1994.

————. "The Mulroney Counter-Revolution, 1984–1993," unpublished paper, Canadian Sociology and Anthropology Association, Learneds. Calgary: University of Calgary, 1994.

————. "Reflections on Canada in the Year 1994," in de Finney, J., et. al., (eds.), *Canadian Studies at Home and Abroad.* Montreal: Association for Canadian Studies, 1995.

Cook, R. *Canada and the French-Canadian Question.* Toronto: Macmillan, 1966.

————. (ed.). *Confederation.* Toronto: University of Toronto Press, 1967.

Coon Come, M. "The Status and Rights of the James Bay Crees in the Context of Quebec Secession from Canada," *Constitutional Forum Constitutionnel,* Fall 1994.

Cornellier, M. *The Bloc.* Toronto: Lorimer, 1995.

Coyne, D. *Roll of the Dice.* Toronto: Lorimer, 1992.

Craig, G.M. (ed.). *Lord Durham's Report.* Toronto: McClelland and Stewart, 1963.

Creighton, D.G. *British North America at Confederation.* Ottawa: Queen's Printer, 1963.

Creighton, D.G. *Dominion of the North: A History of Canada.* Toronto: Macmillan, 1957.

Creighton, D.G. *Empire of the St. Lawrence.* Toronto: Macmillan, 1972.

Dafoe, J.W. *Laurier.* Toronto: McClelland and Stewart, 1963.

Dawson, R. MacGregor. *The Government of Canada.* (revised by Norman Ward). Toronto: University of Toronto Press, 1964 (1947).

den Otten, A.A. *Civilizing the West: The Galts and the Development of Western Canada.* Edmonton: University of Alberta Press, 1982.

Desbarats, P. *René: A Canadian in Search of a Country.* Toronto: McClelland and Stewart, 1976.

Dion, L. *Quebec: The Unfinished Revolution.* Montreal: McGill University Press, 1976.

Dion, S. "The Dynamic of Secession: Scenarios after a Pro-separatist Vote in a Quebec Referendum," *Canadian Journal of Political Science*, September 1995.

————. "Why is Secession Difficult in Well-Established Democracies? Lessons from Quebec," *British Journal of Political Science*, 1995.

Dobbin, M. *Preston Manning and the Reform Party*. Toronto: Lorimer, 1991.

Drache, D. (ed.). *Quebec: Only the Beginning*. Toronto: New Press, 1972.

Drache, D., and Perin, R. (eds.). *Negotiating with a Sovereign Quebec*. Toronto: Lorimer, 1992.

Duhamel, P. "Anglo-Quebec: A Distinct Society." *Report on Business Magazine*, April 1991.

Dunham, A. *Political Unrest in Upper Canada, 1815–1836*. Toronto: McClelland and Stewart, 1963.

Eccles, W.J. *The Ordeal of New France*. Montreal: CBC, 1966.

Flanagan, T. *Waiting for the Wave: The Reform Party and Preston Manning*. Toronto: Stoddart, 1995.

Fournier, P. *A Meech Lake Post-Mortem: Is Quebec Sovereignty Inevitable?* Montreal/Kingston: McGill-Queen's University Press, 1991.

Fournier, P. *The Quebec Establishment*. Montreal: Black Rose, 1976.

Fraser, G. *PQ: René Lévesque and the Parti Québécois in Power*. Toronto: Macmillan, 1984.

Freeman, A., and Grady, P. *Dividing the House: Planning for a Canada without Quebec*. Toronto: HarperCollins, 1995.

Frizzel, A., Pammett, J.H., and Westell, A. *The Canadian General Election of 1993*. Ottawa: Carleton, 1994.

Gagnon, A. (ed.). *Quebec: State and Society*. Toronto: Metheun, 1984.

Gagnon, A.-G., and Rocher, F. (eds.). *Répliques aux détracteurs de la souveraineté du Québec*. Montreal: VLB éditeur, 1992.

Gibson, G. *Plan B: The Future of the Rest of Canada*. Vancouver: Fraser Institute, 1994.

Gourgeon, G. *The History of Quebec Nationalism*. Translated by R. Chodos. Toronto: Lorimer, 1996.

Gourlay, R. *Statistical Account of Upper Canada*. Toronto: McClelland and Stewart, 1974 (1822).

Granatstein, J.L., and Hitsman, J.M. *Broken Promises: A History of Conscription in Canada*. Toronto: Oxford University Press, 1977.

Granastein, J.L., and McNaught, K. (eds.). *"English Canada" Speaks Out*. Toronto: Doubleday, 1991.

Haggart, R., and Golden, A.E. *Rumours of War*. Toronto: Lorimer, 1979.

Harrison, R. *Of Passionate Intensity: Right-Wing Populism and the Reform Party of Canada*. Toronto: University of Toronto, 1995.

Hartt, S.H., et. al. *Tangled Web: Legal Aspects of Deconfederation*. Toronto: C.D. Howe Institute, 1992.

Héroux, M. *The Office of the Commissioner of Official Languages. A Twenty-Year Chronicle from 1970 to Mid-1989*. Ottawa, 1989.

Hughes, E. *French Canada in Transition*. Chicago: University of Chicago Press, 1963.

Keilty, G. (ed.). *1837: Revolution in the Canadas*. Toronto: NC, 1974.

Kwavnik, D. (ed.). *The Tremblay Report*. Toronto: McClelland and Stewart, 1973.

Laidler, D.E., and Robson, W.B. (eds.). *Two Nations, One Money?* Toronto: C.D. Howe Institute, 1991.

Langlois, S., et. al. *Recent Social Trends in Quebec, 1960–1990*. Montreal: McGill-Queen's University Press, 1992.

Language and Society, Special Report, 25th Anniversary of the Royal Commission on Bilingualism and Biculturalism, Summer 1989.

Laurendeau, A. *Witness for Quebec*. Toronto: Macmillan, 1973.

LeDuc, L., and Pamett, J.H. "Referendum Voting: Attitudes and Behaviour in the 1992 Constitutional Referendum," *Canadian Journal of Political Science*, March 1995.

Lemco, J. *Turmoil in the Peaceful Kingdom: The Quebec Sovereignty Movement and Its Implications for Canada and the United States*. Toronto: University of Toronto, 1994.

Lévesque, R. *An Option for Quebec*. Toronto: McClelland and Stewart, 1965.

Lévesque, R. *Memoirs*. Toronto: McClelland and Stewart, 1986.

Lévesque, R. *My Quebec*. Toronto: Methuen, 1979.

Levitt, J. *Henri Bourassa and the Golden Calf: The Social Programme of the Nationalists of Quebec, 1900–1914*. Ottawa: University of Ottawa Press, 1969.

Liberal Party. *Creating Opportunity: The Liberal Plan for Canada*. (The Red Book) Ottawa: Liberal Party of Canada, 1993.

Linteau, P.-A., Durocher, R., and Robert, J.-C. *Quebec: A History, 1867–1929*. Toronto: Lorimer, 1983.

Linteau, P.-A., et. al. *Quebec Since 1930*. Translated by R. Chodos. Toronto: Lorimer, 1995.

Lower, A.R.M. *Colony to Nation*. Toronto: Longmans, Green, 1946.

Macli, C. "Duelling in the Dark." *Report on Business Magazine*, April, 1991.

Mallory, J.R. *The Structure of Canadian Government*. Toronto: Gage, 1984.

Martin, P. "Association after Sovereignty? Canadian Views on Economic Association with a Sovereign Quebec," *Canadian Public Policy*, 1995.

————. "Générations politiques, rationalité économique et appui à la souveraineté au Québec," *Canadian Journal of Political Science*, June 1994.

Masters, D.C. *The Reciprocity Treaty of 1854*. Toronto: McClelland and Stewart, 1963.

McRoberts, K. (ed.). *Beyond Quebec: Taking Stock of Canada*, Montreal/Kingston: McGill-Queen's University Press, 1995.

McRoberts, K., and Monahan, P.J. (eds.). *The Charlottetown Accord, the Referendum and the Future of Canada*. Toronto: University of Toronto Press, 1993.

McRoberts, K., and Postgate, D. *Quebec: Social Change and Political Crisis*. Toronto: McClelland and Stewart, 1980.

McWhinney, E. *Quebec and the Constitution, 1960–1978*. Toronto: University of Toronto Press, 1979.

Milne, D. *The Canadian Constitution*. Toronto: Lorimer, 1991.

Milner, H. *Politics in the New Quebec*. Toronto: McClelland and Stewart, 1978.

Milner, S.H., and Milner, H. *The Decolonization of Quebec: An Analysis of Left-Wing Nationalism*. Toronto: McClelland and Stewart, 1973.

Monahan, P.J. *Cooler Heads Shall Prevail: Assessing the Costs and Consequences of Quebec Separation.* Toronto: C.D. Howe Institute, 1994.

Morin, C. *Le Pouvoir québécois...en négociation.* Montreal: Boréal, 1972.

————. *Quebec vs. Ottawa: The Struggle for Self-Government, 1960–72.* Toronto: University of Toronto Press, 1976.

————. *Les choses comme elles étaient.* Montreal: Boréal, 1994.

Morisson, A. (ed.) *The Canadian Strategic Forecast 1992: Divided We Fall: The National Security Implications of Canadian Constitutional Issues.* Toronto: Canadian Institute for Strategic Studies, 1991.

Morton, W.L. *The Kingdom of Canada.* Toronto: McClelland and Stewart, 1969.

Nash, K. (ed.) *Visions of Canada.* Toronto: McClelland and Stewart, 1991.

Ouellet, F. *Economic and Social History of Quebec, 1760–1850.* Toronto: Carleton University Press, 1980.

Ouellet, F. *Lower Canada, 1791–1840: Social Change and Nationalism.* Toronto: McClelland and Stewart, 1980.

Owram, D. *Promise of Eden: The Canadian Expansionist Movement and the Idea of the West, 1856–1900.* Toronto: University of Toronto Press, 1980.

Parti Québécois. *Quebec in a New World.* Translated by R. Chodos. Toronto: Lorimer, 1995.

Pelletier, G. *The October Crisis.* Toronto: McClelland and Stewart, 1971.

Philpot, R. *Oka: dernier alibi du Canada anglais.* Montreal: VLB éditeur, 1991.

Quebec. *Rapport de la commission d'enquête sur la situation de la langue française et sur les droits linguistiques au Québec.* Gouvernement du Québec, 1972 (Gendron Commission).

————. *Quebec-Canada: A New Deal.* Gouvernement du Québec, 1979.

————. *The Political and Constitutional Future of Quebec.* Gouvernement du Québec, 1992 (Bélanger-Campeau Commission).

————. "Les implications de la mise en oeuvre de la souveraineté: les aspects économiques et les finances pub-
liques." *Exposés et études.* Assemblée Nationale du Québec,
1992 (Vol. 4).

Quebec Liberal Party. *A Quebec Free to Choose.* Quebec City,
1991 (Allaire Report).

Quinn, H. *The Union Nationale: Quebec Nationalism from Duplessis to Lévesque.* Toronto: University of Toronto Press, 1979.

Reid, M. *The Shouting Signpainters.* Toronto: McClelland and
Stewart, 1968.

Resnick, P. *Letters to a Québécois Friend.* Reply by D. Latouche.
Montreal/Kingston: McGill-Queen's University Press, 1990.

————. *Toward a Canada-Quebec Union.* Kingston/Montreal:
McGill-Queen's University Press, 1991.

————. *Thinking English Canada.* Toronto: Stoddart, 1994.

Richler, M. *Oh Canada! Oh Quebec! Requiem for a Divided Country.* Toronto: Penguin, 1992.

Rioux, M. *Quebec in Question.* Toronto: Lorimer, 1978.

Rioux, M., and Martin, Y. (eds.). *French Canadian Society.*
Toronto: McClelland and Stewart, 1964.

Ritchie, G., et. al. *Broken Links: Trade Relations After a Quebec
Secession.* Toronto: C.D. Howe Institute, 1991.

Robin, M. *Shades of Right: Nativist and Fascist Politics in Canada,
1920–1940.* Toronto: University of Toronto Press, 1992.

Rocher, G. "Preface," in Conway, J.F. *Des comptes à rendre.*
Montreal: VLB éditeur, 1995.

Rotstein, A. (ed.). *Power Corrupted: The October Crisis and the
Repression of Quebec.* Toronto: New Press, 1971.

Royal Bank. *Unity or Disunity: An Economic Analysis of the
Benefits and Costs.* Montreal: Royal Bank of Canada, 1992.

Ryerson, S. *1837: The Birth of Canadian Democracy.* Toronto:
Francis White, 1937.

————. *The Founding of Canada.* Toronto: Progress, 1960.

————. *French Canada.* Toronto: Progress, 1953.

————. *Unequal Union.* Toronto: Progress, 1968.

Sarra-Bournet, M. *Le Canada anglais et la souveraineté du Québec:
deux cents leaders d'opinion prononcent.* Montreal: VLB
éditeur, 1995.

Sawatsky, J. *Mulroney: The Politics of Ambition.* Toronto:
Macfarlane, Walter and Ross, 1991.

Saywell, J. *The Rise of the Parti Québécois.* Toronto: University of Toronto Press, 1977.

Scott, F.R., and Oliver, M. (eds.). *Quebec States Her Case.* Toronto: Macmillan, 1964.

Schull, J. *Rebellion: The Rising in French Canada, 1837.* Toronto: Macmillan, 1971.

Seidle, F.L. (ed.). *Seeking a New Canadian Partnership: Asymmetrical and Confederal Options.* Montreal: Institute for Research on Public Policy, 1994.

Sharpe, S., and Braid, D. *Storming Babylon: Preston Manning and the Rise of the Reform Party.* Toronto: Key Porter, 1991.

Siegfried, A. *The Race Question in Canada.* Toronto: McClelland and Stewart, 1966.

Silver, A.I. *The French-Canadian Idea of Confederation, 1864–1900.* Toronto: University of Toronto Press, 1982.

Smith, D. *Bleeding Hearts...Bleeding Country: Canada and the Quebec Crisis.* Edmonton: Hurtig, 1971.

Smith, D.E. *The Regional Decline of a National Party: Liberals on the Prairies.* Toronto: University of Toronto Press, 1981.

Stanley, G.F.G. *The Birth of Western Canada: A History of the Riel Rebellions.* Toronto: University of Toronto Press, 1960.

Stewart, W. *Shrug: Trudeau in Power.* Toronto: New Press, 1972.

Trofimenkoff, S.M. *The Dream of Nation.* Toronto: Gage, 1983.

Trudeau, P.E. *Federalism and the French-Canadians.* Toronto: Macmillan, 1968.

Twigg, J. "Press Reaction to the October 1970 Crisis in Quebec." Unpublished paper, 1971.

Urquhart, M.C., and Buckley, K.A.H. (eds.). *Historical Statistics of Canada.* Ottawa: Statistics Canada, 1983.

Vallières, P. *White Niggers of America.* Toronto: McClelland and Stewart, 1971.

Vallières, P. *Choose!* Toronto: NewPress, 1972.

Vallières, P. *The Assassination of Pierre Laporte: Behind the October '70 Scenario.* Toronto: Lorimer, 1977.

Varcoe, F.P. *The Constitution of Canada.* Toronto: Carswell, 1965.

Wade, M. *The French-Canadian Outlook.* Toronto: McClelland and Stewart, 1964.

Wade, M. *The French-Canadians: 1760–1967.* Toronto: Macmillan, 1968 (Vols. I and II).

Waite, P.B. *The Life and Times of Confederation, 1864–67.* Toronto: University of Toronto Press, 1962.

———. (ed.). *The Confederation Debates in the Province of Canada, 1865.* Toronto: McClelland and Stewart, 1963.

Ward, N. *The Canadian House of Commons.* Toronto: University of Toronto Press, 1950.

Weaver, R.K. (eds.). *The Collapse of Canada?* Washington, D.C.: Brookings Institute, 1992.

Young, R.A. *The Breakup of Czechoslovakia.* Kingston: Queen's University Press, 1994.

———. "How Do Peaceful Secessions Happen?" *Canadian Journal of Political Science,* December 1994.

———. *The Secession of Quebec and the Future of Canada.* Kingston/Montreal: McGill-Queen's University Press, 1995.

The Charlottetown Agreement went much further than Meech in the devolution of powers from Ottawa to the provinces. The new powers the Agreement proposed to extend to the provinces were considerable:

- Exclusive jurisdiction over labour market development and manpower training, including the right to eject the federal government from all activities in the area. Ottawa, however, would still maintain the unemployment insurance program. Surely this was a bizarre idea: Ottawa would pay for unemployment insurance, but Canada could conceivably have ten different manpower development policies unrelated to the national unemployment insurance program.
- Exclusive jurisdiction over culture, but Ottawa would continue to maintain national cultural institutions. How this would work in practice challenged the imagination. Would Ottawa be allowed to pay for and to run the CBC, but with provinces determining provincial programming?
- Exclusive jurisdiction over forestry, mining, tourism, housing, recreation, and municipal and urban affairs. These areas were already considered to be provincial jurisdictions, but Ottawa has not hesitated to act in these areas using the federal spending power. What remained unclear was how much of the federal spending power came with this exclusive jurisdiction.
- The constitutional power to compel Ottawa to negotiate regional development programs. This was an effort to give some force to the already existing constitutional commit-

ment to equalization payments and comparable levels of services and taxes across the country. The new proposal also added a commitment to "comparable economic infrastructures of a national nature," whatever that meant.

- A share in power over immigration, something Quebec already enjoyed by intergovernmental agreement as a result of post-Meech bilateral negotiations between Quebec and Ottawa.
- A share in power over the regulation of the telecommunications industry.
- The right to opt out of new national shared-cost programs with financial compensation.
- A constitutional right to protect future intergovernmental agreements from unilateral change by Ottawa.
- The right to submit a list of names from which Ottawa must select appointees for the Supreme Court.
- A veto over constitutional changes affecting the Senate, the House of Commons, the Supreme Court (except the nomination and appointment process), and the constitutional amending formula.
- A right to opt out, with financial compensation, of any constitutional change that transfers provincial powers to Ottawa.

In addition to these new provincial powers, Charlottetown also proposed to hamstring the federal power. Ottawa's power of disallowance and/or reservation of provincial legislation was to be repealed. Ottawa's power to declare a provincial "work" in the interests of two or more provinces, or the nation as a whole, thereby taking over jurisdiction, was now only to be exercised with the consent of the province in which the "work" was located. These are presently unqualified, clear, and unchallengeable central powers to be exercised at the pleasure and discretion of Ottawa. With these gone, Ottawa would only retain the "peace, order and good government" power, a vague and unsatisfactory central power, subject to arguments about meaning and justification and ultimately arguable in front of the Supreme Court, which, over time, would tilt more and more toward provincial rights.

These were enormous new powers for the provinces and a dramatic shackling of federal power. One can understand why nine premiers, under the decentralizing guidance of Joe Clark and Brian Mulroney, would agree to allow such burdens to be imposed upon them. Interestingly, they also, taken together, more or less amounted to a significant portion of the wish-list Quebec had developed over the past thirty years. The only thing missing, of course, was that the Charlottetown Agreement did not grant each province constitutional recognition as a "distinct society." Only Quebec received that recognition. Now, if this had remained the package on offer — new powers for the provinces, the profound weakening of the federal power, distinct society status for Quebec — then Quebec might have signed on eagerly. If the only way it can get special constitutional status is by giving special status to every other province, then Quebec won't argue. With the support of the prime minister, the nine English-Canadian premiers were playing the same game that the premiers had played during Meech and have more or less played since the Quiet Revolution. If Ottawa wants to solve the Quebec constitutional crisis, the only way it can be done is if each and every concession to Quebec is given to all provinces. In exchange, the nine English-Canadian premiers agreed to yield, reluctantly, on distinct society for Quebec.

The Charlottetown Agreement included commitments to both "the vitality and development of official language minority communities throughout Canada" and the "equality of provinces" in the Canada clause to stand uneasily beside Quebec's distinct society clause. Both proposals struck at the very root of Quebec's continuing grievances. The first was seen as a potential trump card to be used in future Supreme Court tests of Quebec's language laws. It did not take much imagination to anticipate a flurry of challenges by Quebec's English-Canadian minority to many aspects of Quebec's language laws on the grounds that the laws did not respect the vitality and development of the English-speaking minority in Quebec. Public opinion in Quebec would hesitate to accept any measure that appeared to threaten the right of the Québécois to secure and to enhance the French language in Quebec.

The equality of provinces clause was also deeply offensive to many Québécois, though perhaps not as immediately threatening as the minority-language clause. Quebec has always resented being treated as a province just like the others and has always maintained an official position that it is distinctive. Clearly, the equality of provinces clause could be seen as a direct counterweight to Quebec's distinct society clause. But Quebec had long ago learned to live with the uneasy co-existence of the two contradictory concepts in practice. The proposal to insert the equality of provinces provision explicitly in the constitution, however, created agitated concern in Quebec. But given the post-Meech mood, if it had remained merely words, Quebec might well have swallowed the pill in exchange for all the other gains. But Charlottetown proceeded to give that clause substantial effect in a new reformed Senate.

The Senate that was initially proposed in the July Premiers' Accord was unacceptable to Quebec. It was truly Triple-E — equal, elected and effective. It was so large — eight senators for each province, two for each territory, as well as eventual aboriginal representation — that it would have had a significant impact and could conceivably frustrate the will of the House of Commons. As popularly elected politicians, senators would enjoy a power base relatively independent of either the provincial legislatures or the House of Commons, allowing them to become credible brokers and mediators of regional interests in Ottawa. Furthermore, the premiers proposed to give this Senate a great deal of power — a simple majority could veto natural resource taxation measures; a majority of 60 to 70 per cent could force a joint sitting of the two houses to decide any question by a majority vote of the combined chambers; a majority of 70 per cent or more could defeat measures approved by the House of Commons. Although money bills in general were to be immune from the Senate, the 60 to 70 per cent rule would apply to "fundamental policy changes to the tax system." Finally, the Senate would also enjoy the power to ratify or to reject Ottawa's appointments, "of heads of the national cultural institutions, the heads of the federal regulatory boards and agencies," and the governor of the Bank of Canada.

The premiers' Triple-E Senate was flatly rejected by Quebec. It was so large and so powerful that Quebec could never agree to an equal number of senators with the other smaller provinces. Not only was this undemocratic in principle, but, more practically, it would dilute Quebec's voice on behalf of the Québécois in the central government. Furthermore, the prospect of another separately elected, powerful group of potential federalist politicians representing the Québécois was unthinkable. For years, the Quebec government, speaking on behalf of the Québécois through the National Assembly, had had to contend with federalist MPs also speaking for the Québécois and often carrying contradictory messages. To add a third independent and powerful voice to the mix would further reduce the impact of the Quebec National Assembly in Ottawa. Quebec preferred abolition of the Senate or, failing that, the status quo.

In order to overcome Quebec's refusal to accept the loss of so much power at the centre, the premiers' Triple-E Senate proposal was eviscerated and rendered virtually meaningless. In the Charlottetown Agreement, the Senate proposal gave each province six senators and each territory one, for a total of sixty-two senators. The new Senate's powers were strictly limited: a majority vote of the Senate could force a joint sitting where a majority of both Houses would decide an issue; kill a bill approved by the House of Commons regarding natural resource taxation; initiate bills to go to the Commons, other than bills on money matters; veto government appointments of heads of national institutions; and block Commons bills on the French language and/or French culture.

In exchange for accepting equal numbers of senators, the provinces with large populations received additional seats in the House of Commons. Quebec and Ontario each got eighteen additional seats; British Columbia got four in addition to an early redistribution in 1996 to deal with the province's rapidly growing population; and Alberta got two. Thus, the proposed House of Commons was increased by forty-two seats.

In addition, Quebec received a form of special status. Quebec was permanently guaranteed 25 per cent of seats in the House of Commons, essentially freezing and protecting its current share of seats. Furthermore, Quebec was allowed to select its six senators through the National Assembly, ensuring that its Senate seats would be occupied by individuals with the confidence of the National Assembly. Finally, French linguistic and/or cultural matters were subject to a double Senate majority, requiring the approval of both a majority of the sixty-two senators, including a majority of francophone senators. This limited special status, in addition to the distinct society clause, significantly offset the equality of provinces clause and gave Bourassa room to argue in favour of the deal.

In order to obtain Quebec's agreement, native negotiators also made some serious concessions in the final Charlottetown Agreement. In exchange for Quebec's acceptance of the inherent right of self-government for native people, native negotiators and the first ministers agreed that this right would not involve new land rights, and that all native laws would be subordinate to federal and provincial laws in "matters of peace, order and good government." As well, Charlottetown included a guarantee of native representation in the Senate, but the matter of numbers, method of selection and special powers of aboriginal senators were set aside for a future political accord.

On the issue of the creation of new provinces, Quebec failed to obtain a clear veto. Under the Charlottetown Agreement, Ottawa could create new provinces after negotiations with the territories. But each province retained an imperfect partial veto, since the important details of becoming a functioning province, like the details of representation in Senate and the establishment of constitutional rights, required unanimous provincial consent. This, in fact, amounted to a temporary *de facto* veto. As well, Quebec and every other province received a veto over future constitutional changes to the Senate, the House of Commons and the Supreme Court (except for the selection process, which will follow the 7/50 rule — seven provinces with more than 50 per cent of the population).

In the final analysis, the Charlottetown Agreement was a power grab by the premiers. To mollify Quebec, as well as the premiers of the more populous English-Canadian provinces, the Triple-E Senate was gone and replaced by a Single-E Senate — equal. Given the increase in the numbers of Commons seats going to Quebec and Ontario and the dramatic reduction in powers, the proposed Senate ceased to be effective, except on natural resource taxation (the National Energy Program clause). And with Quebec allowed to appoint senators through the National Assembly, the Senate ceased to be elected. Furthermore, though it had yet to be finalized, most premiers other than Bourassa assumed that senators in the nine English-Canadian provinces would be elected on a provincewide basis. This meant that those wishing to have a serious chance at winning a seat would have to get their names included on a central party list. Since the election was to be provincewide, the mechanism for the selection of a party's list of candidates would of necessity be highly centralized and the party leader, particularly if he or she were also premier, would play the key role in determining the names to be included. The senators would thereby owe their first allegiance to the movers and shakers of the provincial party apparatus, not of the federal party apparatus. And if senators wished to be included on the party list the next time around, they would accept the discipline of the provincial party and, most importantly, provincial party leaders. Provincial party leaders, particularly those who were premiers, would thus have exercised enormous power and influence at the centre, power and influence potentially sufficient to frustrate the will of the House of Commons, especially when no party enjoyed a clear majority. Hence, the new Senate was essentially a House of the Premiers.

When the Canada Round was finally over, having brought forth the Charlottetown Agreement, the politicians, civil servants, and negotiators involved, and the journalists covering the process, expressed relief that it was finally over, having complained endlessly and loudly about constitutional fatigue. Many shared this view, especially editorial writers. Many others, however, expressed differing levels of disbelief and shock about the Agreement, since it failed to address many crucial concerns and appeared to have overlooked so many of the views presented both before and after the death of the Meech Lake Accord.

One major strength of the Charlottetown Agreement was the satisfactory inclusion of the inherent right of aboriginal self-government. Another strength was the Social Charter that Ontario's NDP Premier Rae succeeded in obtaining with the support of the other two NDP premiers — Romanow of Saskatchewan and Harcourt of British Columbia. Though declaring a commitment to existing joint federal-provincial programs in health, social assistance, and education; to workers' rights to collective bargaining; and to environmental protection, the Social Charter clause remained toothless since it was not enforceable through the courts, only through a "monitoring mechanism" to be established at a future first ministers' meeting. The inclusion of a Social Charter was a largely meaningless legal victory, though perhaps a positive moral and political one. Finally, a third strength of the Agreement was the inclusion of a mechanism preventing Ottawa from making unilateral reductions in the federal funding share of any future joint programs, or in renewals of agreements in medicare, social assistance, or post-secondary education.

Charlottetown's greatest failure was that it did not address one of the major fears in English Canada that had contributed to the death of Meech — that provincial powers had been unduly enhanced and that the powers of the central government had been unduly diminished. These fears were completely ignored. Indeed, the Charlottetown Agreement went further down the road of decentralization than Meech had gone. After Charlotte-town, the federal government would be left weak and impotent, unable to speak let alone act for Canada by providing effective national leadership. At the centre of this fear had been the conviction that the "opting out/financial compensation" feature of Meech would ensure that no new universal national programs with enforceable national standards could ever again be established. That feature of Meech remained intact in the Charlotte-town Agreement. Provincial governments would be allowed to opt out of any future nationally run shared-cost social programs, yet still receive federal funds in compensation. The only requirement was that to be eligible for federal tax dollars, the province would have to establish a program "compatible with national objectives." But these "national objectives" would not be established and enforced by Ottawa. Rather, they would be set by the first ministers. Ottawa would thereby lose its ability to use the federal spending power to discipline the provinces to adhere to a national program's principles and objectives. Yet, enforcing adherence is something Ottawa has had to do repeatedly, first to establish and then to maintain the integrity of the national medicare program. Under the Charlottetown Agreement, national shared-cost programs like medicare in new areas of urgent public need — such as daycare, for example — could never be established, even if the public demanded them.

Those loudly applauding the Charlottetown Agreement, if only because of constitutional fatigue and a desire to get on with other issues, were also in for a disappointment once they examined the text carefully. Fully twenty-nine separate, complex elements of the Agreement required further negotiations in order to achieve final working arrangements that could be included in future political accords. In other words, the Charlottetown Agreement was a recipe for a continuing and virtually endless negotiating process. The areas requiring these negotiations included not only native self-government, but also every new power transferred to the provinces. This was a "settlement" hardly worth the name. Rather, much of Charlottetown amounted to an agreement to continue negotiating! Canadians who thought that concluding the Agreement had ended the constitutional nightmare were in for a rude awakening.

And what did the West get? Were Western grievances effectively addressed, grievances which had been central in precipitating both the isolation of Quebec in 1981–82 and the unravelling of

Meech? Charlottetown's Single-E Senate allegedly gave the West one clear victory — a simple majority of the new Senate could defeat House of Commons bills relating to natural resource taxation. The substantive meaning of this power remained undefined. In the words of the Agreement, "The precise definition of this category of legislation remains to be determined." If the Agreement were passed, the only real winners in the West would be the natural resource companies, especially the oil and gas interests. Given the Senate's small size and the probability of at-large, provincewide Senate elections, these natural resource companies would do their best to buy all the senators they could. It was a remarkable testimony to the enormous power and influence of the oil and natural gas industry to realize that the only western grievance effectively addressed by the new Senate was that rooted in the industry's deep-seated, continuing anger over Trudeau's National Energy Program. Seldom, if ever, has a single industry's lobbying effort been so effective, not only in creating a Senate but in giving it the single power the lobby wanted.

The apparent gain for the West — and for Atlantic Canada — of an equal Senate was more than offset by the 36 new seats added to central Canada's representation in the House of Commons. Though the Senate could force joint sittings of the combined chambers, the Senate's 62 members, already divided among themselves, would be more than effectively drowned out by the 337 members of the new House of Commons. It seemed hardly worth the estimated annual price tag of $140 million the Charlottetown Senate would cost the taxpayer. Exactly how this new Senate was a victory for the West remained murky.

While the western premiers hailed the transfer of many new powers to the provinces and the "opting out/financial compensation" clause as real victories for the West, many westerners (and Atlantic Canadians) were profoundly uneasy. What good was exclusive provincial jurisdiction in areas like forestry, tourism, housing, culture, and so on, if federal money didn't come with it or if additional fiscal powers were not transferred? What good was the provinces' "opting out/financial compensation" right, if that provided the justification for Ottawa's refusal to bother developing any future national programs in areas of public need? Westerners were well aware that had not access to federal funding been dependent on implementation of an acceptable version of medicare, British Columbia, Alberta, and perhaps Manitoba might never have implemented medicare as we know it. Indeed, a careful examination of western Canadian history informed westerners — and Atlantic Canadians — that the major concessions won over the years of serious and lasting benefit to the people of these regions resulted from decisions made by the House of Commons and enforced by a strong central government in Ottawa. The unemployment insurance program; shared cost programming in health, social assistance, and post-secondary education; and many smaller-scale programs would never have happened had we had as weak a federal government as that proposed in the Charlottetown Agreement. When examined in the clear light of history, and in terms of the real gains of the past, the new provincial powers and the "opting out/financial compensation" clause seemed victories that had more the character of defeats, at least from the perspective of rank-and-file westerners.

Finally, the central question about the Charlottetown Agreement was whether it would be enough to satisfy Quebec. Regardless of what the Allaire Report and the Bélanger-Campeau Commission had demanded as Quebec's minimum — demands seen almost universally in English Canada as outrageous — Bourassa had insisted from the outset that the five elements in the Meech Lake Accord were his bottom line. The Meech minimum had to be conceded to Quebec.

First, Quebec required constitutional recognition as a "distinct society." English-Canadian crankiness about the distinct society clause had been the most significant single factor in the death of Meech. In the post-Meech phase, however, particularly during the elaborate constitutional discussions, English Canadians had become somewhat more receptive to this concession to Quebec. Indeed, many English Canadians had even begun again to toy with the idea of "special status" for Quebec, though preferring the more neutral phrase, "asymmetrical federalism." Still, the hostility to Meech's distinct society clause had emerged abruptly and with surprising ferocity. Therefore, the English-Canadian first ministers approached the issue gingerly. On the other hand, for Bourassa, "distinct society" was non-negotiable — anything less would meet a wall of opposition in Quebec.

Bourassa got the words "distinct society" not once but twice in the Charlottetown Agreement. Section 2.(1)(c) of the Canada clause said, "Quebec constitutes within Canada a distinct society, which includes a French-speaking majority, a unique culture and a civil law tradition," while section 2.(2) said, "The role of the legislature and Government of Quebec to preserve and promote the distinct society of Quebec is affirmed." But these affirmations were twice trumped in the Canada clause, making the distinct society provision of the agreement significantly weaker than that included in Meech. Section 2.(1)(d) committed "Canadians and their governments...to the vitality and development of official language communities throughout Canada." And Section 2.(1)(h) enunciated "the principle of the equality of the provinces," for the first time proposing the constitutionalization of that fundamentally controversial doctrine. In a clash regarding Quebec's language laws, which would prevail, "distinct society" mentioned twice or the double trump? Furthermore, as Clyde Wells put it, a "fence" was put around Quebec's distinct society by specifying its meaning to include only "a French-speaking majority, a unique culture and a civil law tradition," the concessions made to Quebec in the 1774 *Quebec Act*. Meech's distinct society clause had not been so precisely defined, allowing the possibility of expanding upon its meaning and extending its application into new areas. Just days after the Charlottetown Agreement, eight constitutional experts from five Quebec universities published an open letter in *La Presse* and *Le Devoir* emphatically stating "the distinct society clause found in the Charlottetown agreement is of virtually no value for Quebec [ensuring] that the integrity of the Charter of the French Language will be more precarious than ever... We consider that its adoption may even represent a setback with respect to the current situation...The Charlottetown agreement, in defining the distinct society and putting it on an equal footing with the commitment of governments to the vitality and development of the English-speaking minority in Quebec, may put into question what has already been recognized."

Second, Quebec required a veto. In Quebec this was widely seen as a return of Quebec's historic veto given up by Lévesque in order to cement his participation in the Gang of Eight in 1981. Although the Supreme Court had later ruled that no such veto had ever existed, the political convention had indeed prevailed and Quebec had exercised this veto often in the past — most dramatically in 1971 to torpedo the Victoria Charter. Bourassa wanted a Quebec veto over all aspects of the constitution which directly affected Quebec, including the creation of new provinces. Quebec and every other province had obtained such a veto in the Meech Accord.

The Charlottetown Agreement gave all provinces veto power over constitutional changes to the Senate, the House of Commons and all aspects of the Supreme Court, except the nomination and appointment procedure. On the creation of new provinces, Quebec, and every other province, obtained only an imperfect, partial, and temporary veto. This veto was much less than Meech had offered. Again, the issue of the creation of new provinces struck at the heart of one of Quebec's historical anxieties, an anxiety which had increased with the emergence of the doctrine of the equality of provinces. Now one province of ten, Quebec looked forward to an uncertain future when it would become one of eleven, then twelve, then thirteen, as provincial status was granted to Canada's northern territories. The prospect of becoming increasingly marginalized as the one French-speaking province among so many "equal" English-speaking provinces recalled Lord Durham's prescription of gradually pushing the French fact to the margins of society and politics. The Charlottetown Agreement struck an unsatisfactory compromise. Ottawa would have the pre-1982 power to create new provinces following consultation with the first ministers. But each existing province would have a *de facto* veto over the inclusion of the new province in the constitutional amending formula and over any increase in representation in the Senate. Granted, in the realities of political life, such a *de facto* veto could not be used to deny full provincial status forever, but it could provide an important bargaining chip in seeking new concessions. In addition, Bourassa received a backdoor veto he had not requested in the Senate he didn't want — Commons bills affecting the French language and culture required a double majority in the Senate before final approval.

On the third and fourth elements of Meech, there was little controversy. Meech had promised all provinces a significant share in power over immigration if they requested it. This had been such a sore point with Quebec that, after the collapse of Meech, Quebec had received this through direct bilateral negotiations with Ottawa. Charlottetown extended the right to all provinces that wished to pursue it. In Meech Quebec had also gained the constitutional recognition of three of nine members on the Supreme Court, as well as a say in the nomination and selection procedure. Charlottetown easily granted these demands to Quebec as well as granting all provinces the guarantee that Ottawa would only select members of the Supreme Court from lists submitted by the provinces.

Similarly, there was little controversy on the fifth element of Meech crucial for Quebec: opting out and financial compensation.

The Charlottetown Agreement reiterated Meech. Quebec, together with all provinces, could opt out of future national shared-cost programs in areas of provincial jurisdiction and receive financial compensation, as long as the province in question developed a program "compatible with national objectives." Furthermore, a province could opt out in the event of a future constitutional transfer of a provincial jurisdiction to Ottawa with "reasonable compensation." The "national objectives" aspect of the opting-out right caused some continuing anxiety in Quebec, and was seen as a major concession by many Québécois since it allowed Ottawa to maintain a significant role in exercising the federal spending power in the province.

Did the Charlottetown Agreement meet the minimum demands of Meech? At the time, Bourassa and the Agreement's supporters insisted that it did. But on sober reflection, one had to conclude it was nowhere near the Meech minimum. One must recall that at the time Meech was negotiated, the Québécois considered the demands that it addressed as skeletal. After the death of Meech, Québécois demands escalated. With Charlottetown, Quebec was asked not only to accept a watered-down Meech, but at the same time to swallow a Senate it did not want, the entrenchment of aboriginal self-government which created profound unease, a flat refusal even to contemplate a new division of powers based on Quebec's aspirations, and a total rejection of any consideration of "special status" beyond the minimum granted in the 1774 *Quebec Act*. It hardly appeared a serious effort to save or renew Canadian federalism. Granted the English-Canadian premiers had tried to sugar the pill with Quebec's 25 per cent guarantee regarding seats in the House of Commons, the double majority in the Senate on French language and culture, and the right of the National Assembly to select Quebec's six senators. Many in English Canada complained about this "special status" — and it was a kind of special status — but not the kind Quebec wanted. Once again, English Canada had decided virtually unilaterally what the Québécois should have and then imposed it upon them. Certainly, Québécois nationalism could and would use these concessions in the future, as it had with previous concessions, but only as tools to continue to struggle toward one of the two options Québécois nationalism had insisted since the Quiet Revolution constituted the real choices for Quebec and English Canada — real special status involving a new division of powers satisfactory to the Québécois nation or some form of sovereignty. In short, like all earlier accommodations devised and imposed by English Canada, the Charlottetown Agreement really settled nothing, merely attempted once again to postpone the day of final reckoning.

The tragedy for Canada of the Charlottetown Agreement was that the English-Canadian premiers and the prime minister had squandered yet another opportunity to recommend changes that could have taken a large step toward a resolution of the Quebec crisis without jeopardizing the integrity of the whole country. The nine English-Canadian premiers proved unwilling to do so, preferring to use the moment to make a grab for more provincial power under the cover of salvaging Canada. Bourassa was politically vulnerable and desperate for a deal, desperate for any piece of paper he could wave triumphantly as he stepped off the plane at Quebec City. To the surprise of most, including his own top negotiators, Bourassa quickly and easily grasped the straw thrown to him by his colleagues and ushered in another destructive and divisive episode in the history of Québécois–English-Canadian relations.

Index

Aberhart, William, 97
Aboriginal peoples, xii, 7, 9-10, 213, 251; Charlottetown Accord, 157-158; reconciliation, 8; rights, 167, 251; self-government, 140, 141, 143, 167, 170-171, 198, 211, 240; territories, 201, 240
Aboriginal women's rights, 251
Acadia, 7-8, 11
Acadians, 12
Act of Union, 1840, 31-32, 35
An Act to promote the French Language in Quebec, 1969, 67, 70
Action démocratique du Québec (ADQ), 2, 3, 176, 205-206, 207, 214, 232, 233
l'Actualité, 166-167
l'affaire Wilhelmy, 164-165, 166-167
Agreements, intergovernmental, 268
Airports: language dispute, 88-89
Alberta, 37; Charlottetown Accord, 142; energy crisis, 1970s, 103; federal election, 1993, 2, 5, 188; French language rights, 131-132
Alcan, 157
Allaire, Jean, 163, 166, 168, 172, 176, 206
Allaire Report, 138, 161, 276
Alliance for the Preservation of English in Canada, 200
Allophones, 7, 194, 220
American Civil War, 34, 237
American Revolution, 16, 17, 18
Andre, Harvie, 143-144, 172
Anglophone Assault Group, 232
Anglophone intellectuals, 4
Army, Canadian, 57
Arts, Quebec, 55
Asbestos, 91
Assembly of First Nations, 158

l'Association des manufacturiers du Québec, 157
Atlantic Canada, 9, 60, 251; energy crisis, 1970s, 103; federal election, 1965, 65; federal election, 1979, 102; federal election, 1980, 104
Automobile insurance, 91
Axworthy, Lloyd, 196
Bank of Canada, 150
Bank of Montreal, 203
Batoche, 39
le beau risque, 117-119, 189
Beaudoin, Laurent, 236
Bédard, Pierre, 18
Bélanger-Campeau Commission, 138, 161, 276
Bennett, Bill, 179
Bérard, André, 157
Bertrand, Jean-Guy, 228-229
Bilingual sign law dispute, 134-135
Bilingualism, 60, 65-66, 98-99, 137
Bill C-110, 224-225
Bill of Rights, 1689, 208n
Bill 22. See *The Official Languages Act.*
Bill 63. See *An Act to promote the French Language in Quebec.*
Bill 86, 176
Bill 101. *See* Charte de la langue française.
Bill 178, 133-134
Blakeney, Allan, 92; energy crisis, 1970s, 100, 111; federalism, 107; Meech Lake Accord, 134; patriation of the Constitution, 108, 112
Bleus, 35, 46
Bloc Populaire, 188
Bloc Québécois (BQ), 5, 189, 194-195, 220, 249; and Parti Québécois, 213; by-election, 1990, 189; Charlottetown Agreement, 146; federal election,

St. Léonard: crisis, 66-67, 87; federal election of 1993, 194
Saskatchewan, 9, 37; Charlottetown Accord, 142; French language rights, 131; Meech Lake Accord, 132-133
Saturday Night, 231
Sauvé, Paul, 54
Scott, Thomas, 38
Seaton, Lord, 29
Senate, xii, 4, 128, 141, 143, 160, 243-244, 268
Separatism, 60-61, 136
Services, 268
Shaw, Robert, 73
Shawinigan, 61
Sifton, Clifford, 221
Sihota, Moe, 6, 160, 167
Simpson, Jeffrey, 150-151
Social Charter, 251, 273
Social Credit, Alberta, 1930s, 228, 242
Social programs, 247, 249, 251, 276
Somalia affair, 179
"Sovereignty-association," 62, 94-95, 116, 125
Soviet empire, 252
Spending power, federal, 121-122, 250
Spicer Commission, 140, 154
Standard Life Assurance Company, 217
Stanfield, Robert, 64
Statistical Account of Upper Canada, 23-24
Statute of Westminster, 1931, 49
Sugar duties, 33
Sun Life, 96
Sun newspapers, 154
Supreme Court appointments, 121, 122, 268, 277-278
Sydenham, Lord, 31, 32
Task Force on Canadian Unity, 1979, 7
Taxation, 267-268
Taylor, Allan, 149, 150
Telecommunications industry, 242, 268
"Ten Resolutions," 28
Terrana, Anna, 231
Thirteen Colonies, 11, 12, 16
Timber duties, 33
Toronto Necropolis, 25
Toronto Stock Exchange, 170
Tourism, 267

Trade unions, 52, 74, 153
Treaty of Utrecht, 1713, 12
Tremblay, André, 164-165
Tremblay, Gerald, 234
Triple-E Senate, 4, 140, 141, 172, 243-244
Trois Rivières, 61
Trudeau, Pierre, 59-60, 119, 127-128, 197; and sovereignty, 90; bilingualism, 70; Charlottetown Agreement, 152, 153, 154, 165-166, 168, 170, 173, 178, 195, 250; election, 63-65; equality of provinces doctrine, 242-243; federalism, 53, 70, 90, 235; Meech Lake Accord, 137, 153; multiculturalism, 70, 239; National Energy Program, 105; October crisis, 1970, 72, 73, 75-76, 78, 80, 83, 84; patriation of Constitution, 108-111; re-election, 1980, 104; resignation, final, 1984, 116; resignation, first, 1979, 103
Turner, John, 116-117
Twenty Realities of Secession, 225-226
"Two Nations" concept, 58, 240
Unemployment insurance, 267, 276
Unilingualism petition, Victoria, B.C., 135
Union Jack, 49
Union Nationale, 50, 52, 54, 93, 119; Conscription crisis, World War II, 46; French language, 55, 67, 87; Quebec provincial election, 1966, 61-62; Quebec provincial election, 1970, 70, 71
Union of B.C. Chiefs, 157
Union Populaire, 188-189
United Empire Loyalists, 18-19
"Unity or Disunity: An Economic Analysis of the Benefits and Costs," 149-150
Unity rally, Canada Place, Montreal, 219
University of Quebec, 217
Upper Canada, 18, 20. *See also* Canada West; Ontario.; rebellion, 23-25; responsible government, 22, 31, 33
Urban affairs, 267
Ursuline nuns, 12
Valcourt, Bernard, 178
Vallières, Pierre, 56, 82